Ark of the Broken Covenant

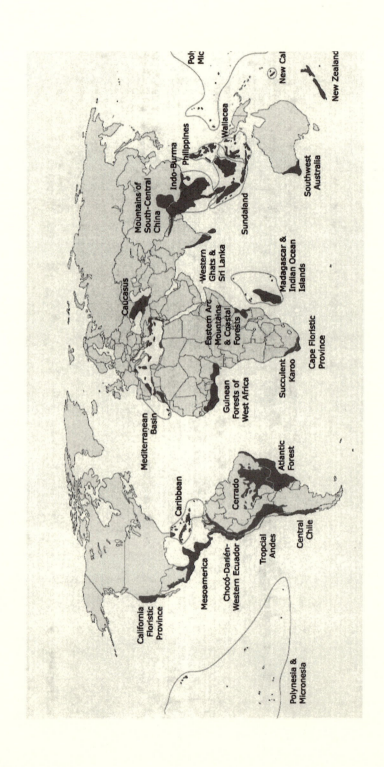

Biodiversity Hotspots of the World. © Conservation International, 2002. Used with permission.

Ark of the Broken Covenant
Protecting the World's Biodiversity Hotspots

John Charles Kunich

Issues in Comparative Public Law
Edward J. Eberle, Series Editor

 PRAEGER

Westport, Connecticut
London

Library of Congress Cataloging-in-Publication Data

Kunich, John C., 1953–
    Ark of the broken covenant : protecting the world's biodiversity hotspots / John
Charles Kunich.
        p.   cm.—(Issues in comparative public law)
    Includes bibliographical references and index.
    ISBN 0–275–97840–0 (alk. paper)
      1. Environmental law.   2. Biological diversity.   I. Title.   II. Series.
    K3585.K86   2003
    333.7′2—dc21   2002029766

British Library Cataloguing in Publication Data is available.

Library of Congress Catalog Card Number: 2002029766
ISBN: 0–275–97840–0

First published in 2003

Praeger Publishers, 88 Post Road West, Westport, CT 06881
An imprint of Greenwood Publishing Group, Inc.
www.praeger.com

Printed in the United States of America

The paper used in this book complies with the
Permanent Paper Standard issued by the National
Information Standards Organization (Z39.48–1984).

10 9 8 7 6 5 4 3 2

Contents

Dedication
and Acknowledgments

The author thanks his dear wife, Marcia Vigil, and their wonderful daughters, Christina Laurel Kunich and Julie-Kate Marva Kunich, for their unending love and support. This book is dedicated to all the species we have driven into extinction without ever even giving them a name.

Series Foreword

John Kunich's book is a welcome edition to the Praeger Series on Issues in Comparative Public Law. The series provides a forum for the examination of issues of major importance to contemporary society, discussed from a comparative perspective.

Kunich's book is an important contribution to environmental awareness and comparative literature. He shines the light on an important global problem that has been underappreciated, if not neglected; namely, whether to protect the increasingly few areas left in the world where life-forms live and, hopefully, will continue to thrive. Kunich calls these areas "hotspots" because they contain within their relatively small area a disproportionately large share of all life-forms on the earth. These hotspots contain extraordinary ecological richness, including remaining habitats of plant species, nonfish vertebrate species, and other life-forms.

Hotspots are under grave threat due to forces of industrialization, globalization, and civilization. Humans are encroaching dramatically on the kingdoms of plants and animals, much to their peril. According to scientific thought, we are currently in the midst of a major extinction spasm that could rival the few other disastrous epochs in our planet's history that claimed the lives of millions of species. As we consider globalization—its merits and demerits—Kunich reminds us that we need to at least take a moment, amidst the hustle of the marketplace, to consider what to do with the many remaining species that share the earth with us.

Kunich makes the case why the survival of these species is a matter of the highest importance. The life-forms and natural wonders within these hotspots possess untold riches, including incalculable benefits for humans and the environment in medicine, food production, pest control, and many other fields. With the advent of genetic engineering, the DNA of every species may hold the keys to great advancements in other species and for humankind as well. These reasons, alone, should give us pause. But as higher level thinkers, we should also consider the moral obligation we have to preserve living things. Ultimately, how we act in life will count for more than what we consume or produce.

Surveying existing legal regimes, internationally and nationally, as they relate to biodiversity, Kunich finds them wanting in addressing the concerns of hotspots. Accordingly, he proposes an innovative solution to the problem, drawing upon money, human ingenuity, and the better qualities within us. His proposal is a call for action, a call hopefully that is not too late. The book is pathbreaking, focusing a lens on a matter of seminal importance for all of us who inhabit the globe. Kunich discusses hotspots comprehensively, through consideration of science, law, public policy, and ethics, nationally and comparatively. He offers a blueprint on how effectively to fashion our future. Kunich's book is an inspiration to present and future generations dedicated to preserving and protecting living habitats.

Edward J. Eberle

Preface

What would be the appropriate legal course of action if credible scientific evidence surfaced showing that most of the earth's species are concentrated in only a few poorly protected regions? What response would be prudent if it came to light that this planet's remaining biodiversity is in no way evenly distributed, but rather is overwhelmingly confined to certain key, imperiled areas? What legal and policy options would we invoke if we learned that our best chance to save thousands, even millions of species from extinction is to focus on the fate of approximately 25 zones of immense ecological significance?

These are not hypothetical questions taken from a law school class on environmental law. They are not ripped from the pages of an overly imaginative final examination in a natural resources law course. On the contrary, they are based on fact. The answers to these questions may spell the difference between survival and extinction for an immense number of species in existence today.

Tragically, the answers thus far are all wrong. No new comprehensive legislation has been proposed. There has been no attempt to amend existing statutory or regulatory law to address the issue on a systematic basis. Virtually nothing has been done through diplomatic means. Political officials have made no effort to bring the situation to the attention of other world leaders or the general public. In short, to the very limited extent people in positions of power are aware of the phenomenon at all, the universal response has been to leave the status quo entirely undisturbed.

If he had been a present-day environmentalist, Mark Twain might have said, "Everybody talks about saving biodiversity, but nobody does anything about it." So many trees have been felled in printing the numerous books and articles debating the problem that cynics might suggest this whirlwind of words itself is a factor in the demise of some species. Unfortunately, after decades of academic criticism and congressional debate, a collection of "protected area" laws and individual "endangered species" laws in the various nations, and a few nonbinding international agreements, remain essentially alone in the legal fight to preserve global biodiversity. This patchwork safety net has not been equal to the task.

This is more than just another case of failing to see the forest for the trees. In many instances, it is a matter of failing to see the endangered species for the rainforest. There is persuasive evidence that a great many species exist, and go out of existence, in the tropical forests and other most vital habitats of the world without human beings ever being aware of them.

In this book I will examine briefly the scientific facts concerning extinction and the magnitude of the worldwide extinction threat today. I will highlight a major recent scientific breakthrough—the identification of a few ecologically significant regions, called biodiversity hotspots, within which most of the earth's species are concentrated—as the key to understanding and countering the threat to biodiversity. I will then set forth the first comprehensive published account of the legal protections now in place with regard to each of the most likely hotspots, and the efficacy of these safeguards, both internationally and nation by nation. Finally, I will propose a pathbreaking legal solution that could spell the difference between extinction and survival for untold multitudes of species in some of the ecologically richest yet most poorly understood regions on this planet.

The title of this book, *Ark of the Broken Covenant*, is an allusion with several layers of meaning. According to well-known ancient traditions, all life on earth was long ago preserved from a disastrous global extinction event by safeguarding representatives of each species on a single large boat, Noah's Ark. The biodiversity hotspots can be analogized to Noah's Ark, because collectively they represent the best chance we have to save not all, but a large number, of the world's living things by protecting them in the small enclaves in which they now seek refuge. If the Ark sinks, as is the current trend if the hotspots remain devoid of effective legal protection, the many species that depend on that literal/figurative lifeboat will die.

Ark has a second meaning as well. Another age-old tradition holds that a special container, called the Ark of the Covenant, was the repository for the commandments God had given to humankind. The Ark of the Covenant was considered to be of immense importance and was to be treated with the utmost reverence and respect. The hotspots may similarly be viewed, in the aggregate, as the vessel that holds perhaps the earth's greatest treasure—its living species. If there is a modern-day Ark of the Covenant, it is not any box of human making but rather the few handfuls of land where so much of life is confined.

The hotspots concept also embraces the idea of a global version of the Public Trust doctrine, that people have a duty to exercise responsible stewardship over the natural resources they own, possess, or use. The Public Trust doctrine implies that human beings are bound by an unwritten covenant—an agreement or contract of significance far beyond that of ordinary pacts—to take good care of the pieces of nature that come within our dominion and control. But the very fact that the hotspots are so small compared to their original size is powerful evidence that we, the people of the world, have broken that covenant. We have failed to be good stewards of the hotspots and have breached our duty to preserve them for the future. Far from revering, treasuring, and diligently guarding the hotspots, we have exploited them for our own temporary gain and allowed others to use them and abuse them to the brink of ruination.

The Noah's Ark of today is rapidly sinking. The 21st century Ark of the Covenant has been dropped, and we are the ones who dropped it. And the covenant all the world's people have inherited, to protect the myriad living things with which we share this planet, has been broken—by us. Thus, the hotspots are indeed the Ark of the Broken Covenant.

But the primary thesis of this book is that it is still not too late. This book brings a message of hope, not despair. Our modern, very real, living Noah's Ark can be repaired before it forever disappears into oblivion, despite the fact that we have been breaking our covenant until now. We can begin carrying our Ark of the Covenant with honor and respect. And we can commit ourselves to abiding by our mutually shared covenant, the global Public Trust, to treat the treasures of nature as something to save, not something to spend. It is with this mission of hope in mind that this book was written.

• 1 •

Extinction and the Biodiversity Hotspots

The world is now in the midst of a major extinction event, even a mass extinction. Many species are at risk, including numerous species unknown to humankind. To say the least, this is very bad news indeed. However, the primary thrust of this book is optimistic, in the sense that it is not too late. There is an opportunity to intervene in a focused, cost-effective way that could do much to ameliorate the situation, by directing our efforts at those relatively few threatened eco-regions, or hotspots, in which a disproportionate share of life on earth is concentrated.

In this chapter, I will briefly examine the current scientific thought on extinction, both in terms of its historical record and the causes and magnitude of the present-day extinction threat. I will then explore why we should care about the loss of species, particularly when we have never even given many of them a name. Finally, I will introduce the concept of the biodiversity hotspots and begin a discussion of why they could be a vital component of a comprehensive response to the modern extinctions taking place today.

Some of the material in this chapter will be rather heavy on the science side. I am presenting it in some detail for sake of completeness and to serve the interests of specialists who might want supporting documentation. For the average layperson, it will be sufficient if you glean the main points. It is not my intention to make you relive the disturbing mix of anxiety, confusion, and boredom you may have felt in your science classes back in high school or college, I assure you.

EXTINCTIONS THROUGH THE AGES

I do not intend to set forth an exhaustive, all-encompassing account of the massive scientific literature on the history of extinction, nor the nature and extent of the contemporary extinction event. Many entire books and scholarly journal articles have been devoted to these complex and difficult topics, and there are important areas within this field in which much scientific research remains to be done. I intend rather to offer a concise summary of some of the salient points on which modern science has come to some common understanding, and in so doing, to lay the foundation for the remainder of this book.

Extinction is, of course, a normal event in the life cycle of a species, much as death is a part of life for any individual organism. Some species persist much longer than others, just as the members of any group enjoy divergent life spans. This natural ebb and flow of life has always been an intrinsic element of the living planet.

It is when extinctions occur at a rate significantly higher than the normal or background level that something extraordinary is evidently at work. These events are known as "mass extinctions" (or "extinction spasms"), which have been defined, with deliberate vagueness, as the extinction of a significant proportion of the world's biota in a geologically insignificant period of time.[1]

It is generally accepted that there have been no fewer than five mass extinctions in the earth's history, at least during the Phanerozoic Eon (the vast expanse of time which includes the present day). These "big five" mass extinctions occurred at the boundaries between the following geological periods: Ordovician-Silurian (O-S); near the end of the Upper Devonian (D) (usually known as the Frasnian-Famennian events, or F-F); Permian-Triassic (P-Tr); Triassic-Jurassic (Tr-J); and Cretaceous-Tertiary (K-T).[2] In terms of millions of years ago (Mya), the mass extinctions have been placed at roughly 440 for O-S, 365 for F-F, 245 for P-Tr, 210 for Tr-J, and 66 for K-T,[3] with the mass extinctions taking place over a span of time ranging from less than 0.5 to as long as 11 million years.[4] There is some support for other mass or near-mass extinctions in addition to the big five, including events near the end of the Early Cambrian (about 512 Mya) and at the end of the Jurassic and Early Cretaceous, among several others.[5]

How much was biodiversity diminished during the mass extinctions? One estimate is that the following percentages of then-existing families, genera, and species, respectively, were lost during the big five. For the O-S, 26, 60, and 84–85; for F-F, 22, 57, and 79–83; for P-Tr, 51, 82, and 95; for Tr-J, 22, 53, and 79–80; and for K-T, 16, 47, and 70–76.[6] As can be seen from these data, and not surprisingly, mass extinctions claim a greater share of species than of higher taxa, in a predictable pattern. That is, the lower the taxonomic category, the more it was diminished, with species being reduced the most, and classes and phyla the least.[7] Also, there has been considerable selectivity in the mass extinctions, with some regions, for example, the tropics, and some taxa generally suffering more severely than others.[8]

It may be difficult for us to conceptualize the magnitude of the losses inflicted during the mass extinctions. The numbers alone cannot convey adequately the sweeping away of so many entire families of living things, let alone the lower taxa. When, in the end-Permian mass extinction, 51 percent of all families disappeared, and with them 95 percent of all species, there was an enormous setback for the biodiversity of that time that dramatically affected the whole future course of evolution. Yet, as we shall soon discuss, we who are alive today are able to witness for ourselves what a mass extinction looks like.

There are myriad aspects to the body of scientific thought germane to the phenomenon of mass extinctions, despite the fact that modern scientific study in this area began to any significant extent only in the 1950s and 1960s.[9] There are questions regarding the duration of the extinction spasms, and whether they occurred in multiple stages over a prolonged period or more or less in one large "pulse." Some seem to fit much better in the pulse category than others. Some may have been the result of one or more sudden catastrophic changes such as massive extraterrestrial impacts or volcanic eruptions, while others could be attributable to less dramatic, much more gradual shifts in global temperature, sea level, or other environmental factors.[10] There is also an intriguing debate concerning the periodicity of mass extinctions. Some researchers have noted that some, perhaps most, periods of heightened extinction rates (at least during the latest 250 million years) appear to follow a cycle, recurring roughly every 26 million years, but there has been considerable controversy over this point.[11] If this periodicity of mass extinctions is genuine, is it some bizarre coincidence on a grand scale, or is it linked to some recurring cause? Such issues represent fascinating aspects in the advances made by modern science regarding decidedly premodern phenomena, but I will not discuss them further here.

Of greatest significance to our purposes in this book is the cause or causes of these mass extinctions. If we can discern what brought about the destruction of such a large share of life on this planet during the great extinctions of the past, perhaps we can take steps to counteract any contemporary extinction spasm. At a minimum, we will be aware of the dangerous factors that can spur a mass extinction, and be alert for them.

Unfortunately, this is no small feat. It is a daunting piece of detective work indeed to identify with any degree of confidence the culprit or culprits responsible for the death of these myriad taxa so many millions of years ago. Various theories have been propounded, often challenged by alternative explanations and a great deal of intense scientific debate. It is sufficient for our purposes briefly to mention the possibilities most often discussed as causal factors for one or more of the mass extinctions. The following are the "usual suspects," keeping in mind that any particular mass extinction might have been sparked by more than one factor, or multiple incidents of the same factor acting in concert, possibly over an extended period of time. Additionally, the prior condition of the world and its biota might have been an important factor in determining the consequences of a particular stressor at a particular point in time.[12]

Bolide Impact

The high-velocity collision of large objects from beyond our own planet, such as meteors or comets, has been advanced in recent decades as a causal agent in some or even all mass extinctions and perhaps many other extinctions as well.[13] Although the theory is controversial and has been the subject of towering stacks of scholarly articles, there is substantial evidence that bolide impact significantly contributed to at least the K-T mass extinction.[14]

The theory is that one or more large bolide impacts may have thrown enormous quantities of dust into the atmosphere, generated huge tsunamis, and sparked massive wildfires, and the resulting smoke wrapped the surface of the earth in a silt layer laced with iridium and led to widespread and prolonged acid rain as well as significant alteration of the climate.[15] Climatic alteration could have been either global cooling, caused by the immense amounts of particulate matter and smoke shrouding the planet, or global warming, provoked by this shroud trapping heat in like a greenhouse.[16] Thus, in addition to the cataclysmic initial impact, which immediately would have devastated everything anywhere near the "strike zone," bolide impact would have caused much more global damage due to multiple secondary effects.

Volcanic Activity

Large-scale volcanic eruptions have also been proffered as a likely cause of some mass extinctions. Some phenomenally powerful eruptions are known to have occurred, such as the one in the center of northern Sumatra about 75,000 years ago that created a depression in the earth 65 kilometers long and blew out 1,000 cubic kilometers of solid material.[17] There are some similarities between the effects postulated from the largest eruptions and those mentioned in the context of bolide impact.

As in the case of an extraterrestrial strike, the destructive effects of the initial eruption—massive lava flow, wildfires, shock waves, and the like in the vicinity—may have been dwarfed by the secondary phenomena. Huge volcanic eruptions might have released large quantities of particulate matter as well as carbon dioxide and sulphur dioxide into the atmosphere, leading to acid rain, perhaps a period of global darkness, change in global temperature (probably warming due to increased carbon dioxide), and/or possibly oceanic anoxia/dysoxia brought about by global warming.[18] Such events, either alone or together with other factors, have been linked to the K-T event and, by some, to all post-Paleozoic mass extinctions.[19]

Climate Changes

Widespread warming or cooling is, of course, one of the effects thought to be generated by both bolide impact and volcanism and thus in some cases would not be the actual primal cause of the extinction but rather one of the secondary effects of the primal cause. However, it is possible that other factors may also be at least partially responsible for some of the historical perturbations in the planet's climate.

The most likely cause of most instances of global cooling during earth's history is continental drift, in which the world's land mass(es) moved, and sometimes split apart, carrying some habitats closer to the poles where extensive glaciation occurred.[20] High-latitude cooling could have caused the restriction of tropical fauna to more limited habitats and increased their risk of extinction, as in the O-S mass extinction.[21] Other instances of global cooling, such as might have been caused either by smoke or particulate matter blocking out the sun's light or by a drawdown of atmospheric carbon dioxide, could have virtually eliminated tropical habitats, as in the K-T and F-F events.[22]

Global warming, on the other hand, which is generally attributed to an increase in greenhouse gases such as carbon dioxide, may eliminate or greatly reduce polar habitats. Of more significance to the planet as a whole, global warming may also affect oceanic circulation and cause a decrease in the solubility of oxygen, thus leading to anoxia/dysoxia. For this reason, widespread warming has been considered an important factor spurring the O-S, P-Tr, and perhaps other mass extinctions.[23]

Marine Regression

It seems clear that there is a strong correlation between major declines in sea level and marine mass extinctions, as well as with the big five mass extinctions generally and perhaps others.[24] Particularly where a global drop in sea level has been rapid and large, a strong link to mass extinctions is evident from the fossil record. Some have argued that the shrinkage in the area of epicontinental sea habitat may have led to widespread extinction, as is typical for situations in which available habitat is drastically diminished.[25] However, there is support for the proposition that the key factor in some mass extinctions may have been less the falling sea levels than the reduction in habitat area provoked by the development of anoxic waters during the subsequent transgression.[26] That brings us to the last major cause of mass extinctions historically.

Anoxia

Anoxia, that is, significant lowering of the oxygen content in sea water, as during marine transgression when the sea level rises following a regression, is widely believed to be the primary cause of most marine extinctions. When anoxia prevails in shallow as well as deep waters, numerous extinctions are predictable. Anoxia leads, inter alia, to changes in nutrient levels (particularly reductions), and a collapse in marine productivity would cause many extinctions.[27] Evidence exists linking anoxia with most if not all of the major extinction spasms in the Phanerozoic Eon.[28] It is unclear, however, what the ultimate cause or causes of these great incidents of anoxia were; a possible link to global warming has been suggested.[29]

Clearly, these possible causes of mass extinction are not independent, nor are they mutually exclusive. There are links between and among them, in various combinations. For any particular mass extinction event, one or more of these factors may have been predominant, and multiple causes may have been significant. My main point here is to identify these as the chief factors that have been implicated in the great extinction spasms of the prehuman phase of the earth's history. We will now examine the situation today and discuss the likely causes of contemporary extinctions. In so doing, we will see the similarities and differences between the big five mass extinctions and the present circumstances.

ADDING TO THE BIG FIVE: A CONTEMPORARY MASS EXTINCTION?

It is extremely difficult to arrive at a satisfactory estimate of the magnitude of the current extinction crisis. One problem is that we know so little about life on earth today in the first place. If we do not know how many species exist, we cannot know precisely how many are ceasing to exist; respectable estimates as to the number of species now extant vary by an order of magnitude. Moreover, for many of the species we have identified, we know very little about their range, their habits, their life cycles, and other details important to an understanding of their health or risk status.

Although there is some scientific dispute, the most widely held view is that the earth is now in the midst of a mass extinction that rivals the great disappearances of ages past, that is, a sixth mass extinction.[30] According to this theory, the vast majority of species will be extinct long before scientists have even identified and named them.

In his seminal work on the extinction situation decades ago, renowned British ecologist Norman Myers of Oxford University hypothesized the current extinction crisis, primarily a result of habitat destruction and other human actions.[31] Myers warned that the world could soon suffer an "extinction spasm accounting for 1 million species." Tragically, his estimates may have been overly optimistic, as he himself now recognizes.[32] To put this in historical context, the background or natural rate of extinction has been estimated to average only a few species per million years for most taxonomic groups.[33]

Predictions of a contemporary mass extinction are generally derived by extrapolation. Larger, more well known species, such as mammals and birds, are more visible, more easily studied, and much more thoroughly identified and catalogued than most aquatic life-forms and invertebrates. Mammals and birds also are well represented in the fossil record, enabling scientists to craft better estimates of their historical extinction rates than with groups that do not lend themselves as well to fossilization.[34] Thus, mammals and birds can be used as indicators or proxies for other groups' extinction rates and histories, because they are

1. taxonomically relatively well known,[35]
2. easily observed, and
3. prominently etched in the fossil history.

Mammals and birds, however, constitute a small minority of the community of living things, both in terms of number of species and in terms of number of individuals. Invertebrates, particularly members of the phylum Arthropoda and, within it, the class Insecta, account for the vast majority of described species. Somewhat in excess of one million species of insects have been given scientific names.[36] Enormous as this total is, though, some have opined that this may amount to less than 10 percent of insect species, with particularly large numbers of unknown species presumed to reside in the tropics.[37]

It has been estimated that the ratio of unknown to known species may be as high as 21 to 1, with 30 million undescribed species versus the approximately 1.75 million that have been identified and taxonomically categorized by people.[38] Some biologists hold that the great majority of the species of insects, nematode worms, and fungi have yet to be discovered.[39] Although no one knows for certain, there seems to be an emerging scientific consensus that the total number of species on earth today is somewhere in the range of 7 to 13 million, with the best "rule of thumb" estimates centering on 10 million species, very roughly speaking.[40]

It is in the vast, largely unknown and unstudied shadows of the great tropical habitats and the oceans that many experts postulate both myriad unidentified species and the precipitous extinction thereof.[41] It is undisputed that, as one expert puts it, "Our ignorance of the natural world is enormous," and that, as we struggle with our response to the plight of our fellow organisms on this planet, "[i]f we do not even know who the players are, our understanding of how well they are playing is far more deficient."[42]

One reason there is no precise figure even for formally identified species is that there is no recognized single central register of names for described species across all taxonomic categories, nor a comprehensive and effective means of ascertaining whether a given species has previously been described by someone else.[43] Laypersons may be surprised to learn that there is no handy master list of our current species inventory, but when one considers the sheer numbers involved and the difficulty of cross-checking descriptions, it becomes quite understandable that this task remains on the global "to-do" list.

Even for the species we "know," we know very little about very many. Virtually nothing is known about most of the roughly 1.75 million "described" species other than the name someone has given them, where they were collected, and what they look like; there is a paucity of information relevant to assessing the role species play within their ecosystems.[44] Most of what we know falls into the realm of bean counting, such as totaling the number of species identified within each of the major taxonomic groups.[45] As to how many additional species still await identification, a variety of extrapolation factors have been proposed, with the aforementioned widely differing estimates of the total number of species on earth.[46]

So can we draw any reasonable conclusions as to the magnitude of the extinction threat today? The answer is yes. Two-time Pulitzer Prize winner Edward O. Wilson of Harvard summarized the contemporary extinction situation as follows:

In the small minority of groups of plants and animals that are well known, extinction is proceeding at a rapid rate, far above prehuman levels. In many cases the level is calamitous: the entire group is threatened.[47]

Wilson cited several examples and noted that, where we do have enough information to gain a clear picture of the current situation, we usually see extinction in progress.[48] But some skillful analysis is necessary to discern the true nature of the problem. It is possible selectively to consider certain data and reach very different conclusions from those drawn by Wilson and most other notable scientists as to the reality of the sixth extinction now in progress.

For example, the most recent list of species officially recognized by the widely respected International Union for Conservation of Nature and Natural Resources as having become extinct since the year 1600 contains the names of only 1,104 species.[49] If extinction rates are as high as many experts claim, the skeptics can ask why there is so little empirical evidence of actual as opposed to hypothetical or invisible extinctions?

One important point is that it is very difficult to determine when the last individual member of a species has died—a feat akin to proving a negative—and that for hosts of small and obscure species it is virtually impossible to monitor their fate, particularly when the species exist only within a remote, inaccessible wilderness.[50] Also, there can be a long lag time between the point at which a species becomes committed to extinction and the point at which it actually becomes extinct—a key point relevant to the ultimate effects of rampant habitat destruction.[51] In other words, a species may be given a death sentence by such pressures as habitat constriction, thereby condemned to death long before its ultimate extinction, and spend many years languishing on "death row." The "living dead" in this situation are not yet extinct but are irreversibly on the way there, a nonhuman variation of the "dead man walking" theme. I will discuss this again shortly in connection with the species-area curve.

Within the scientific community, there are multiple methods used to estimate the current extinction rate, and tremendous differences as to the results obtained. Depending on the assumptions, the benchmarks, the taxa focused on, and the data chosen, most experts have posited anywhere from 0.6 to 10 percent global species loss per decade, with some controversial estimates even higher.[52] Such wide variation in estimates has provided ample citation fodder for whichever point of view a person wishes to advocate, and some tendency for one camp or another to censor dissenting viewpoints. The spread of the "political correctness"[53] philosophy to the world of science is an unfortunate development, because an issue as serious as the current extinction problem desperately needs a full and free interchange of ideas and data if a workable solution is to be developed.[54]

One of the more widely accepted methods of estimating species loss is based on the theory of island biogeography, developed using data from actual islands. Given that many of the living and dying species are localized in the tropical rainforests and other remote areas, and thus do not lend themselves to ready observation, scientists are forced to use mathematical models based on the "species-area curve." To state the proposition very simply, this recognizes that each species needs a habitat in which to live, and a larger habitat can support more species than a smaller one.[55]

If we imagine each habitat as an island, to some extent separated from other habitats by such barriers as water, mountains, differing vegetation, or areas of human development, the living things on each island are in a very real sense contestants in a large-scale high-stakes game of *Survivor*, the popular television program. Which ones will be voted off the island? Which will win the latest immunity challenge? Who or what sits as a member of the tribal council and passes judgment on the next to be driven from survival to extinction? Island biogeography studies such questions and attempts to identify the factors that determine which (or how many) torches soon will be extinguished and which will remain burning for a while longer.

Island biogeography theory, among other things, has developed the formula that

$$S = CA^z$$

where S is the number of species, C is a constant, A is the area in the habitat, and the exponent z is another constant. The value of z varies according to the type of organisms involved and the distance between the habitat in question and other neighboring life-containing areas. It ranges among the various life-forms in the world from about 0.15 to 0.35, holding constant for a given group of organisms in a given location but changing when we consider a different group of organisms and/or a different location.[56] A general rule of thumb for the "area effect" is that a tenfold increase in habitat area will result in a doubling of the number of species; that is, the usual value of z is about 0.30.[57]

Extinction curves are calculated by inverting the relationship, that is, treating habitats of whatever type as "islands" and calculating what happens to species as the island shrinks. For purposes of the rule of thumb, this means that a 90 percent *loss* of habitat area in many cases would be expected to cause an eventual *reduction* of species in the area of roughly 50 percent.[58] I say "eventual" because it may take many years for species to die out entirely within a diminished habitat area. Survivors of some, even many, species will crowd into the remaining area and may doggedly persist there, clinging to survival in lowered numbers, for a long time. They are not now extinct, and thus are properly excluded from all lists of extinct species. But the fact that such species are not immediately driven into extinction may be only a comforting illusion. Once the number of individuals—especially, of course, reproductively capable individuals in an appropriate mix of males and females—falls beneath a certain level, the species is in grave danger of ultimate extinction. There is an impoverished gene pool, and there is less room to weather the inevitable seasons of drought, disease, violent storms, fires, floods, and many other destructive agents that would not cause the extinction of a more populous species.[59]

This phenomenon, in which rampant habitat destruction forces many species into a situation of inevitable but not immediate extinction, is especially insidious. Because the ultimate extinction of most species is postponed, perhaps for many years, people may be misled that all is well. But these species that are doomed to die—the "living dead"—*will* become extinct in due course, and by the time the actual extinctions commence in large numbers, it will be too late. Like an immense balloon payment on a mortgage that only comes due at the very end of a long period of living on borrowed time, we could be on the road to a deluge of dying species.

The area effect is important, whatever the precise values it yields in any individual instance, because it describes a problem central to the loss of biodiversity in the world today—habitat destruction. Habitat loss may initially cause few extinctions, and then many more as the last remnants of a particular habitat are destroyed. Thus, we may not observe the ultimate peak of the contemporary extinction event for decades.[60] Wilson and others have estimated that current rates of habitat destruction imply an eventual loss of approximately 30,000 species worldwide each year, a rate enormously higher than the typically accepted background rate of about 1 species lost per million years, and more than enough in terms of sheer numbers to qualify this as another mass extinction.[61] Indeed, even when deliberately selecting the most conservative scientifically justified parameters, carefully chosen to draw a *maximally optimistic* conclusion, Wilson calculates that the number of species currently doomed each year is 27,000, 74 each day, 3 each hour.[62]

That is what a mass extinction looks like. Ironically, although it is happening right now, most of these extinctions are invisible to us. In many cases we do not even know the species ever existed in the first place. They have been living, and are now dying out, beyond our view.

We will now consider habitat destruction and other factors usually associated with modern extinctions. A basic understanding of the primary threats to biodiversity today is a prerequisite to any intelligent attempt to intervene.

CAUSES OF CONTEMPORARY EXTINCTIONS

There is one obvious difference between the current extinction event and the mass extinctions of the past: Human beings are present and most definitely accounted for. Unlike the situation in the classic big five mass extinctions, *Homo sapiens* has no airtight alibi this time. Indeed, we are the prime suspect. The evidence indicates that we are doing an excellent job mimicking the devastation previously wrought by extraterrestrial impacts and titanic volcanic eruptions.[63] It is equally obvious that people, whatever our faults, have not brought about any latter-day catastrophic meteor strikes or epidemic in volcanism, nor have we managed to cause a dramatic drop in sea level. So how are we generating a modern sequel to the great disasters of earth's history?

Human beings are changing this planet in ways comparable to the cataclysmic events linked to the big five mass extinctions, but by what means? The actual triggering mechanisms may be less dramatic and less abrupt than some of the factors that brought about the big five, but the result is familiar. The main human-induced causes of the contemporary extinction crisis, in probable order of importance, are:

1. direct habitat destruction,
2. overexploitation/overkill, and
3. introduced or invasive species along with the diseases carried by these exotic animals and plants.[64]

These causes should not be thought of as unrelated. They may operate synergistically, combining their effects to drive species and populations to the brink of extinction and beyond.[65]

Habitat destruction—today's biodiversity enemy number one—includes deliberate deforestation or other harmful modification to make room for agriculture, grazing, mining, human habitation, roads, and other developmental activities. It also includes habitat degradation and deleterious alteration due to air and water pollution.[66] The species-area curve points to dire consequences of the phenomenal rate of habitat destruction attributed to modern human actions, as I mentioned in the previous section.

Prior to recent decades, overharvesting of biological resources, as in excessive hunting and fishing, was probably the chief means by which humans caused the extinction of other life-forms. There are many well-known examples, particularly of large animals and birds, that were hunted into oblivion, dating back perhaps to the Pleistocene.[67] But this generally is more limited than other extinction factors because it operates on purposefully selected species one at a time. Sometimes, a species hunted out of existence will take with it other species dependent on it that were not specifically targeted, but this phenomenon is still more limited than the degree of devastation wrought by habitat destruction, which sweeps out virtually all species in one giant, indiscriminate assault.

The third main human-linked cause of extinction is our introduction, whether intentional or accidental, of exotic species and all that accompanies them. Especially on islands and other isolated habitats, nonindigenous species can swiftly drive native species out of existence. They are sometimes called invasive species because their initial introduction into a previously unexploited habitat can indeed take on many of the features of a military invasion. The spread of the invasive species in the new habitat can be remarkably swift and extensive in the absence of natural predators or other controls that normally exist for native species, and the concomitant destruction of preexisting species can be equally precipitous. This can occur through the new species outcompeting the others; bringing new and devastating diseases with them (including diseases carried by humans themselves); and/or altering through their actions the habitat crucial for the survival of indigenous species.[68] The effect of the invasive nonindigenous species on native species is often rapid and horrific, as well as economically costly.[69]

Human beings may also be on the road to recreating another main cause of the big five mass extinctions, that is, climate alteration, especially global warming. Potentially, this could be more deadly than all of the other extinction drivers combined because of its effects on the entire planet and all habitats worldwide. The political and scientific controversies surrounding the contemporary global warming issue are both heated (sorry!) and well known, and it is not my aim to replicate them here. However, if events bear out some of the predictions of human-induced global warming through intense production of greenhouse gasses, we may be inadvertently reenacting a catastrophe of profound proportions.[70] In addition, human-induced acid rain and increased levels of UV-B radiation may have profound and wide-ranging effects on habitats and biodiversity.[71]

I should note that not all species are equally vulnerable to extinction, including mass extinctions.[72] Important for our purposes in this book is the fact that there are species that are perfectly well adapted to a specific niche, often in a narrow habitat range, which find themselves so locked in to their adaptations that they are unable to adjust when their habitat is altered. Because of their narrow survival strategy, these species might be considered biologically predisposed to extinction, although they may survive indefinitely if their niche is undisturbed.[73] There are many examples of situations in which adaptations that were phenomenally successful in filling a particular ecological niche suddenly become maladaptive in the wake of human interactions with that niche.[74]

Habitat restriction, such as where a species is endemic to a particularly limited region, can greatly increase a species' vulnerability to extinction.[75] When the geographic range of a species contracts, the members are crowded into a less diverse area that is more prone to natural disaster and human-made alteration. There is also intensified competition for scarce resources, and for mates. And aside from the simple interrelationship of species and area, the nature of the lost areas is important. As habitat is fragmented, smaller remnants will in some cases be incapable of supporting the requisite diversity of life-forms, and a domino effect of local extinctions, known as faunal collapse, may result.[76] I will return later to the subject of endemism and discuss its role in the current biodiversity crisis, but first we should devote some attention to answering the question, "So what?"

THE IMPORTANCE OF SAVING SPECIES

In a world dominated by humans, in which the needs of humans are, not surprisingly, seen as preeminent by most members of that species, it is important to examine the question of why we should be concerned with the extinction of other life-forms.[77] Before they can be convinced to do anything to intervene, people will need to understand what benefits they can expect to derive from the bargain. The reasons for humans to attempt to prevent the extinction of other creatures can be bundled into four main categories, each of which subsumes considerable complexity:

1. present practical value;
2. potential future practical value;
3. intangible value; and
4. moral duty.

I will summarize each of these briefly.

First, many species of plants and animals currently provide *Homo sapiens* with a variety of tangible, practical benefits of real and immediate value to people.[78] A host of domesticated animals and crop plants are obvious examples, directly supplying nutrients for the human diet. People can derive this nutrition directly, by consuming all or part of the plant or animal itself, or indirectly, by eating substances produced by the plant or animal, such as eggs, milk, honey, fruit, grains, vegetables, and foods made therefrom. In addition to food, plants and animals are the producers of essentials such as cotton, wool, silk, leather, wood, paper, dyes, and their ancillary commodities. However, only 20 species provide 90 percent of the global food supply today, and three species (corn, wheat, and rice) contribute more than half of the total. Countless other species, currently known or unknown, could perhaps "be bred or provide genes to increase production in deserts, saline flats and other marginal habitats" to feed the world's expanding population in the future.[79]

Plants are the source of many medicinal drugs, and about half of all prescription drugs in the United States come from wild organisms, of a total value estimated to exceed $14 billion per year.[80] Our antibiotics, anticancer agents, painkillers, and blood thinners have been derived thus far from only a few hundred species, leaving the biochemistry and genetic components of millions of other species unexplored and untapped as a potentially colossal reservoir of new medicines and healing agents. Why? According to Edward O. Wilson,

The reason is to be found in the principles of evolutionary biology. Caught in an endless arms race, these species have devised myriad ways to combat microbes and cancer-causing runaway cells. We have scarcely begun to consult them for the experience stored in their genes.[81]

The role of animals in medical and other scientific research has been of inestimable worth, and largely the contribution of such otherwise insignificant or despised creatures as the common mouse, rat, and fruit fly.[82] Less obvious but still practical benefits come from creatures that facilitate the production of other plants or animals that in turn are consumed or otherwise used. This includes a vast array of insects, which pollinate many flowering plants, including fruit-bearing varieties, and which are the primary food source for many birds; it also includes annelids (earthworms) and other burrowing organisms, which similarly play an unobtrusive yet vital role in aerating soil, making it suitable for producing plant life.

Ecological benefits conferred by living things are sometimes overlooked by laypersons but are of paramount importance.[83] In addition to all of the human-centered practical reasons for preserving species as individual species, there are tangible synergistic benefits produced by species interactions on an ecosystem level. The concept of "ecosystem services" is fairly new, but several enormously significant examples have been identified.[84] These include the decomposition and detoxification of organic matter and other wastes, which is mostly performed by the smallest, least charismatic organisms in any ecosystem—the living things we might call the "enigmatic microfauna" to distinguish them from the famous "charismatic megafauna" that often attract most of our attention.[85] Without the microorganisms and insects that effectuate the decomposition process for organic material, the world would quickly be buried in its own waste. Other examples are generation and renewal of soil, mitigation of floods, purification of air and water, and partial stabilization of climate.[86] Some commentators place an extremely high value on these and other ecosystem services.[87]

Among the most fundamental of ecosystem services is the photosynthetic process of most plants, which not only fixes, or converts, solar energy into usable nutrients but also converts carbon dioxide into oxygen, literally the life-breath of our species. And the exquisitely intricate natural system of checks and balances by which various species keep one another's populations, including those of pest and disease-causing organisms, within manageable limits is far more effective and safe than any pesticide program.[88]

Most previously identified species that provide obvious, practical benefits to humans are not in danger of extinction. In fact, many are actively safeguarded, raised, cultivated, and otherwise managed to maximize their productivity. There have been some cases of overharvesting of such species, but for the most part this type of species is safe due to our own self-interest. Of course, this presupposes that humans have

1. discovered the species and
2. learned of the benefits the species has to offer.

In the case of the postulated myriad unidentified species inhabiting the world, neither of these presuppositions pertains.

The species that are less ostentatious about their value to people, moreover, may be even less fortunate. In some cases, for example, it is not even known which species of insects pollinate which useful plants, or which species are depended on by birds, fish, and other creatures for their sustenance, so humans may destroy or allow the destruction of these insects without realizing the consequences.

A second basic reason for humans to preserve species is that they may have potential *future* practical value to people. New uses are continually being discovered for living things as technology advances and science progresses, often transforming apparently inconsequential species into valuable assets.[89] By definition, of course, it is impossible to know which or how many species fall into this category at any point in time. But it should be evident that modern technology and research methods are powerful tools for unleashing the power of helpful genies (and genes) from the most unassuming, unlikely magic lamps. Given some of the important benefits now being derived from uncharismatic and previously unimportant species, it would be wise to preserve as many as possible to provide future investigators with the raw material for their experiments.[90]

The value of all of the unknown species must fall into this category, other than the ecosystem services many of them undoubtedly perform without our knowledge. Until we discover any particular species, we cannot hope to discern any practical use for it. The vertiginously high numbers of unknown species thought to exist today, with most credible estimates holding that between 3 million and 12 million species still are hidden from us, should be enough to move any rational utility-maximizing person to invest in their discovery and study. We have glimpsed some of the immense value derived from the species we already know. There may well be unimaginable treasures hidden in those countless nameless species, waiting like a vast collection of magic lamps for someone to find them and learn their secrets.

Each living species can be viewed as the end product of countless years of research and development, the culmination of eons of experimentation in nature's laboratory. As Wilson has stated, "each species of higher organism is richer in information than a Caravaggio painting, Bach fugue, or any other great work of art."[91] Each species represents a successful set of strategies for meeting some of life's challenges and threats. Much can be learned from the collective experience of these myriad generations in assisting people with their own problems. And with the advent of genetic engineering, wherein it is increasingly possible to transfer genetic material from one taxonomic group to another (even across the kingdom barrier) to confer previously lacking biological traits (such as greater productivity, reduced need for water, increased hardiness, and natural resistance to disease and insect pests), each species is potentially a significant genetic resource. This genetic wealth, in millions of different forms, could be as vital in tomorrow's society as wood and paper in today's.[92]

In addition to the unknown species, it is possible, even probable, that some currently known but "insignificant" species could take on a crucial role in the ecosystems of the future.[93] For example, wild relatives of current crop species can be an invaluable source of genetic diversity in the event the monoculture-cultivated plants fall prey to disease or other environmental conditions. And if environmental conditions change, through global warming, increased pollution, or other habitat alterations, some other species may possess traits that will prove preadapted to these new circumstances. Some species that occupy key positions in today's ecosystems may be unable to adapt, and unless other species are available to fill their niche, the ecosystems may suffer catastrophic degradation. The redundancy provided for by millions of years of natural selection cannot be fully understood and appreciated unless and until it is needed.[94] It is not necessarily the large, obvious life-forms that play these pivotal roles; in fact, the "lower" levels of the food web are the foundation upon which all other components of each ecosystem depend.[95]

The biosphere that is the planet Earth may be conceptualized as an exceedingly complex "computer program" with millions of parts, each of which is evolving. It would be foolish indeed to destroy, or to allow the destruction of, the program's codes, because we do not and cannot know their importance, whether at present or in some unforeseeably altered world of the future. Extinction shuts doors and deprives us forever of the option to discover value in that which we previously found valueless.[96]

A corollary of this is the principle that some species may be valuable precisely because they are endangered or threatened. A particularly vulnerable species within a given habitat may someday provide an early warning signal that there are problems that may eventually affect far more species. This has been termed the "canary in the mine" syndrome.[97] For such species, their strength is in their weakness.

A third main reason to preserve species is their intangible value. Although less practical, and less susceptible to reduction to a dollars-and-cents bottom line, there is real wealth in living things. Many people find great beauty in nature, and nowhere else is the maxim more true that beauty is in the eye of the beholder.[98] Depending on one's individual preferences, species as diverse as a house cat, a fern, a goldfish, a beetle, and a paramecium can be works of art, supplying emotional sustenance. Entire industries are tailored for the loyal human aficionados of these living art forms.[99]

Certain species also serve symbolic functions, for nations, states, schools, sports teams, and other organizations. In this capacity, they tend to inspire and motivate the members of the human organizations, as the symbol of their majesty, courage, power, or speed. From the grandeur of our national bird, the American bald eagle, to the questionable yet strangely appropriate imagery of the bear cub as symbol of Chicago's National League professional baseball team,[100] species represent a spectrum of attributes to which humans aspire.

Other life-forms also have intangible value as educational tools and entertainment sources. The persistent popularity of zoos, circuses, and televised nature programs is evidence of the deep-seated fascination other species hold for their human admirers. Indeed, other species can be viewed as a living history, available for study by people and a source of inspiration. Similar to the satisfaction many persons derive from the study of their own genealogy, tracing the roots of their lineage, an appreciation for humanity's place in the family tree of all earth's life-forms can be very fulfilling.

Finally, fourth, and least pragmatic, is the *moral duty* not to exterminate our fellow passengers on the spaceship that is this planet.[101] With its origins at least as ancient as the biblical injunction to "replenish" the earth as its caretakers,[102] this moral duty has strong precedential support. Although most people accept the propriety of human use of other species for food, clothing, and other purposes, they likely would draw the line at exploiting these species into extinction. If nothing else, this smacks of killing the proverbial goose that laid the golden egg. On a higher plane, it places an upper limit on our freedom to exploit other living things.

The moral duty may be seen as an obligation to refrain from "murdering" another species in its entirety because that species has in some sense a right to exist. Additionally, people may want to preserve other species as a living legacy for their children and grandchildren, feeling it is wrong to deprive posterity of a heritage their own ancestors had passed down to them. For many, this sense may be confined to certain particularly renowned and beloved species such as the tiger, or bald eagle, or panda. For others, there may be a more encompassing notion that we need to preserve as much as we can of the world we inherited and hand it on to the next generation in turn, undiminished—that we have no right to remove entirely any other species from this planet we all share.

Taken alone or together, the reasons outlined above provide powerful justification for the cause of preserving species. Whether one is motivated solely by immediate self-interest, long-term self-interest, sentiment, altruism, or moral imperative, or by some concatenation of these, the answer to the question "So what?" is clear. It is important to preserve biodiversity, perhaps more important than anything else.[103] It is unimaginably costly not to do so.

THE BIODIVERSITY "HOTSPOTS" AND THE CURRENT MASS EXTINCTION

Many of the unknown species, as well as many of the ones previously identified, are now widely believed to be concentrated in what has been termed "hotspots." These hotspots are pockets of nature that contain multitudinous species, including many rare and endangered species found nowhere else, that have also been threatened to a significant degree by human activities. Thus, the hotspots are "hot" not only because they contain so much unique biodiversity but also because they are at risk and are urgently in need of protection. They are where the action is in the current mass extinction.

Norman Myers introduced the threatened biodiversity hotspots concept in two groundbreaking papers published in 1988[104] and 1990.[105] Myers recognized that a modest number of hotspot regions, which occupy only a small (and ever shrinking) total land area—most often, but not always, in tropical forest areas—account for an exceedingly high percentage of global biodiversity and an amazing degree of species endemism. He selected vascular plants as the primary indicators of overall biodiversity within a region, supplemented with data from other taxa, where available.

Another illustrious early proponent of the hotspots concept is Edward O. Wilson. Wilson has written,

From the coastal sage of California to the rainforests of West Africa, the hottest of the terrestrial hotspots occupy only 1.4% of the world's land surface yet are the exclusive home of more than a third of the terrestrial plant and vertebrate species. Similarly, from the streams of Appalachia to the Philippine coral reefs, aquatic hotspots occupy a tiny fraction of the shallow water surface.[106]

Wilson also indicates that the tropical rainforests are believed by some biologists to harbor more than half of the world's species.[107] Indeed, from these "natural greenhouses" many world records of biodiversity have been reported, including 425 species of trees in a single hectare of Brazil's Atlantic forest and 1,300 butterfly species from one corner of the Manu National Park in Peru.[108] This astonishing profusion of diverse life-forms within very small geographical confines illustrates the importance of preserving hotspots, my own proposal for which I will cover subsequently in this book in the last two chapters.

Because the hotspots sustain such an extraordinary concentration of species, including very likely large numbers of species unknown to humankind, I have used this idea to formulate a phrase that appears in various parts of this book—a phrase that I hope helps people to conceptualize what the hotspots are as well as their importance. If the hotspots are the small but vital portions of the earth in which so many species are nurtured, including so many new to us, then it is quite appropriate to call the hotspots the "womb of the unknown species."

There is a viscerally satisfying parallel between the phrase "womb of the unknown species" and the well-known "tomb of the unknown soldier." Just as the tomb of the unknown soldier contains the remains of unidentified American soldiers who died in various wars, the hotspots are both the womb and, potentially, the tomb for species we cannot call by name even as we kill them. The unidentified species the hotspots harbor are, like the identity of the unknown soldiers, "known but to God." And just as the tomb of the unknown soldier pays homage to individuals to whom the United States owes its freedom, the womb of the unknown species is emblematic of the ineffable importance the hosts, indeed probably millions, of nameless species may have for life in all the nations of the world. But how can we know the unknown species? How can we determine how many species exist, or are at risk, or what their significance might be? Is there any way to eliminate or reduce the scientific uncertainty that, in part, has prevented meaningful legal protection for so much of the biodiversity on this planet?

As discussed earlier, there is contemporary scientific debate concerning the number of known species, the number of species yet to be discovered, and the magnitude of the current extinction crisis. There are persistent problems of too few taxonomists and ecologists, too little funding, and too low a priority, whether political or scientific, to make much of a dent in the task of resolving these questions.[109] The basic question of how many species exist on earth will remain wide open to divergent opinions, based as much on conjecture as on empirical evidence. Unavoidably, then, any estimates of what fraction of living species is or will soon be going extinct cannot be very precise, because the denominator is itself to some extent a product of guesswork, more or less educated as the case may be. Whatever the numbers, the hotspots are the focal point of much of the concern. Therefore, in the next chapter, I will delve into the hotspots in more detail.

NOTES

1. A. HALLAM and P.B. WIGNALL, MASS EXTINCTIONS AND THEIR AFTERMATH, 1 (Oxford, 1997) (hereinafter MASS EXTINCTIONS). An alternative definition is any substantial increase in the amount of extinction suffered by more than one geographically widespread higher taxon during a relatively short interval of geological time, resulting in at least temporary decline in their standing diversity. *Id.* (citing Sepkoski).

2. *See, e.g.*, Eric Buffetaut, *The Relevance of Past Mass Extinctions to an Understanding of Current and Future Extinction Processes*, 82 Palaeogeography, Palaeoclimatology, Palaeoecology 169, 171 (1990). *See also* M.J. Benton, *Diversification and Extinction in the History of Life*, 268 Science 52 (Apr. 7, 1995).

3. *See* EDWARD O. WILSON, THE DIVERSITY OF LIFE, 29 (Belknap, Harvard 1992).

4. *See* Douglas H. Erwin, *The End and the Beginning: Recoveries from Mass Extinctions*, Tree 344, 347 (Table 1), vol. 13, no. 9 (Sept. 1998). Of course, the fossil record does not permit us to pinpoint the duration of such distant events, and there is considerable imprecision in these estimates.

5. Buffetaut, *supra* note 2, at 171. *See* J.J. Sepkoski, *Phanerozoic Overview of Mass Extinctions*, 277–95, in PATTERNS AND PROCESSES IN THE HISTORY OF LIFE (D.M. Raup and D. Jablonski, eds., Springer-Verlag, 1986) for a discussion of many of the noted extinction spasms in addition to the big five.

6. MASS EXTINCTIONS, *supra* note 1, at 4 (Table 1.1). Living things, of course, are classified taxonomically into the following major groupings, or taxa, listed in order from the broadest/highest to the narrowest/lowest: kingdom, phylum, class, order, family, genus, and species.

7. Wilson, *supra* note 3, at 191.

8. David Jablonski, *Mass Extinctions: Persistent Problems and New Directions*, Geological Society of America Special Paper 307, 3–4 (1996).

9. MASS EXTINCTIONS, *supra* note 1, at 3–4. *See, e.g.*, N.D. Newell, *Paleontological Gaps and Geochronology*, 36 Journal of Paleontology 592–610 (1962); D.M. Raup and J.J. Sepkoski, *Mass Extinction in the Marine Fossil Record*, 215 Science 1501–3 (1982).

10. *See* Erwin, *supra* note 4, Table 1.

11. Much has been written on the periodicity issue, and various intervals have been posited during the decades-long debate about the correct period between major extinction events (including more than the big five), ranging from about 32 million years to less than 26 million years. Several scholars have questioned the validity of the concept itself and/or suggested that it is an artifact of various factors rather than a genuine phenomenon. *See, e.g.*, D.M. Raup and J.J. Sepkoski, *Periodicity of Extinctions in the Geologic Past*, 81 Proceedings of the National Academy of Sciences USA, 801–5 (1982); D.M. Raup and J.J. Sepkoski, *Periodic Extinctions of Families and Genera*, 231 Science 833–6 (1986); A. Hoffman, *Patterns of Family Extinction Depend on Definition and Geological Time-Scale*, 315 Nature 659–62 (1985); M.J. Benton, *Diversification and Extinction in the History of Life*, 268 Science 52–8 (1995); MASS EXTINCTIONS, *supra* note 1, at 4–12.

12. *Id.* at 3.

13. For the more extreme view as to the importance of bolide impact as a cause of extinction events, *see generally*, D.M. RAUP, EXTINCTION: BAD LUCK OR BAD GENES?

(W.W. Norton, 1991). For evidence of large craters evidently caused by bolide impact during the Phanerozoic Eon, *see* R.A.F. Grieve, *Terrestrial Impact Structures,* 15 Annual Reviews of Earth and Planetary Sciences 245–70 (1987).

14. MASS EXTINCTIONS, *supra* note 1, at 243.

15. Wilson, *supra* note 3, at 25–30.

16. *Id.* at 26.

17. *Id.* at 24–25.

18. MASS EXTINCTIONS, *supra* note 1, at 245.

19. *Id.* at 245–46.

20. *See* Wilson, *supra* note 3, at 31. Drifting of the original supercontinent, Pangaea, or portions thereof may have caused some of the mass extinctions. *Id.*

21. *Id. See* MASS EXTINCTIONS, *supra* note 1, at 247.

22. MASS EXTINCTIONS, *supra* note 1, at 246–47.

23. *Id.* at 247–48.

24. *See generally* A. HALLAM, PHANEROZOIC SEA-LEVEL CHANGES (Columbia, 1992).

25. N.D. Newell, *Revolutions in the History of Life,* 89 Geological Society of America Special Paper, 63–91 (1967).

26. MASS EXTINCTIONS, *supra* note 1, at 250.

27. Of course, catastrophic reduction in nutrient supplies is one of the most important secondary effects of all of the major causes of mass extinctions. *See* Ronald E. Martin, *Catastrophic Fluctuations in Nutrient Levels as an Agent of Mass Extinction: Upward Scaling of Ecological Processes?* 405–29, in BIODIVERSITY DYNAMICS: TURNOVER OF POPULATIONS, TAXA, AND COMMUNITIES (Michael L. McKinney and James A. Drake, eds., Columbia, 1998).

28. MASS EXTINCTIONS, *supra* note 1, at 250–51.

29. *See* H.C. Jenkyns, *Cretaceous Anoxia Events: From Continents to Oceans,* 137 Journal of the Geological Society of London, 171–88 (1980). *See also* R.V. TYSON, SEDIMENTARY ORGANIC MATTER (Chapman & Hall, 1995); P.B. WIGNALL, BLACK SHALES (Oxford, 1994).

30. *See, e.g.,* Wilson, *supra* note 3, at 243–80; Niles Eldredge, *Cretaceous Meteor Showers, the Human Ecological "Niche," and the Sixth Extinction,* 1–15, in EXTINCTIONS IN NEAR TIME: CAUSES, CONTEXTS, AND CONSEQUENCES, 2 (Ross D.E. MacPhee, ed., Kluwer, 1999); Christopher Humphries, Paul Williams, and Richard Vane-Wright, *Measuring Biodiversity Value for Conservation,* 26 Annual Review of Ecology and Systematics 93, 94 (1995); Paul Ehrlich, *Extinction: What Is Happening Now and What Needs to be Done,* in DYNAMICS OF EXTINCTION, 157 (David Elliott, ed. 1986); Stuart L. Pimm and Thomas M. Brooks, *The Sixth Extinction: How Large, How Soon, and Where?,* in NATURE AND HUMAN SOCIETY: THE QUEST FOR A SUSTAINABLE WORLD, 46–62 (Peter Raven, ed., NRC 1997).

31. *See generally,* NORMAN MYERS, THE SINKING ARK: A NEW LOOK AT THE PROBLEM OF DISAPPEARING SPECIES (1979). *See also* THE GLOBAL 2000 REPORT TO THE PRESIDENT: ENTERING THE TWENTY-FIRST CENTURY 37 (1980), which projected the extinction of between 0.5 and 2 million species (considered by the authors to amount to 15 to 20 percent of all species on earth) by the year 2000, mostly as a result of habitat destruction, but also in part because of pollution. This mass extinction was described as without precedent in human history. The authors hypothesized that insects, other invertebrates, and plant species, many of which are unclassified and unexamined by scientists, would bear the brunt of the losses.

32. Norman Myers, *The Biodiversity Outlook: Endangered Species and Endangered Ideas*, in SOCIAL ORDER AND ENDANGERED SPECIES PRESERVATION, xxviii–xxix (J.F. Shogren and J. Tschirart, eds., Cambridge, 2001) (arguing that we are already in the midst of a major mass extinction, even by conservative estimates).

33. David Jablonski, *Mass Extinctions: New Answers, New Questions* in THE LAST EXTINCTION, 43–61 (Les Kaufman et al., ed. 1986).

34. Ehrlich, *supra* note 30, at 158–9.

35. Occasionally, previously unknown species of mammals or birds are discovered even today. For example, during the 1960s, a small population of an undescribed species of cat was found on the island of Iriomote, near Okinawa. *Id.* And four species of mammals have recently been discovered in the remote Annamite Mountains along the border between Vietnam and Laos, including a large cowlike animal called a saola or spindlehorn. Edward O. Wilson, *Vanishing Before Our Eyes*, Time, April–May 2000, at 29–30. Generally, though, the size and diurnal lifestyle of most mammals and birds makes it less likely that they can exist without being detected by humans.

36. Nigel E. Stork, *The Magnitude of Global Biodiversity and Its Decline*, in THE LIVING PLANET IN CRISIS: BIODIVERSITY SCIENCE AND POLICY, at 7 (Joel Cracraft and Francesca T. Grifo, eds. 1999) (hereinafter LIVING PLANET).

37. Ehrlich, *supra* note 30, at 158–9.

38. Wilson, *supra* note 35, at 34.

39. *Id. See* Edward O. Wilson, *The Current State of Biological Diversity*, in BIODIVERSITY 3–18 (1988).

40. For some recent estimates, *see, e.g.*, Robert M. May, *The Dimensions of Life on Earth*, in NATURE AND HUMAN SOCIETY: THE QUEST FOR A SUSTAINABLE WORLD, 30–45 (Peter Raven, ed., NRC 1997) (estimating 7 million species worldwide, with a range from 5 to 15 million plausible); Stork, *supra* note 36, at 10–21 (employing various factors, taxon by taxon, in arriving at a rough estimate of 13.4 million species); Paul Williams, Kevin Gaston, and Chris Humphries, *Mapping Biodiversity Value Worldwide: Combining Higher-Taxon Richness from Different Groups*, 264 Proceedings of the Royal Society, Biological Sciences 141–148 (1997) (crediting an estimate of 13.5 million species); Humphries, et al., *supra* note 30, at 94–5 (accepting a range of 5–15 million species); T. Erwin, *Tropical Forests: Their Richness in Coleoptera and Other Arthropod Species*, 36 Coleopt. Bull. 74–75 (1982); Benton, *supra* note 2; P.M. Hammond, *The Current Magnitude of Biodiversity*, in GLOBAL BIODIVERSITY ASSESSMENT, 113–28 (V.H. Heywood, ed., Cambridge, 1995) (estimating 12 million species total); Norman Myers, *Questions of Mass Extinction*, 2 Biodivers. & Conserv. 2–17 (1993) (mentioning several estimates and concluding that we can be fairly certain that there are at least 10 million species today).

41. *Id.*

42. Hunter, *Coping with Ignorance: The Coarse-Filter Strategy for Maintaining Biodiversity*, in BALANCING ON THE BRINK OF EXTINCTION, 266–7 (Kathryn Kohm ed. 1991).

43. Stork, *supra* note 36, at 6–9.

44. *See* J. Lawton, *On the Behaviour of Autecologists and the Crisis of Extinction*, 67 Oikos 3–5 (1993); R. Vane-Wright, C. Smith, and P. Williams, *What to Protect? Systematics and the Agony of Choice*, 55 Biol. Conserv. 235, 251 (1991) (mentioning the order-of-magnitude uncertainty as to the global number of species and the dearth of information as to the species already described).

45. Stork, *supra* note 36, at 21. For example, humans have described roughly the following numbers of species at present: 1,000,000 insects; 300,000 algae; 75,000 arachnids; 70,000 fungi; 70,000 molluscs; and, for all vertebrates, i.e., chordates combined, 45,000. *Id.*

46. *Id.*

47. Wilson, *supra* note 3, at 255 (emphasis in the original).

48. *Id* at 255–59.

49. Stork, *supra* note 36, at 25.

50. *Id.*

51. *Id. See* V.H. Heywood et al., *Uncertainties in Extinction Rates*, 368 Nature 105 (1994).

52. Stork, *supra* note 36, at 24, Table 1.9. The lowest generally accepted number is about 1 percent loss per decade; when applied even to the approximately 1.75 million currently identified species, this amounts to the extinction of at least 17,500 species per decade. This is certainly enough to constitute a major crisis. And if one allows for the existence of additional unidentified species, perhaps in large numbers, and perhaps somewhat more than 1 percent loss per decade, the figures quickly become far more alarming.

53. The political correctness movement's influence has become so pervasive that I almost felt compelled to avoid the use of conceivably judgmental or anthropocentric terms such as "animal" or "lower life-forms" in this book. However, my favorite politically correct euphemisms, "differently speciated" and "evolutionarily challenged," have yet to gain popular acceptance.

54. For additional discussion of the extinction controversy, *see* Richard Tobin, The Expendable Future: U.S. Politics and the Protection of Biological Diversity 2–4 (1990); Thomas Lovejoy, *Species Leave the Ark One by One*, in The Preservation of Species: The Value of Biological Diversity 13–16 (Bryan Norton, ed. 1986).

55. *See, e.g.*, S.L. Pimm et al., *Bird Extinctions in the Central Pacific*, in Extinction Rates, at 75–97 (J.H. Lawton and R.M. May, eds. 1995) (suggesting that 50 percent or more of the bird species on many Pacific islands are missing, endangered, extinct, or known only from bones).

56. Wilson, *supra* note 3, at 221, 277.

57. *Id.*

58. *Id.*

59. *Id.* at 278–80. *See* Thomas Brooks, Stuart Pimm, and Joseph Oyugi, *Time Lag between Deforestation and Bird Extinction in Tropical Forest Fragments*, 13 Conserv. Biol. 1140–50 (1999).

60. *See* Stuart L. Pimm and Peter Raven, *Extinction by Numbers*, 403 Nature 843 (24 Feb. 2000).

61. Eldredge, *supra* note 30, at 2. *But see* Buffetaut, *supra* note 2, at 172–73 for the proposition that, to qualify as a true mass extinction, there should be a global cause, akin to bolide impact, and that thus far, human-generated extinctions have been of local dimension, albeit numerous . . . unless one considers the ultimate cause of contemporary extinctions to be the appearance of *Homo sapiens* itself.

62. Wilson, *supra* note 3, at 280. *See also* Andy Purvis, et al., *Nonrandom Extinction and the Loss of Evolutionary History*, 288 Science 328–30 (Apr. 14, 2000). (Stating that current and projected extinction rates exceed geologically normal background

rates by several orders of magnitude and constitute an extinction episode equivalent to the mass extinctions of the paleontological past.) *Accord*, Russell Lande, *Genetics and Demography in Biological Conservation*, 241 Science 1455 (16 Sept. 1988); Stuart Pimm et al., *The Future of Biodiversity*, 269 Science 347 (Jul. 21, 1995).

63. Eldridge, *supra* note 30, at 4. (Terming the contemporary situation as the "sixth extinction," i.e., worthy to be placed alongside the big five mass extinctions.)

64. *Id. See* Wilson, *supra* note 3, at 253–54; Stuart L. Pimm, *Extinction*, in CONSERVATION SCIENCE AND ACTION, 20, 29–30 (William J. Sutherland, ed., 1998) (stressing the importance of introduction of alien species as well as habitat loss as leading causes of contemporary extinctions); Russell Lande, *Anthropogenic, Ecological, and Genetic Factors in Extinction*, in CONSERVATION IN A CHANGING WORLD: INTEGRATING PROCESSES INTO PRIORITIES FOR ACTION, 29–51 (G. Mace, A Balmford, and J. Ginsberg, eds., Cambridge University Press, 1998) (discussing how the main anthropogenic factors interact disastrously with other factors not directly related to human activities to cause "extinction vortices.").

65. Myers, *supra* note 40, at 7–9.

66. Wilson, *supra* note 3, at 253–54. Wilson cites IUCN data for the proposition that habitat destruction has been an important factor in over 90 percent of recent cases of species imperilment.

67. Eldredge, *supra* note 30, at 4–5.

68. *Id.* at 5. *See* I. Atkinson, *Introduced Animals and Extinctions*, in CONSERVATION FOR THE TWENTY-FIRST CENTURY, 54–69 (D. Western and M. Pearl, eds., Oxford, 1989); R.D.E. MacPhee and P.A. Marx, *The 40,000-Year Plague: Humans, Hyperdisease, and First-Contact Extinctions*, 169–217, in NATURAL CHANGE AND HUMAN IMPACT IN MADAGASCAR (S. Goodman and B. Patterson, eds., Smithsonian, 1997).

69. *See* David Pimentel et al., *Environmental and Economic Costs of Nonindigenous Species in the United States*, 50 Bioscience 53–65 (2000) (estimating the annual environmental damage and losses caused by the approximately 50,000 nonindigenous species in the United States as $50 billion).

70. Wilson, *supra* note 3, at 271–72.

71. Myers, *supra* note 40, at 11–12.

72. Michael L. McKinney, *Extinction Vulnerability and Selectivity: Combining Ecological and Paleontological Views*, 28 Annu. Rev. Ecol. Syst. 495–516 (1997) (extensively discussing traits that promote extinction vulnerability, including specialized diet, large body size, high trophic level, low fecundity, limited mobility, slow growth/development, and migratory habits, inter alia; specialization/narrow adaptation is arguably the most fundamental factor).

73. Humphrey, *How Species Become Vulnerable to Extinction and How We Can Meet the Crises*, in ANIMAL EXTINCTIONS, 9–12 (R.J. Hoage, ed. 1985).

74. Examples include a population of about 35,000 gray bats (*Myotis grisescens*) in a cave in Tennessee. These specialized creatures require a summer habitat in which they can forage over water bodies for aquatic insects. This renders them vulnerable to water-quality problems in their cave, which could diminish or poison their summer food supply. Another adaptive/maladaptive trait is large body size. Although effective in deterring predators in the wild, such size carries with it the requirement for many resources, in large quantities, any one of which might fall victim to man's activities. A high trophic level (at or near the top of a food chain or food web) also makes a species vulnerable to loss of lower level species. *Id.*

75. *See* Terborgh and Winter, *Some Causes of Extinction*, in CONSERVATION BIOLOGY: AN EVOLUTIONARY-ECOLOGICAL PERSPECTIVE 119–33 (Michael Soule and Bruce Wilcox, eds., 1980) (discussing several factors that can increase the risk of extinction for a given species).

76. Humphrey, *supra* note 73, at 13.

77. *See* Myers, *supra* note 31, at 46–48, 57–81; William E. Kunin and John H. Lawton, *Does Biodiversity Matter? Evaluating the Case for Conserving Species*, in BIODIVERSITY: A BIOLOGY OF NUMBERS AND DIFFERENCE, 283–308 (Kevin J. Gaston, ed., Blackwell, 1996) (discussing the various reasons for people to preserve biodiversity). *See also* Oliver A. Houck, *Why Do We Protect Endangered Species, and What Does That Say About Whether Restrictions on Private Property to Protect Them Constitute "Takings"?*, 80 Iowa L. Rev. 297 (1995).

78. *See* John B. Loomis and Douglas S. White, *Economic Benefits of Rare and Endangered Species: Summary and Meta-Analysis*, 18 Ecological Econ. 197, 199 (1996); Wilson, *supra* note 3, at 281–310; PAUL M. WOOD, BIODIVERSITY AND DEMOCRACY: RETHINKING SOCIETY AND NATURE, 49–57 (UBC Press, 2000).

79. Wilson, *supra* note 35, at 31.

80. Tobin, *supra* note 54, at 11–12. In addition to the medicinal contributions from wild plants, some snake venoms provide nonaddictive painkillers, and blowfly (Calliphoridae) larvae secrete a substance that aids the healing of deep wounds. *Id.* at 12.

81. Wilson, *supra* note 35, at 31; Mark J. Plotkin, *Nature's Gifts: The Hidden Medicine Chest*, Time, April–May 2000, at 34.

82. The science of genetics owes many of its modern advancements to the work done on the fruit fly, *Drosophila melanogaster*, which in other contexts is considered a troublesome pest of cash crops. Some of the very features that render creatures such as the fruit fly, mouse, and rat pests also make them extremely useful as experimental subjects: quick reproductive cycle, large numbers of offspring, ubiquity, and general adaptability to varying ambient conditions.

83. Tobin, *supra* note 54, at 11–14; Jared des Rosiers, Note, *The Exemption Process Under the Endangered Species Act: How the "God Squad" Works and Why*, 66 Notre Dame L. Rev. 825, 827–34 (1991).

84. Barton H. Thompson, Jr., *People or Prairie Chickens: The Uncertain Search for Optimal Biodiversity*, 51 Stan. L. Rev. 1127, 1136–37 (1999).

85. Gretchen C. Daily, *Introduction: What Are Ecosystem Services*, in NATURE'S SERVICES: SOCIETAL DEPENDENCE ON NATURAL ECOSYSTEMS, at 1–4 (Gretchen C. Daily, ed. 1997).

86. *Id.*

87. *See* Robert Costanza et al., *The Value of the World's Ecosystem Services and Natural Capital*, 387 Nature 253, 259 (1997) (estimating the total global value of ecosystem services at $33 trillion). However, this phenomenally high estimate has been criticized. *See* David Pearce, *Auditing the Earth*, 40 Env't 23, 25–28 (1998). But even lower, more conservative estimates tend to be immense. *See* David Pimentel et al., *Economic and Environmental Benefits of Biodiversity*, 47 Bioscience 747–57 (1997) (placing the annual global value of environmental or ecosystem services at $2.9 trillion, with annual benefits of $300 billion within the United States alone).

88. NILES ELDREDGE, THE MINER'S CANARY: UNRAVELING THE MYSTERIES OF EXTINCTION 220 (1991).

89. Thomas Lovejoy, *Species Leave the Ark One by One*, in THE PRESERVATION OF SPECIES: THE VALUE OF BIOLOGICAL DIVERSITY, 16–18 (Bryan Norton, ed. 1986). The *Penicillium* mold is a classic example. Useless or an annoyance for thousands of years, this inconspicuous, humble mold was then found to ward off competitive fungi, which made it useful in producing and preserving Roquefort cheese. This use was then the foundation for the profound antibiotic medical advancements that have in large part catapulted the human race out of the era of early death. Similarly, aspirin, or salicylic acid, consists of an organic molecule originally derived from a willow, *Salix*. *Id*. *See also* William Barrett, *Delaying Tactics*, Forbes, Mar. 1998, at 68 (stating that the Pacific yew plant, which was once burned as a pest in the Northwest old growth forests, was discovered to be the source of the anticancer drug Taxol and now brings the Bristol-Meyers Squibb Company $1.3 billion per year).

90. *Id*. at 17. For example, the pharmaceutical industry often uses ideas drawn from naturally occurring substances to guide their research in the development and synthesis of new medical drugs. Even where the mass-produced medicines ultimately are synthetic replicas of the natural chemicals, the original impetus for the concept comes from living species. *See* Mark Sagoff, *On the Preservation of Species*, 7 Colum. J. Envtl. L. 33, 52 (1980); David Ehrenfield, *The Conservation of Non-Resources*, 64 Am. Scientist 648, 648–51 (1976).

91. Edward O. Wilson, *The Biological Diversity Crisis*, 35 Bioscience 701 (1985).

92. Even a common mouse could provide "enough genetic information to fill every edition of the *Encyclopedia Britannica* published since 1768! This means that each time humans hasten an extinction, they forfeit information of inestimable value." Tobin, *supra* note 54, at 10. *See generally* John C. Kunich, *Mother Frankenstein, Doctor Nature, and the Environmental Law of Genetic Engineering*, 78 Wash. U. L. Q., Number 4 (2001).

93. Holly D. Doremus, *Patching the Ark: Improving Legal Protection of Biological Diversity*, 18 Ecology Law Quarterly 265, 271 (1991).

94. "To keep every cog and wheel is the first precaution of intelligent tinkering." ALDO LEOPOLD, *The Round River*, in A SAND COUNTY ALMANAC 188, 190 (enlarged ed., 1966).

95. Such uncharismatic species as phytoplankton (in the marine context) and insect larvae (in the terrestrial context) occupy an indispensable niche in their respective ecosystems. By serving as the primary, and perhaps exclusive, food source for the array of species above them in the food web, they constitute the underpinnings of their ecosystems. If the highest levels of the food web (the dominant predators) are removed, it is commonly understood that overpopulation of their prey species will likely result. But as damaging as this can be, its danger is exceeded by that caused by removal of the lowest levels of the food web, because when the nutritional base is destroyed, the entire biostructure depending thereon must either find some substitute or follow the lower species into extinction.

96. *See* FRANCES CAIRNCROSS, COSTING THE EARTH: THE CHALLENGE FOR GOVERNMENTS, THE OPPORTUNITIES FOR BUSINESS 132 (1991).

97. *See* John Copeland Nagle, *Playing Noah*, 82 Minn. L. Rev. 1171, 1210–15 (1998); Zygmunt J.B. Plater, *The Embattled Social Utilities of the Endangered Species Act—A Noah Presumption and Caution Against Putting Gasmasks on the Canaries in the Coalmine*, 27 Envtl. L. 845, 875 (1997).

98. *See generally* THE BIOPHILIA HYPOTHESIS (Stephen R. Kellert and Edward O. Wilson, eds., 1993). Wilson suggests that, through millions of years of co-evolution, a formidable bond has formed between people and other life-forms, and that bond is manifested in many ways.

99. Doremus, *supra* note 93, at 271–3.

100. The choice of an immature ursine animal, with its inherent weakness, clumsiness, helplessness, and vulnerability to stronger adversaries, was perhaps prophetic for the Chicago Cubs. In a demonstration of futility unrivaled in professional sports, the Cubs have failed to win the World Series since 1908, when the famed Tinker-to-Evers-to-Chance double play combination overcame the burden of the team's mascot to win the world championship. The Cubs have not even been in a World Series since 1945, even as the losing team.

101. Doremus, *supra* note 93, at 273–5; ALDO LEOPOLD, A SAND COUNTY AL-MANAC 262 (enlarged ed., 1966) DAVID EHRENFELD, THE ARROGANCE OF HUMAN-ISM 207–10 (1978); Bryan Norton, Commodity, Amenity, and Morality: The Limits of Quantification in Valuing Biodiversity, in BIODIVERSITY (E.O. Wilson, ed., 1988) at 200–01; Patrick Parenteau, *Rearranging the Deck Chairs: Endangered Species Act Reforms in an Era of Mass Extinction*, 22 Wm. & Mary Envtl. L. & Pol'y Rev. 227, 243–46 (1998).

102. Genesis 1:26, 28 (King James).

103. Wood, *supra* note 78, at 130–76.

104. Norman Myers, *Threatened Biotas: "Hot Spots" in Tropical Forests*, 8 Environ. 1–20 (1988) (identifying 10 tropical rainforest hotspots that contain, inter alia, about 13 percent of all plant species in just 0.2 percent of earth's total land area).

105. Norman Myers, *The Biodiversity Challenge: Expanded Hot-Spots Analysis*, 10 Environ. 243–56 (1990). Originally, Myers often used two separate words to describe these eco-regions, i.e., "hot spots," but that soon evolved into a hyphenated term, "hot-spots," and then into a single word, "hotspots." For reasons of consistency and economy, i.e., saving precious blank spaces and scarce hyphens, I will use the single, unhyphenated term "hotspots." Additionally, this usage will help to distinguish the concept at issue in this book from other common uses of the term "hot spot."

106. Wilson, *supra* note 35, at 34. Although there is no reason why marine hotspots should not also receive legal recognition and protection, this book will focus on terrestrial hotspots because they fall within the territorial limits of identifiable sovereign nations, are somewhat better known, and lend themselves more to legal preservation measures than those that lie beneath international waters. *See also* Wilson, *supra* note 3, at 260–70.

107. *Id.* at 29.

108. *Id.* Both figures are at least 10 times greater than the number of species found in comparable sites in Europe and North America, illustrating the hotspot phenomenon.

109. *See* Erwin, *supra* note 4, at 348.

• 2 •

The Hotspots

LISTING THE HOTSPOTS

I will now list the regions selected by the originator of the hotspot concept, Norman Myers, as well as those subsequently chosen by Conservation International (CI), the leading international nongovernmental environmental organization in the realm of hotspots preservation. The following is a summary and harmonization of those two lists. Myers identified 10 hotspots in his 1988 study[1] and 8 more in his 1990 work.[2] CI has adopted or incorporated most of these and added several more in consultation with Dr. Myers.

As the hotspots concept has evolved, the criteria are now as follows. To be considered a hotspot, the region must exhibit at least 0.5 percent of total global vascular plant species endemic to the area (*species endemism*), based on an estimated global total of approximately 300,000 vascular plant species (revised upward from the previous estimate of 250,000 based on recent data). That means a region must contain roughly 1,500 endemic species of vascular plants to qualify as a hotspot. The sheer numbers of such species (*species diversity*) are also considered. Secondarily, there should be a significant extent of endemism and diversity among "non-fish vertebrates," that is, birds, mammals, reptiles, and amphibians, of which there are some 27,298 worldwide; where available, invertebrate data also should be evaluated.[3]

Vascular plants are used as a major indicator of overall biodiversity in the hotspots approach, as well as in some other prominent methods of priority setting to be discussed later in this chapter, because they are found throughout the regions and habitats of the planet. They have dispersed and diversified to fill virtually every niche and so are there to serve as barometers of biodiversity. They are comparatively well known as to their distribution and range, with reasonably reliable information as to their conservation status.[4] They are also obviously linked to very many other life-forms because they are the primary fixers of solar energy and the food source for all herbivores as well as an important nutrient source for many omnivores; as such, plants are essential to the survival of most other organisms. They are also connected to many other species through the processes of pollination and seed/fruit dispersal. And because of the large number of described species of vascular plants, there is a statistically reliable basis for data-driven analysis of rates of endemism and other key attributes.

Endemism is the main criterion, as complemented by species diversity and ecosystem diversity, because endemic species are often the first to be driven into extinction by human activities due to the narrowness of their adaptation to one particular area.[5] Also, endemic species clearly highlight the importance of a region because, by definition, they are found nowhere else; their survival is directly linked to the hotspot in question, with no room for equivocation.[6]

Hotspots analysis supplements vascular plant data with similar information regarding nonfish vertebrates and, where available, invertebrates. Many of these are, like the higher plants, among the better known, more well-understood life-forms and provide a useful additional window into the overall biodiversity of any given region. The analysis is primarily species-based (species endemism and species diversity), as is the case with most but not all of the alternative approaches discussed hereafter, because the species is the most basic, recognizable taxon that lends itself to biodiversity analysis. However, hotspots methodology also acknowledges the importance of considering phyletic or *higher-taxa diversity*, usually at the family level, as well as *beta/ecosystem diversity*, and such information is used in concert with the other data where available.[7]

In addition to these biological criteria, there is a criterion pertaining to the *degree of threat* to the area, that is, whether it has already lost 75 percent or more of its original primary natural vegetation cover. The biological criteria are used to arrive at a first-cut list of regions, which is then refined using degree of threat during a second level of analysis.[8] Social, economic, and political factors combine to influence the degree of threat, with the most severely imperiled regions garnering the most urgent attention, all else being equal. As a secondary analytical layer, consideration of these factors is useful in determining the appropriate conservation strategy, but the biological criteria are always paramount in hotspots analysis. In other words, no area should be left out on the basis of political difficulty or a judgment that it is futile to intervene in light of so much prior devastation.[9]

Scientific difficulty is another matter. Thus far, hotspots analysis has remained focused on terrestrial rather than marine habitats. Philosophically, there is no reason not to include marine regions, even the depths of the ocean, within the global list of vital biodiversity centers. Indeed, Conservation International has begun to focus on "key marine areas" in addition to the terrestrial hotspots.[10]

Whether there is currently sufficient scientific information about the marine realm to enable us to assess with some confidence the relative importance of its vast, multitudinous habitats is a matter open to vigorous debate. We do know that human-induced threat is more direct, intense, and immediate in the terrestrial regions, at least insofar as there are no people living in, and comparatively few working in, the marine portions of the planet. Oil spills and other forms of pollution, overharvesting of commercially valuable fish and other species, and other forces do, of course, take a heavy toll on marine biodiversity. Undoubtedly, the deep oceans are among the last true frontiers of the globe, largely unexplored, and the repositories of some of the greatest secrets of life among their presumably legion unknown species. Consequently, over time, key marine regions may in fact be added to the hotspots list as another vital part of the womb of the unknown species.

The following list of hotspots is the result of years of analysis along the lines I have outlined. The list is presented in no particular hierarchical order.

1. Madagascar. Myers (1988) identified the eastern rainforest region, while CI includes all of the large island of Madagascar plus the nearby Indian Ocean islands, including the Seychelles, as part of one hotspot.[11] Most of the plant and animal species in Madagascar evolved apart from the rest of the world and are unique to the island; it features spectacular endemism not only at the species level but also in the genus and family categories. It has been called "a unique evolutionary experiment, a living laboratory unlike any place else on Earth."[12] Of the estimated 10,000–12,000 species of flowering plants, more than 80 percent are endemic to Madagascar,[13] and a stunning total of 260 genera and 10 families are also endemic.[14] This spectacular hotspot also features 250 endemic species of butterflies, 78 endemic mammals, 115 endemic birds, 274 endemic reptiles, and 176 endemic amphibians.[15]

2. Atlantic Coast Brazil/Atlantic Forest Region. Myers (1988) focused on the coastal lowlands portion of Brazil's Atlantic rainforest. CI expands this hotspot to include the interior portions of the Atlantic forest, especially the mountains of the Serra do Mar and associated ranges inland from the coast, plus western extensions of the Atlantic forest into eastern Paraguay and the Province of Misiones in Argentina.[16] This is one of the two major rainforest areas within Brazil and can be ranked among the top five of all hotspots on a wide variety of factors; plant diversity alone includes some 6,000 endemics.[17] Geographically isolated from the Amazonian forests to the north and west, this is one of the greatest centers of biodiversity in the world.[18] Of the region's 280 amphibian species, 253 are endemic—an incredible 90.4 percent endemism rate.[19]

3. Western Ecuador/Chocó-Darien-Western Ecuador. Myers (1988) identified the lowland rainforests, which CI expanded to include the dry forests, as well as the

continuation of these forests into northwestern coastal Peru and the Chocó region of Colombia, the latter of which was considered a separate hotspot by Myers.[20] A great variety of ecosystem types present in this limited geographic area has given rise to high levels of diversity and endemism.[21] The forested regions of the lowlands and foothills of Ecuador west of the Andes once contained about 10,000 plant species but have been almost totally deforested, bringing this area to an extreme crisis situation.[22]

4. Western Amazonia Uplands/Tropical Andes. Myers (1988) highlighted the enormous importance of this hotspot, terming it "a kind of global epicenter of biodiversity." CI calls this region "the Tropical Andes" and expands it to include higher altitude areas as well as several Andean outliers such as the Sierra de la Macarena and the Sierra Nevada de Santa Maria, plus portions of the northern Venezuela montane.[23] This one hotspot alone is home to at least 45,000 plant species (15 to 17 percent of the world's total), of which 20,000 are endemic (7.4 percent of the global total)—by far the highest of any hotspot.[24] This means that about 7 percent of all the world's vascular plants are endemic to just 0.8 percent of the planet's land surface.[25] There is also an amazing degree of diversity and endemism among amphibians, reptiles, and birds; overall, this hotspot harbors 3,389 known species of nonfish vertebrates, of which 1,567 (46.2 percent) are endemic.[26] It should be obvious why this has been called "the richest and most diverse biodiversity hotspot on Earth."[27]

5. Eastern Himalayas/Mountains of South-Central China. Myers's (1988) hotspot was divided by CI into two hotspots, the Mountains of South-Central China[28] and Indo-Burma.[29] CI also adds much more territory to both. As defined by CI, the Mountains of South-Central China include about 3,500 species of endemic vascular plants, as well as great diversity and endemism among vertebrates and other taxa.[30]

6. Peninsular Malaysia/Northern Borneo/Sundaland. Myers's (1988) hotspot was combined by CI with the large islands of western Indonesia and East Malaysia to form one very large hotspot that CI calls Sundaland.[31] Sundaland defies precise estimates of biodiversity, but reasonable extrapolations from available data indicate that this is one of the hottest of the hotspots. A conservative estimate is that Sundaland is home to 15,000 endemic vascular plant species and 115 endemic mammals, and its endemism rates in other taxa are very high as well.[32]

7. Philippines. Myers (1988) and CI agree that the 7,000-plus islands of the Philippines, in their entirety, should be considered a hotspot.[33] This is undoubtedly one of the preeminent hotspots, featuring 518 endemic species of nonfish vertebrates, approximately 50 percent endemism among its 8,000-plus species of plants, and 352 endemic butterfly species.[34] The biodiversity of the Philippines is especially amazing in light of its relatively small land mass. It is by far the smallest of the top nine hotspots that have within their borders at least 2 percent of higher plants and/or 2 percent of nonfish vertebrates, worldwide, as endemics.[35] Tragically, this hotspot is "at the edge of a full-scale biodiversity collapse."[36]

8. New Caledonia. As with the Philippines, Myers (1988) and CI concur in deeming the entire entity a hotspot.[37] Island-derived extinction rate predictions should apply. One of the smallest of the hotspots, this region features some of the highest

levels of endemism, particularly among plants. It contains 3,322 vascular plant species, of which an amazing 2,551 (76.8 percent) are endemics, and there are five entire families of plants endemic to this hotspot—truly impressive considering the smallness of the geographical area.[38]

9. Southwestern Ivory Coast/Guinean Forests of West Africa. Myers (1990) focused on the Tai Forest, while CI adds all of the Guinean Forests of West Africa, plus four islands in the Gulf of Guinea.[39] The islands alone contain large numbers of endemic species, and the endemism rate overall for this hotspot is very high.[40] The forest is severely threatened, with extreme habitat fragmentation and degradation throughout most of the region.[41]

10. Eastern Arc Mountains and Coastal Forests of Tanzania/Kenya. CI expands Myers (1990) by including the Coastal Forests of Tanzania and neighboring portions of Kenya.[42] This hotspot contains 13 percent of all mainland tropical Africa's 30,000 plant species in just 0.1 percent of the region's expanse, along with a 35 percent endemism rate among its 1,400 plant species.[43]

11. Western Ghats of India and Sri Lanka. CI modifies the work of Myers (1988, 1990) by combining this area with Sri Lanka and considering the resulting region a single hotspot.[44] As defined by CI, the combined hotspot contains at least 4,780 species of vascular plants, of which about 2,180 (45.6 percent) are endemic.[45]

12. Cape Floristic Province of South Africa. Myers (1990) and CI concur on the global importance of this hotspot.[46] This region boasts the greatest extratropical concentration of higher plant species on the planet, with 8,200 species, 5,682 of which are endemic. There is also a phenomenal endemism rate at the genus and family levels, equaled only by Madagascar and New Caledonia.[47]

13. Southwestern Australia. CI slightly expands Myers (1990) as to this hotspot.[48] Millions of years of isolation have produced extremely high levels of endemism, including 79.2 percent of plant species (4,331 endemics out of a total of 5,469).[49]

14. California Floristic Province. Myers (1990) and CI agree.[50] This Mediterranean-type ecosystem is one of the few that are situated mainly within the borders of a developed country. It is home to 4,426 species of higher plants, of which 48 percent are endemic, as well as more than 30 percent of all known insect species in North America north of Mexico.[51] It also contains about 25 percent of all the plant species found in the United States and Canada combined.[52]

15. Central Chile. Myers (1990) limited this hotspot to the Mediterranean-type area of Central Chile, while CI includes the Winter Rainfall Desert region as well.[53] It contains 3,429 identified species of plants, of which 46.8 percent are endemic.[54]

16. Hawaii/Polynesia/Micronesia. Myers (1988) recognized the significance of this region, and CI has included it in the larger Polynesia/Micronesia hotspot.[55] The Hawaiian Islands alone contain 386 wetlands. The biodiversity in Hawaii is under intense pressure and has already experienced severe losses.[56] Overall, the combined Polynesia/Micronesia hotspot boasts 3,334 endemic species of plants out of a total of 6,557 (an endemism rate of 50.8 percent), and 223 endemic nonfish vertebrates of a total of 342 (a 65 percent rate).[57]

17. Mesoamerica. Added by CI, this hotspot includes all tropical and subtropical natural plant formations from the Panama Canal west and north through Costa Rica, Nicaragua, Honduras, El Salvador, Guatemala, and Belize, and extending into southern and central Mexico as far as the middle of the Sierra Madre Oriental.[58] In terms of global biodiversity, it is one of the most significant of all the hotspots, ranking with the Tropical Andes and Sundaland.[59] There are an estimated 24,000 vascular plant species, of which about 5,000 (21 percent) are endemic, and 521 mammal species, with an extremely high 210 (40.3 percent) endemic.[60] Overall, this hotspot harbors 2,859 nonfish vertebrate species, of which an astonishing total of 1,159 (40.5 percent) are endemic.[61]

18. Caribbean. Added by CI, the Caribbean encompasses all of the Greater and Lesser Antilles, the Bahamas, the Turks and Caicos Islands, plus subtropical Florida from Lake Okeechobee south through the Everglades and into the Florida Keys.[62] Island-derived extinction rate predictions should apply. Plant diversity and endemism are both very high, with an estimated 7,000 endemic species out of a total of 12,000 (58 percent endemism).[63] For nonfish vertebrates, 779 out of 1,518 species are endemic (51 percent), including 164 of 189 amphibians (86.7 percent).[64]

19. Brazilian Cerrado. Added by CI. Occupying the central Brazilian plateau, this is the only hotspot that consists mostly of savanna, woodland/savanna, and dry forest ecosystems.[65] Total plant diversity has been estimated at 10,000 species, with 44 percent endemic to this hotspot.[66]

20. Mediterranean Basin. Added by CI, this is a huge hotspot, encompassing all of Cyprus and most of Greece, Lebanon, and Portugal, as well as smaller parts of France, Algeria, Libya, Spain, Israel, and Morocco.[67] The Mediterranean Basin hotspot features some 13,000 endemic plant species (4.8 percent of the global total) and an overall 25,000 species of plants.[68]

21. Caucasus. Added by CI. It includes portions of Azerbaijan, Georgia, Chechenia, Ingushetia, Northern Osetia, Kabardino-Balkaria, Karachai-Cherkesia, and Adigea Autonomous Republics, plus northeastern Turkey and a small part of northwestern Iran.[69] About 6,300 plant species have been recorded in this hotspot, with at least 1,600 of them endemic.[70]

22. New Zealand. Added by CI, this large island is the only hotspot that encompasses the entire land area of a developed nation.[71] Although the absolute numbers of species are relatively modest for both plants and vertebrates, there are extremely high endemism rates. At least 2,085 species of plants (approximately 61 to 68 percent endemism) are found here and nowhere else,[72] as are 136 nonfish vertebrates (62.7 percent endemism).[73]

23. Succulent Karoo of South Africa. Added by CI, this is the only hotspot that is entirely arid.[74] It is home to 4,849 species of vascular plants, of which 1,940 (40 percent) are endemic. It is also a center of diversity for many kinds of invertebrates and reptiles.[75]

24. Wallacea. Added by CI, Wallacea includes the large island of Sulawesi, the various islands to the east of Sulawesi (generally known as the Moluccas or Spice Islands or Maluku), and the "Banda Arc" of islands, the Lesser Sundas or Nusa

Tenggara, situated to the south of Sulawesi and the Moluccas.[76] This hotspot consists mostly of tropical rainforest, inhabited by 201 mammalian species with an endemism rate of at least 61.2 percent. Wallacea also features 697 species of birds, with a 35.7 percent endemism rate.[77]

25. Indo-Burma. Modified and expanded by CI from Myers's Eastern Himalayas hotspot (1988). This consists of tropical Asia east of the Indian subcontinent, excluding the Malesian region. It encompasses the nations of Vietnam, Cambodia, Laos, Thailand, and Myanmar/Burma, inter alia.[78] There are approximately 13,500 species of higher plants here, of which some 7,000, or 51.9 percent, are endemic.[79] The nonmarine vertebrate fauna is also very diverse, with 73 species and 8 genera of endemic mammals, 1,170 species of birds, 484 species and 143 genera of reptiles, and a host of others.[80] This region is not well studied, and, because of the large amounts of heavily forested territory, there may be many species yet to be identified.

What are some of the most remarkable features of these most remarkable regions? These hotspots encompass *all* of the remaining habitats of 133,149 identified plant species (44 percent of the world's total) and 9,645 nonfish vertebrate species (35 percent of the world's total).[81] These endemic species are crowded into an aggregate expanse of 2.14 million square kilometers, or only 1.44 percent of the earth's land surface, while at one time they occupied 17.4 million square kilometers, 11.8 percent of the planet's land surface.[82] The hotspots' remaining *global area* is roughly equivalent to that of Alaska and Texas combined.[83] They have already lost 88 percent of their primary vegetation and are likely, absent greatly increased conservation efforts, to lose much more in the foreseeable future.[84]

These hotspots feature a great diversity of habitat type. Most contain some tropical forest, which appears in 15 of the hotspots. Nine are mainly or entirely made up of islands, and almost all tropical islands belong in a hotspot. Sixteen hotspots are in the tropics, three consist of temperate forest and grasslands, and five are in Mediterranean-type zones.[85]

Ecologists generally place a great deal of emphasis on degree of endemism as the principal criterion for hotspot status because endemics are entirely dependent on a single area for survival.[86] Endemics, because of their restricted ranges, are often among the most vulnerable species in any ecosystem and are most in need of swift and effective conservation action. The hotspots listed here contain at least 44 percent of all identified plant species as endemics—an enormous number of species found only in the hotspots *and nowhere else.*[87] Also, 53.8 percent of all known species of amphibians, 37.8 percent of reptiles, 29.2 percent of mammals, and 27.8 percent of birds are *entirely limited* to the hotspots.[88] The hotspots are home to 81.6 percent of endangered bird species and 57.5 percent of endangered mammal species.[89] If we develop, contaminate, or otherwise damage the 1.44 percent of the earth's land surface on which these hotspots cling to life, we can expect the concomitant loss of incredible numbers of species.

OTHER APPROACHES TO BIODIVERSITY PRESERVATION

As I have mentioned, the hotspots concept has been part of the debate only since 1988. There are certainly other scientifically valid methods of setting priorities for biodiversity preservation, and the hotspots approach must be considered within this broader context. I will briefly summarize some of these alternatives here. There is a large body of scientific literature within which the relative strengths and limitations of the various priority-setting approaches have been examined in depth, and I will cite some examples.

All of the area-based (as opposed to single-species) approaches to assessing priorities involve either explicit or implicit judgments about the relative importance of several attributes of biodiversity within any given region. These include the *richness* of the region, that is, how many different species live within it; the *representativity*, or how well it holds the key habitats and species that are representative of a wider area; the *uniqueness*, as in the number of endemic species present or the number of limited-extent ecosystems; the *degree of threat*, as often expressed in numbers of endangered and threatened species present and/or the extent to which original habitat has been reduced; its *genetic contribution*, as reflected in some calculation of the taxonomic distinctiveness of the species present; and its *population value*, as demonstrated by the numbers of individuals present for the species contained in the region.[90]

The World Wide Fund for Nature (WWF) and the World Conservation Union (IUCN) have cooperated to develop a list of "centers of plant diversity," or CPDs.[91] This list of the most vital concentrations of plant species on a global basis is the result of a massive project involving numerous experts and workshops, including many on a national/local level. A total of 234 centers of plant diversity have been identified by WWF and IUCN worldwide.[92] Of these, 6 are located in North America (apart from Mesoamerica, which has 20), 9 in Europe, 14 in Australia and New Zealand, 21 in China/East Asia, 30 in Africa, 41 in Southeast Asia/Malesia, and 46 in South America, among others.[93]

The criteria for a CPD are principally that a given area is evidently species-rich in plants, even though the number of species present may not be accurately known, and that the area is known to contain a large number of endemic plant species.[94] In addition to these criteria, consideration is also given to the degree and imminence of threat to the site of large-scale devastation and the extent to which the site contains an important gene pool of plants of current or potential value to humans, a diverse range of habitat types, and/or a significant proportion of plant species adapted to special conditions.[95] Plants were chosen as indicators of global biodiversity for CPDs, as with the hotspots, mainly because they are virtually ubiquitous across the entire range of terrestrial habitats in all regions of the world and constitute the "background habitat" for vast numbers of other species, serving as food sources for most and interacting with many in pollination and fruit/seed dispersal.[96]

A similar method along the general lines of the centers of plant diversity, and another significant alternative to the hotspots approach, has been advanced by BirdLife International.[97] This organization focuses on "restricted-range" bird species, the approximately 2,623 species (27 percent of all birds) that have breeding ranges of less than 50,000 square kilometers.[98] In other words, these are birds endemic to fairly limited regions. Birds are considered valuable indicators of biodiversity because they have dispersed to and diversified in all of the world's regions and nearly all types of terrestrial habitats, are the best known and documented major taxonomic group, are represented by a manageable number of species (about 10,000 avian species worldwide as compared to at least 250,000 species of vascular plants), are sensitive to environmental disturbance, and enjoy widespread popular appeal, thereby making good flagship species for rallying public support.[99]

BirdLife International has used a multistep method to compile a list of 218 Endemic Bird Areas (EBAs) of primary importance that are home to about 93 percent of the restricted-range bird species, as well as 138 Secondary Endemic Bird Areas of somewhat lesser importance, and to rank the overall priority of EBAs as critical, urgent, or high, according to numerical scores for biological importance and current threat level.[100] The EBAs are located throughout the world, but 77 percent are in the tropics and subtropics, and the dominant habitat is forest (83 percent).[101] The top countries for EBAs, with more than 10 each, are Indonesia, Mexico, Brazil, Peru, Colombia, Papua New Guinea, and China.[102]

A third prominent alternative is posited by the World Wildlife Fund and the World Wide Fund for Nature, which have published the "List of Global 200 Eco-regions."[103] The Global 200 list attempts to include representatives of significant biome types, both terrestrial and aquatic, including marine areas. The WWF list of 200 priority areas includes 136 terrestrial, 36 freshwater, and 61 marine zones, or eco-regions.[104] The central idea behind this "representation" approach is that by conserving the broadest variety of the world's habitats, we can conserve the broadest variety of the world's species and most endangered wildlife, as well as higher expressions of life on earth—whole communities and ecosystems, wherever they might be situated. The inclusion of marine eco-regions sets Global 200 apart from hotspots analysis and the other main paradigms outlined herein.

The Global 200 approach differs from that reflected in the hotspots and other methods mentioned in another key respect in that it emphasizes breadth of genetic variation and representation of outstanding examples of each major habitat type (MHT) (such as coral reefs, tropical dry forests, large lakes, etc.)[105] rather than the greatest concentrations of endemic species, total numbers of species, and/or the most threatened areas. Within each

MHT and biogeographic realm, these factors do play a role, for eco-regions are classified on the basis of their biological distinctiveness as determined by species richness, endemism, taxonomic uniqueness, unusual ecological or evolutionary phenomena, and global rarity of MHT.[106]

Global 200 is guided by the idea that it may be more important to preserve the widest possible range of taxonomic variation as opposed to the most species, and that, at a minimum, we should ensure that all major ecosystem and habitat types are represented within our conservation strategies. The concept is that, in terms of protecting and possibly using genetic resources, saving representatives of many different species, genera, and families evolutionarily adapted for life within well-chosen representatives of the various MHTs could be of more value than focusing largely on tropical ecosystems that might contain numerous endemic species but not necessarily an extraordinary number of higher taxa.[107] This method is designed to integrate the goal of maintaining species diversity with another level of conservation action, that is, the preservation of distinct ecosystems and ecological processes.

Some researchers have advanced the concept of "complementary areas" as an aid to selecting high-priority areas for conservation.[108] The idea is that where the identities of species or other biodiversity surrogates are known, we should select areas that in combination have the highest representation of diversity.[109] Complementarity analysis attempts to determine the most efficient methods of including substantially all of a given set of species within a particular network of protected areas, that is, that represent a maximum of diversity in the minimum number of sites.[110] Several computerized algorithms have been developed to perform this analysis on any scale, usually by first choosing the most diverse area, then the area with the largest number of selected species not included within the first area, and so on until all applicable species are represented.[111] This is related to "gap analysis," wherein additional conservation areas are chosen to fill gaps in biodiversity representation left by other protected areas.[112]

There are other notable alternatives as well, such as those advocated by The Nature Conservancy, the World Resources Institute, the British Natural History Museum,[113] and other organizations.[114] Each of these approaches has value, and each looks at somewhat different factors on the road to arriving at somewhat different conclusions and recommendations. There is certainly room for considerable disagreement as to which areas qualify for top priority in conservation efforts and what the boundaries of those areas should be.

Differences in approach notwithstanding, there is a fair degree of similarity between the results yielded by hotspots analysis and those from the other main alternatives. For example, of the 234 Centers of Plant Diversity, 192 are either partially or entirely within the hotspots as defined herein, as are 144 of the 218 Endemic Bird Areas and 69 of the 138 Secondary Endemic

Bird Areas.[115] Similarly, 79 out of 136 Global 200 eco-regions overlap to some extent with the hotspots.[116] This suggests that each approach has some merit, as well as opportunities for further scientific advancement in evaluating conservation priorities.

Scientists can and do differ as to which factors are most appropriate in determining the optimal regions for expenditure of scarce conservation resources, as well as how much emphasis to place on the various factors that are considered.[117] Are birds the best species to choose as indicators of overall biodiversity, or are vascular plants preferable? Is a higher-taxa approach (perhaps focusing on families) or a habitats-based analysis better than any method that focuses on numbers and distribution of species?[118] What are the most important criteria to use in making hard choices about what areas to protect?

It is not the purpose of this book to resolve these and other related, very complex questions but only to examine in detail one credible approach to biodiversity preservation. I do not suggest, with quasi-religious zeal, that the hotspots are the one and only true way to salvation for life on earth . . . only that they are one way that deserves further attention.[119] The proposal I set forth in Chapter 5 is flexible enough to accommodate the divergent strands of scientific thought, whether on the hotspots as currently understood, on some other current alternative, or on a new variation that borrows from the best options. The Ark of the Broken Covenant can be conceptualized as the hotspots, Global 200, EBAs, or any number of other means of evaluating life on earth. The key is to begin somewhere, and to shake the status quo, before it is too late.

NOTES

1. Norman Myers, *Threatened Biotas: "Hot Spots" in Tropical Forests*, 8 Environ. 1–20 (1988).

2. Norman Myers, *The Biodiversity Challenge: Expanded Hot-Spots Analysis*, 10 Environ. 243–56 (1990).

3. RUSSELL A. MITTERMEIER, NORMAN MYERS, AND CRISTINA GOETTSCH MITTERMEIER, HOTSPOTS: EARTH'S BIOLOGICALLY RICHEST AND MOST ENDANGERED TERRESTRIAL ECOREGIONS at 29–31 (2000) (hereinafter HOTSPOTS).

4. Myers, *supra* note 2, at 244.

5. Stuart Pimm and R.A. Askins, *Forest Losses Predict Bird Extinctions in Eastern North America*, 92 Proceedings of the National Academy of Sciences 9343–47 (1995).

6. HOTSPOTS, *supra* note 3, at 27.

7. *Id.*

8. *Id.* at 29–31.

9. *Id.* at 29.

10. *See* <http://www.conservation.org/xp/CIWEB/strategies/marine_ecosystems/marine_ecosystems.xml>.

11. HOTSPOTS, *supra* note 3, at 30, 189–200.

12. *Id.* at 189.

13. EDWARD O. WILSON, THE DIVERSITY OF LIFE, 267 (Belknap, Harvard 1992).

14. HOTSPOTS, *supra* note 3, at 189–90.

15. *Id.* at 190. This means that Madagascar contains as endemics 2.8 percent of all the nonfish vertebrates of the world. Only the Tropical Andes, the Caribbean, and Mesoamerica have a higher percentage. *Id.*

16. *Id.* at 30, 137–44.

17. *Id.* at 137.

18. Wilson, *supra* note 13, at 264–6.

19. HOTSPOTS, *supra* note 3, at 137.

20. *Id.* at 30, 123–30. CI calls the combined hotspot Chocó-Darien-Western Ecuador. *Id.*

21. *Id.* at 124.

22. Wilson, *supra* note 13, at 264.

23. HOTSPOTS, *supra* note 3, at 30, 69–82.

24. Russell A. Mittermeier, Norman Myers, et al., *Biodiversity Hotspots and Major Tropical Wilderness Areas: Approaches to Setting Conservation Priorities*, 12 Conserv. Biol. 516, 518 (Jun. 1998).

25. HOTSPOTS, *supra* note 3, at 73.

26. *Id.* at 73–74. As a point of comparison, these vertebrate numbers are 530 more total species and 408 more endemics than are found in the next richest hotspot. *Id.* at 74.

27. *Id.* at 69. *See* Wilson, *supra* note 13, at 264.

28. *Id.* at 30, 339–50.

29. *Id.* at 30, 319–34. As defined by CI, the Indo-Burma hotspot is an area of great unknowns, but a conservative estimate is that the hotspot contains about 13,500 species of vascular plants, with an endemism rate of 51.9 percent. The vertebrate fauna is also very diverse. *Id.* at 321.

30. *Id.* at 341. *See* Wilson, *supra* note 13, at 267.

31. *Id.* at 30, 279–90.

32. *Id.* at 281–82. *See* Wilson, *supra* note 13, at 268.

33. *Id.* at 30, 309–15.

34. *Id.* at 310.

35. *Id.* at 311.

36. *See* Wilson, *supra* note 13, at 268–9.

37. HOTSPOTS, *supra* note 3, at 30, 367–76.

38. *Id.* at 367. *See* Wilson, *supra* note 13, at 269.

39. *Id.* at 30, 239–49.

40. *Id.* at 240.

41. *Id.* at 247. *See* Wilson, *supra* note 13, at 266.

42. *Id.* at 30, 205–13.

43. *Id.* at 205.

44. *Id.* at 30, 353–63.

45. *Id.* at 354–57. *See* Wilson, *supra* note 13, at 267–8.

46. *Id.* at 30–31, 219–26.

47. *Id.* at 219.

48. *Id.* at 31, 405–14.

49. *Id.* at 407.

50. *Id.* at 31, 177–84.

51. *Id.* at 177–78.

52. *See* Wilson, *supra* note 13, at 261.

53. HOTSPOTS, *supra* note 3, at 31, 161–71.

54. *Id.* at 161. *See* Wilson, *supra* note 13, at 261.

55. *Id.* at 31, 391–401. As defined by CI, the entire Polynesia/Micronesia hotspot includes about 6,557 species of vascular plants, of which 3,334 (51 percent) are endemics. *Id.* at 392.

56. *Id.* at 392.

57. *Id.* at 37.

58. *Id.* at 31, 87–102.

59. *Id.* at 87.

60. *Id.* at 88–89.

61. *Id.* at 89.

62. *Id.* at 31, 109–20.

63. *Id.* at 111.

64. *Id.* at 37.

65. *Id.* at 31, 149–55.

66. *Id.* at 149–51.

67. *Id.* at 31, 255–65.

68. Mittermeier, Myers, et al., *supra* note 24, at 518.

69. HOTSPOTS, *supra* note 3, at 31, 269–73.

70. *Id.* at 270.

71. *Id.* at 31, 379–87.

72. *Id.* at 380.

73. *Id.* at 37.

74. *Id.* at 31, 229–34.

75. *Id.* at 229.

76. *Id.* at 31, 297–304.

77. *Id.* at 298–300.

78. *Id.* at 319.

79. *Id.* at 321.

80. *Id.*

81. Norman Myers, Russell A. Mittermeier, et al., *Biodiversity Hotspots for Conservation Priorities*, 403 Nature 853, 855 (Feb. 2000).

82. *Id.*

83. HOTSPOTS, *supra* note 3, at 34.

84. Myers, Mittermeier, et al., *supra* note 81, at 855.

85. *Id.*

86. Mittermeier, Myers, et al., *supra* note 24, at 517.

87. *Id.*

88. HOTSPOTS, *supra* note 3, at 37.

89. *Id.* at 58. These data include species listed as either critically endangered or endangered by the International Union for Conservation of Nature and Natural Resources.

90. *See* A.J. STATTERSFIELD, ET AL., ENDEMIC BIRD AREAS OF THE WORLD: PRIORITIES FOR BIODIVERSITY CONSERVATION, Birdlife Conservation Series 7, at 16–18 (BirdLife International, Cambridge, U.K., 1998).

91. STEPHEN D. DAVIS, VERNON H. HEYWOOD, ET AL., CENTRES OF PLANT DIVERSITY: A GUIDE AND STRATEGY FOR THEIR CONSERVATION, 3 volumes (IUCN Publications, Cambridge, 1994–97). Volume 1 (1994) covers Europe, Africa, Southwest Asia, and the Middle East. Volume 2 (1995) examines Asia, Australasia, and the Pacific. Volume 3 (1997) deals with the Americas.

92. *Id.* Vol. 1, at 3–7.

93. *Id.* at 7. The CPDs are presented, in tabular form, at 10–36, with a summary of information pertaining to each.

94. *Id.* Vol. 1, at 6.

95. *Id.* at 6–10.

96. *Id.* at 1. These same factors are why the hotspots approach relies heavily on endemism rates and diversity of vascular plants in arriving at first-order lists of possible hotspots.

97. *See* Stattersfield, *supra* note 90, at 50. About 70 percent of the centers of plant diversity overlap in some way with endemic bird areas, and 60 percent of endemic bird areas overlap with centers of plant diversity. However, only about 10 percent actually match, and the most common relationship is one of only partial overlap. *Id.*

98. *Id.* at 21–23.

99. *Id.* at 45.

100. *Id.* at 19–38, 39–43.

101. *Id.* at 10–11, 29–31.

102. *Id.* at 10, 36–38. In terms of the highest numbers of threatened restricted-range bird species, the list is topped by the Philippines, Indonesia, Brazil, Colombia, Peru, Ecuador, China, the United States, Madagascar, and Mexico.

103. David M. Olson and Eric Dinerstein, *The Global 200: A Representation Approach to Conserving the Earth's Most Biologically Valuable Ecoregions*, 12 Conserv. Biol. 502–15 (1998).

104. *Id.* at 509. Eco-regions are defined as relatively large units of land or water containing a characteristic set of natural communities that share a large majority of their species, dynamics, and environmental conditions. *Id.* at 502.

105. *Id.* at 502. Researchers in this field have identified 12 MHTs in the terrestrial realm, 3 in the fresh water, and 4 in the marine realm, which have been further subdivided by biogeographic realm. *Id. See* WWF, Global 200 Eco-regions (map) (World Wildlife Fund, Washington D.C., 1997).

106. *Id.* at 509. Biological distinctiveness is used to evaluate the relative importance and rarity of each eco-region and estimate the urgency of conservation action based on the opportunities for saving distinct areas around the world. Eco-regions are classified as either globally outstanding, regionally outstanding, bioregionally outstanding, or locally important. *Id.*

107. *Id.* For a comparison of BirdLife International's EBAs and the Global 200 eco-regions, *see* Stattersfield, *supra* note 90, at 48.

108. *See, e.g.*, Paul Williams, *Key Sites for Conservation: Area-Selection Methods for Biodiversity*, in CONSERVATION IN A CHANGING WORLD: INTEGRATING PROCESSES INTO PRIORITIES FOR ACTION, 224–30 (G. Mace, A Balmford, and J. Ginsberg, eds.,

Cambridge University Press, 1998); Peter C. Howard, et al., *Complementarity and the Use of Indicator Groups for Reserve Selection in Uganda*, 394 Nature 472–75 (1998); C.R. Margules and R.L. Pressey, *Systematic Conservation Planning*, 405 Nature 243–53 (2000); R.L. Pressey et al., *Beyond Opportunism: Key Principles for Systematic Reserve Selection*, 8 Trends Ecol. Evol. 124–28 (1993).

109. *See, e.g.*, R. Vane-Wright, C. Smith, and P. Williams, *What to Protect? Systematics and the Agony of Choice*, 55 Biol. Conserv. 235–54 (1991); B. Csuti et al., *A Comparison of Reserve Selection Algorithms Using Data on Terrestrial Vertebrates in Oregon*, 80 Biol. Conserv. 83–97 (1997).

110. R.L. Pressey and A.O. Nicholls, *Efficiency in Conservation Evaluation: Scoring Versus Iterative Approaches*, 50 Biol. Conserv. 199–218 (1989).

111. Stattersfield, *supra* note 90, at 17; Ana S. Rodrigues, J. Orestes Cerdeira, and Kevin J. Gaston, *Flexibility, Efficiency, and Accountability: Adapting Reserve Selection Algorithms to More Complex Conservation Problems*, 23 Ecography 565–74 (2000). *See also* Kevin J. Gaston, et al., *Complementary Representation and Zones of Ecological Transition*, 4 Ecol. Letters 4–9 (2001); Ana S. Rodrigues, Kevin J. Gaston, and Richard D. Gregory, *Using Presence-Absence Data to Establish Reserve Selection Procedures That Are Robust to Temporal Species Turnover*, 267 Proc. R. Soc. Lond., 897–902 (2000); Ana S. Rodrigues, Richard D. Gregory, and Kevin J. Gaston, *Robustness of Reserve Selection Procedures Under Temporal Species Turnover*, 267 Proc. R. Soc. Lond. 49–55 (2000). Each of the latter three sources identify some shortcomings in minimum representation sets and recommend an alternative that incorporates viability concerns.

112. *See, e.g.*, A.R. Kiester, et al., *Conservation Prioritization Using GAP Data*, 10 Biol. Conserv. 1332–42 (1996); M.D. Jennings, *Gap Analysis: Concepts, Methods, and Recent Results*, 15 Landscape Ecol. 5–20 (2000); J.M. Scott, et al., *Gap Analysis: A Geographic Approach to the Protection of Biological Diversity*, 123 Wildlife Monogr. 1–41 (1993). The Gap Analysis Program in the United States currently uses a form of complementarity.

113. The Natural History Museum uses an on-line map of the world (the "Worldmap") to highlight various priority areas for biodiversity conservation. It shows the distribution of some of the most highly valued terrestrial biodiversity worldwide (mammals, reptiles, amphibians, and seed plants), using family-level data for equal-area grid cells. It implements the complementarity principle to find a priority sequence of regions which will represent all taxa by identifying the maximum increment of unrepresented biodiversity possible at each step. The Worldmap can be viewed at <http://www.nhm.ac.uk/science/projects/worldmap/>. *See* R. Vane-Wright et al., *supra* note 108.

114. *See generally*, The Nature Conservancy, *Designing a Geography of Hope: Guidelines for Ecoregion-Based Conservation* (The Nature Conservancy, Arlington VA, 1997); G.M. Mace, *It's Time to Work Together and Stop Duplicating Efforts*, 405 Nature 393 (25 May 2000).

115. Hotspots, *supra* note 3, at 65–66.

116. *Id.* at 66.

117. *See, e.g.*, Colin Bibby, *Selecting Areas for Conservation*, in Conservation Science and Action, 176–201 (William Sutherland, ed., 1998); David Lees, C. Kremen, and L. Andriamampianina, *A Null Model for Species Richness Gradients: Bounded Range Overlap of Butterflies and Other Rainforest Endemics in Madagascar*,

67 Biological Journal of the Linnean Society 529–554 (1999); Ashbindu Singh, *Application of Geospatial Information for Identifying Priority Areas for Biodiversity Conservation*, in NATURE AND HUMAN SOCIETY: THE QUEST FOR A SUSTAINABLE WORLD, 276–80 (Peter Raven, ed., NRC 1997); Christopher Humphries, Paul Williams, and Richard Vane-Wright, *Measuring Biodiversity Value for Conservation*, 26 Annual Reviews of Ecology and Systematics 93–111 (1995); Williams, *supra* note 107, 211–49; Norman Myers, *Global Biodiversity Priorities and Expanded Conservation Policies*, in CONSERVATION IN A CHANGING WORLD: INTEGRATING PROCESSES INTO PRIORITIES FOR ACTION, 273–85 (G. Mace, A Balmford, and J. Ginsberg, eds., Cambridge University Press, 1998).

118. Paul Williams, Kevin Gaston, and Chris Humphries, *Mapping Biodiversity Value Worldwide: Combining Higher-Taxon Richness from Different Groups*, 264 Proceedings of the Royal Society, Biological Sciences 141–148 (1997); Paul H. Williams and Kevin J. Gaston, *Measuring More of Biodiversity: Can Higher-Taxon Richness Predict Wholesale Species Richness?*, 67 Biol. Conserv. 211–17 (1994).

119. In fact, the hotspots approach has begun to receive increased levels of attention in the popular media as well as in the conservation science field. For example, *National Geographic* magazine launched a projected two-year series of articles dealing with the hotspots beginning with the January 2002 issue.

• 3 •

Burn Control? Current International Law Relevant to Hotspots Preservation

I will now examine the current legal regime—first on an international[1] and then, in Chapter 4, on an individual-nation level—that at least peripherally touches on the preservation of the hotspots. I will begin with the handful of global international agreements, including those often categorized as multilateral environmental agreements (MEAs), that have some relevance to the hotspots.

Let me warn you, however, that if you are expecting to find an international agreement that specifically addresses the hotspots, or any of the alternative methods of setting biodiversity conservation priorities, you will wear out the pages of this book searching in vain. You might as well take your binoculars, pack a picnic basket, and stroll off into the nearest public park looking for wild unicorns. You would be about as successful, and at least you would enjoy some fresh air and a tasty snack while you are en route to disappointment. If you are reading this book in the mistaken belief that you have picked up a mystery whodunit, I am reluctant to give away the surprise O. Henry–like ending . . . but there is no such law in existence. The most you will find is an occasional international agreement that rustles the leaves of the hotspots as it passes by in the night. But because that is all we have, that is what we will discuss.

INTERNATIONAL LEGAL MECHANISMS

Convention on Biological Diversity

At the 1992 United Nations Conference on Environment and Development (the "Earth Summit") in Rio de Janeiro, leaders of many nations gathered to discuss "sustainable development," and one product from that meeting was the Convention on Biological Diversity (CBD).[2] Certainly, the name itself seems promising for those who are hoping to find international legal protection for the hotspots. Over 150 governments signed the document at the Rio conference, and there are now 183 parties.[3] But does the CBD live up to the promise of its name?

The CBD establishes three main goals: the conservation of biological diversity, the sustainable use of its components, and the fair and equitable sharing of the benefits from the use of genetic resources.[4] In contrast to earlier treaties, it does not include any lists or annexes of protected species or areas but deals with the problem of biodiversity in a more comprehensive fashion, addressing all aspects of biodiversity, including access to biological resources, biotechnology, and financial resources.[5] The CBD identifies the problem of dwindling biodiversity, sets overall goals and policies and general obligations, and organizes technical and financial cooperation. As an overall approach to conservation, this is a huge improvement over earlier models. Unfortunately, this advance is tempered by the fact that the responsibility and discretion for achieving its goals rests largely with the countries that sign and ratify it.

For example, Article 6 states that signatories are required, in accordance with their "particular conditions and capabilities," to "develop national strategies, plans or programmes for the conservation and sustainable use of biodiversity," and to integrate "as far as possible and as appropriate, the conservation and sustainable use of biological diversity" into broader national plans for environment and development.[6] This is a laudable idea, but the caveats and conditional clauses weaken it considerably. Nations are left to decide for themselves whether they have the "conditions and capabilities" that generate these duties, and whether any given actions are "possible" or "appropriate."

Similarly, Article 7 provides that each signatory shall "as far as possible and as appropriate" "identify components of biological diversity important for its conservation and sustainable use" and monitor them, "paying particular attention to those requiring urgent conservation measures and those which offer the greatest potential for sustainable use."[7] In identifying these key areas, nations are to consider, inter alia, ecosystems and habitats

containing high diversity, large numbers of endemic or threatened species, or wilderness; required by migratory species; of social, economic, cultural or scientific importance; or, which are representative, unique or associated with key evolutionary or other biological processes.[8]

This description certainly is broad enough to embrace the hotspots, if a nation is so inclined. But when is it "possible" for a developing nation to divert scarce resources to the identification and monitoring of key pockets of biodiversity? When is it "appropriate" to make such an investment in biodiversity, in light of all the other pressing needs poorer nations must try to meet? The answer, in the real world, is "not very often."

Article 8, pertaining to in situ conservation, includes the same escape hatch, "as far as possible and as appropriate," in directing each signatory, inter alia, to establish "a system of protected areas or areas where special measures need to be taken to conserve biological diversity"; develop guidelines for their selection, establishment, and management; "[r]egulate or manage biological resources important for the conservation of biological diversity whether within or outside protected areas, with a view to ensuring their conservation and sustainable use"; "[p]romote the protection of ecosystems, natural habitats, and the maintenance of viable populations of species in natural surroundings"; "[p]romote environmentally sound and sustainable development in areas adjacent to protected areas with a view to furthering protection of these areas"; and "[r]ehabilitate and restore degraded ecosystems and promote the recovery of threatened species . . . through the development and implementation of plans or other management strategies."[9]

The concept of sustainable use appears again in Article 10. Once more, "as far as possible and appropriate," signatories are to, inter alia, "[i]ntegrate consideration of the conservation and sustainable use of biological resources into national decison-making"; "[a]dopt measures relating to the use of biological resources to avoid or minimize adverse impacts on biological diversity"; encourage cooperation between government and the private sector in developing methods for sustainable use; and "[p]rotect and encourage customary use of biological resources in accordance with traditional cultural practices that are compatible with conservation or sustainable use requirements."[10]

As with many other international agreements, in order to attract signatories, the CBD was festooned with caveats, conditional clauses, and reservations that rob its good ideas of much of their real power. These problems aside, the CBD was a breakthrough in a way, because the text of Stockholm Principle 21 appears verbatim as Article 3, marking the first time this language had appeared in binding international law rather than in "customary law" or "soft law."[11] Article 3 reads:

States have, in accordance with the Charter of the United Nations and the principles of international law, the sovereign right to exploit their own resources pursuant to their own environmental policies, and the responsibility to ensure that activities within their jurisdiction or control do not cause damage to the environment of other States or of areas beyond the limits of national jurisdiction.[12]

Thus, the traditional concept of national sovereignty over resources is, at least in principle, balanced within the CBD by the requirement that each party accept its responsibility not to harm the territory of any other state or the territory beyond its own national jurisdiction.[13] This could be significant for hotspots preservation, given the global significance of these eco-regions and the persistent problem of individual nations exploiting them and/or failing to afford them adequate protection.

The CBD also contains a progressive provision in terms of funding. In recognition of the practical concerns and needs of many countries, CBD-related activities by developing countries are eligible for support from the financial mechanism of the CBD, that is, the Global Environment Facility (GEF).[14] Each party is to provide financial support according to its available resources and commensurate with the national objectives undertaken to meet the CBD's directives.[15] GEF projects, supported by the United Nations Environment Program (UNEP), the United Nations Development Program (UNDP), and the World Bank, are to help forge international cooperation and finance actions to address four critical threats to the global environment: biodiversity loss, climate change, depletion of the ozone layer, and degradation of international waters. By the end of 1999, the GEF had contributed nearly $1 billion for biodiversity projects in more than 120 countries.[16] Undoubtedly, many of these projects have made a valuable contribution to the cause of biodiversity.

This is a promising feature of the CBD. It acknowledges the need to provide positive financial incentives for biodiversity conservation in contrast to the traditional fear-driven command-and-control model.[17] It also recognizes that some nations are more capable than others of funding environmental protection and seeks to level the playing field. Without a meaningful infusion of resources, including and especially money, many developing nations will lack the wherewithal to effect real progress within their borders, no matter how devoted they may be to the ideal of environmental protection.

Building on the understanding that developing nations must develop more intelligently to be eco-friendly, one of the most important portions of the CBD is the provision for technical and scientific cooperation and the creation of a mechanism to collect, manage, and disperse information and statistics on global biodiversity.[18] Article 18 provides for a clearinghouse whereby technical and scientific information concerning biodiversity can be shared among nations to help further conservation efforts.[19] This, too, is a worthwhile initiative that could advance the state of knowledge globally. Developing nations might gain a head start on their own conservation programs if they can build on the lessons learned by other, more resource-rich, developed countries.

The CBD is a broad document that also features some very controversial provisions on intellectual property and biotechnology, including "genetic resources." For example, Article 19 provides in part:

Each Contracting Party shall take all practicable measures to promote and advance priority access on a fair and equitable basis by Contracting Parties, especially developing countries, to the results and benefits arising from biotechnologies based upon genetic resources provided by those Contracting Parties. Such access shall be on mutually agreed terms.[20]

Similarly, Article 16 provides for access to and transfer of technology, including biotechnology, such that developing countries "which provide genetic resources are provided access to and transfer of technology which makes use of those resources, on mutually agreed terms, including technology protected by patents and other intellectual property rights."[21] Such terms have been of great concern to the United States, to the extent that President Clinton did not even seek Senate ratification of the CBD. The specter of claims by developing nations on the financial profits arising from the exploitation and development of natural resources and on highly valuable and expensively acquired intellectual property, including biotechnology, being siphoned off by other nations has haunted the CBD and has frightened off the United States and some other developed nations.[22] Yet it is precisely these parts of the CBD that most astutely address the underlying pressures driving the current mass extinction.

The United States' hesitancy notwithstanding, many key hotspots nations have signed and ratified or otherwise approved the CBD, including Brazil, Madagascar, Papua New Guinea, Democratic Republic of the Congo, China, India, Indonesia, and others.[23] In theory, then, the CBD could be a useful tool for hotspots preservation. However, there are some serious shortcomings, as we have already begun to see.

First, the CBD does not actually create enforceable legal obligations. Instead, it directs its signatories to enact legislation within their jurisdiction consistent with the CBD objectives. If a nation fails to do this, there are no real consequences. Under the CBD, parties have very few obligations, and most of these are eviscerated with the phrases "as far as possible and as appropriate," or "in accordance with [a party's] capabilities."[24] For developing nations, implementing measures are further contingent on commitments from First World parties to provide technology and funding.[25] In addition, no mechanism exists to assess the substantive adequacy and consistency of national biodiversity plans, and thus it is practically impossible to detect any breach of CBD obligations.[26]

The GEF has been criticized as well. Some have noted the conflict inherent in the involvement of the World Bank as the managing partner of the GEF, which might impose a prodevelopment inclination on CBD actions.[27] Additionally, critics have pointed out a possible GEF/World Bank bias toward supporting projects that redound to the benefit of developed nations instead of devoting more attention to developing countries where most of the real action should be.[28]

Also, the CBD does not focus on hotspots per se, nor any of the other methods for ranking biodiversity resources, but only instructs signatories to identify and monitor important biodiversity resources and take some steps toward preserving them. This is very general guidance, and compliance is very much in the eye of the beholder.[29] There is no overarching priority scheme for either identifying or protecting the most vital pockets of biodiversity. Worthwhile initiatives may be fostered by the CBD, nation by nation, one park or preserve at a time, but this is too haphazard and idiosyncratic to be a substitute for specific, big-picture legislation with real enforcement capabilities.

World Heritage Convention

The Convention Concerning the Protection of the World Cultural and Natural Heritage (the World Heritage Convention, or WHC)[30] was adopted by the General Conference of UNESCO in 1972. The WHC provides an international framework for the protection of natural and cultural areas of "outstanding universal value."[31] To date, some 172 countries have adhered to the WHC, out of the 189 Member States of the United Nations including key hotspots nations. As with the CBD, the name of the WHC is intriguing, and seems to imply the type of overarching legal protection of the world's hotspots that we are searching for. Are our hopes to be illusory once again?

The Preamble states with clarity the core principles relevant to the preservation of all resources that are locally situated yet have global significance. Although neither the term "biodiversity hotspot," nor any of the alternative means for establishing biodiversity conservation priorities (e.g., Global 200, Endemic Bird Areas, Centres of Plant Diversity, WORLDMAP), specifically appear anywhere in the WHC, the vexing challenges that assail such natural treasures are nonetheless recognized in the Preamble:

[T]he cultural heritage and the natural heritage are increasingly threatened with destruction not only by the traditional causes of decay, but also by changing social and economic conditions which aggravate the situation with even more formidable phenomena of damage or destruction . . . deterioration or disappearance of any item of the cultural or natural heritage constitutes a harmful impoverishment of the heritage of all the nations of the world . . . protection of this heritage at the national level often remains incomplete because of the scale of the resources which it requires and of the insufficient economic, scientific, and technological resources of the country where the property to be protected is situated . . . existing international conventions, recommendations and resolutions concerning cultural and natural property demonstrate the importance, for all the peoples of the world, of safeguarding this unique and irreplaceable property, to whatever people it may belong . . . parts of the cultural or natural heritage are of outstanding interest and therefore need to be preserved as part of the world heritage of mankind as a whole . . . in view of the magnitude and gravity of the new dangers threatening them, it is incumbent on the international community as a whole to participate in the protection of the cultural and natural heritage of outstanding universal value, by the granting of collective assistance which, although not taking the place of action by the State concerned, will serve as an efficient complement thereto . . . [and] it is essential for this purpose to adopt new provisions in the form of a convention establishing an effective system of collective protection of the cultural and natural heritage of outstanding universal value, organized on a permanent basis and in accordance with modern scientific methods . . . .[32]

Building on this philosophical and factual predicate, the WHC establishes, as its centerpiece, a list of specific places in the world that meet its overarching criterion of "outstanding universal value." The World Heritage List is the compendium of sites, in either the "natural heritage"[33] or "cultural heritage"[34] category, that have been recognized formally according to the terms of the WHC.

The WHC defines the type of natural or cultural sites that can be considered for inclusion in the World Heritage List and sets forth the duties of states parties in identifying potential sites and their roles in protecting them. Specifically with regard to "natural heritage" sites, the WHC supplies the following criteria:

[N]atural features consisting of physical and biological formations or groups of such formations, which are of outstanding universal value from the aesthetic or scientific point of view; geological and physiographical formations and precisely delineated areas which constitute the habitat of threatened species of animals and plants of outstanding universal value from the point of view of science or conservation; natural sites or precisely delineated natural areas of outstanding universal value from the point of view of science, conservation, or natural beauty.[35]

The Convention, in Article 4, places the primary "duty of ensuring the identification, protection, conservation, presentation and transmission to future generations of the cultural and natural heritage" sites on the World Heritage List with the nation that is host to each site.[36] Each host nation is to "do all it can to this end, to the utmost of its own resources.[37] Additionally, where appropriate, each host nation may also draw upon "any international assistance and co-operation, in particular, financial, artistic, scientific and technical, which it may be able to obtain."[38]

Article 6 is at the core of the WHC. It begins with an important caveat:

Whilst fully respecting the sovereignty of the States on whose territory the cultural and natural heritage . . . is situated, and without prejudice to property rights provided by national legislation, the States Parties to this Convention recognize that such heritage constitutes a world heritage for whose protection it is the duty of the international community as a whole to cooperate.[39]

Article 6 further provides that signatories undertake "to give their help in the identification, protection, conservation and preservation of the cultural and natural heritage . . . if the States on whose territory it is situated so request,"[40] and "not to take any deliberate measures which might damage directly or indirectly the cultural and natural heritage . . . situated on the territory of other States Parties to this Convention."[41]

Article 5 states that signatories "shall endeavour, in so far as possible, and as appropriate for each country," inter alia, "to develop scientific and technical studies and research and to work out such operating methods as will make the State capable of counteracting the dangers that threaten its cultural or natural heritage,"[42] and "to take the appropriate legal, scientific, technical, administrative and financial measures necessary for the identification, protection, conservation, presentation, and rehabilitation of this heritage."[43]

This is an ambitious agenda, but one rendered hostage to the whims of the leadership within each State Party. Nations that are predisposed to take effective action to preserve their natural and cultural heritage will do so, and perhaps would do so even absent Article 5 of the WHC. Those that lack this predisposition will find ample room for discretion and exception in the introductory clause to justify a very comfortable inaction. As a result, the efficacy of these provisions is questionable even within the confines of Article 5 itself. Other, more overarching, problems with the WHC, have further impaired the Convention in its implementation and enforcement, as will be discussed shortly.

The WHC includes the well-intentioned but controversial concept of transitional zoning, or "buffer zones." The idea is that listed World Heritage sites should be surrounded by concentric regions of graduated restrictiveness to provide a margin of safety around the sites themselves. Whenever necessary for proper conservation, "an adequate 'buffer zone' around a property should be provided and should be afforded the necessary protection. A buffer zone can be defined as an area surrounding the property which has restrictions placed on its use to give an added layer of protection."[44] Of course, by expanding the territory subject to increased regulation beyond the actual formal boundaries of a listed site, such as a national park, wildlife refuge, or wilderness area, the buffer zone principle can be seen as an encroachment on the private property rights of individual landowners. This then contributes to the disputatious nature of many WHC listing proposals, as citizens fight to defend their property interests from indirect erosion.[45]

The application for a site to be inscribed on the World Heritage List must come from the country itself.[46] Moreover, no site may be placed on the list without the consent of the nation concerned.[47] An application must include a plan detailing how the site is managed and protected in national legislation. The World Heritage Committee[48] meets once a year and examines the applications on the basis of technical evaluations. These independent evaluations of proposed cultural and natural sites are provided by two advisory bodies, the International Council on Monuments and Sites (ICOMOS) and the World Conservation Union (IUCN), respectively.[49]

The World Heritage List has grown to a formidable size. As of September, 2002, the list included 730 sites of "outstanding universal value" in 125 nations.[50] Of these 730 sites, 563 are denominated as "cultural," 144 as "natural," and 23 as "mixed."[51] One of the 31 new sites added to the World Heritage List in December, 2001 was an area within the Brazilian Cerrado hotspot consisting of the Chapada dos Veadeiros and Emas National Parks,[52] which, although certainly not encompassing the entirety of this important hotspot, is a positive development illustrative of the potential for the WHC to assist in hotspot identification and preservation.

The World Heritage List includes other sites that fall within the hotspots, albeit sites that usually amount to only a small fraction of the territory that each hotspot actually embraces on the basis of the scientific evidence alone. Notably, given the prominent representation of tropical forests in the hotspots, the list features 41 separate tropical forest sites, which in the aggregate encompass 30.6 million hectares of territory.[53] Of these sites, 23 are national parks within their respective nations, and over a dozen more are reserves or sanctuaries of one type or another. In this way, the WHC has often functioned to lend some degree of additional support to areas that had previously been identified and set apart by the host nation as an important natural property.

There is a World Heritage Fund established under Article 15 that provides limited financial support to nations in furtherance of the WHC's purposes. The fund is to receive compulsory and voluntary contributions from the WHC signatories and several other sources.[54] Requests for international assistance for the preservation of WHC properties are made under Article 19, and the funds are to be granted only for duly listed sites, pursuant to Article 20. Technical assistance and training are also available,[55] which, if offered in conjunction with sufficient levels of financial aid, might be instrumental in effecting meaningful protection for World Heritage Sites.

The World Heritage Fund is set up as a trust fund.[56] Specifically, Article 15.3 provides, in pertinent part:

The resources of the Fund shall consist of: (a) compulsory and voluntary contributions made by States Parties to this Convention; (b) contributions, gifts or bequests which may be made by: (i) other States; (ii) the United Nations Educational, Scientific and Cultural Organization, other organizations of the United Nations system, particularly the United Nations Development Programme or other intergovernmental organizations; (iii) public or private bodies or individuals; (c) any interest due on the resources of the Fund; (d) funds raised by collections and receipts from events organized for the benefit of the fund; and (e) all other resources authorized by the Fund's regulations, as drawn up by the World Heritage Committee.[57]

This enables the World Heritage Fund to receive contributions from a wide range of donors, including private individuals, non-governmental organizations, and any nation. The WHC also directs States Parties to "consider or encourage the establishment of national public and private foundations or associations whose purpose is to invite donations for the protection of the cultural and natural heritage"[58] as defined in the WHC. The overarching concept is to broaden the scope of possible funding sources and empower the WHC to employ innovative and unconventional ideas to augment the funds available for preservation of the natural and cultural resources it seeks to safeguard. Although this is at present still largely untapped potential, the potential is spelled out in the WHC nonetheless, which sets the foundation for future progress.

The World Heritage Committee determines the acceptable uses for the Fund's resources, and "may accept contributions to be used only for a certain programme or project, provided that the Committee shall have decided on the implementation" of such an initiative.[59] No political conditions may be attached to contributions made to the Fund.[60] In other words, interested individuals and groups, including nongovernmental organizations (NGOs), have some ability to target their donations to certain favored proj-ects, such as the preservation of a particular sector of a hotspot. This could be a useful tool for harnessing the power and money of activists, philanthropists, and public interest groups in the WHC's efforts to assist certain sites on the World Heritage List.

With regard to the signatories to the WHC, the amount of "compulsory" contributions to the Fund is discussed in Article 16, paragraph 1:

Without prejudice to any supplementary voluntary contribution, the States Parties to this Convention undertake to pay regularly, every two years, to the World Heritage Fund, contributions, the amount of which, in the form of a uniform percentage applicable to all States, shall be determined by the General Assembly of States Parties to the Convention, meeting during the sessions of the General Conference of the United Nations Educational, Scientific and Cultural Organization. This decision of the General Assembly requires the majority of the States Parties present and voting, which have not made the declaration referred to in paragraph 2 of this Article. In no case shall the compulsory contribution of States Parties to the Convention exceed 1% of the contribution to the regular budget of the United Nations Educational, Scientific and Cultural Organization.[61]

However, Article 16, paragraph 2, allows Parties to issue a "declaration" that they will not be bound to contribute to the World Heritage Fund in the manner provided by paragraph 1. The United States is one of the nations that has exercised the option to excuse itself from contributing to the World Heritage Fund under Article 16.1. Strangely, paragraph 4 directs that contributions from Parties that have made this declaration "shall be paid on a regular basis, at least every two years, and should not be less than the contributions which they should have paid if they had been bound by the provisions of paragraph 1 of this Article."[62] In any event, sanctions for non-payment of either "voluntary" or "compulsory" contributions are quite limited:

Any State Party to the Convention which is in arrears with the payment of its compulsory or voluntary contribution for the current year and the calendar year immediately preceding it shall not be eligible as a Member of the World Heritage Committee. . . . [63]

Requests for international assistance for the preservation of WHC properties are made under Article 19, and the funds are to be granted only for duly listed sites, pursuant to Article 20. There is also technical assistance and training available,[64] which, if offered in conjunction with sufficient levels of financial aid, might be instrumental in effecting meaningful protection for World Heritage Sites. Article 22 specifies that assistance to sites on the World Heritage List may take the form of: studies concerning the artistic, scientific and technical problems raised by the protection, conservation, presentation and rehabilitation of the site; provision of experts, technicians and skilled labor to ensure that the approved work is correctly carried out; training of staff and specialists at all levels in the field of identification, protection, conservation, presentation and rehabilitation of the site; supply of equipment which the nation concerned does not possess or is not in a position to acquire; low-interest or interest-free loans which might be repayable on a long-term basis; and the granting, "in exceptional cases and for special reasons, of non-repayable subsidies."[65]

Could the quantum of assistance provided under the WHC suffice to make an outcome-determinative difference for any site, including a hotspot? The language of the Convention is characteristically vague:

International assistance on a large scale shall be preceded by detailed scientific, economic and technical studies. These studies shall draw upon the most advanced techniques for the protection, conservation, presentation and rehabilitation of the natural and cultural heritage and shall be consistent with the objectives of this Convention. The studies shall also seek means of making rational use of the resources available in the State concerned.[66]

The text does not define the key terms "large scale," "detailed" studies, and "most advanced techniques." The imprecision of the standards leaves important decisions on the appropriate degree of help to the discretion of the World Heritage Committee. Similarly, the restriction in Article 25 to the effect that "only part of the cost of work necessary shall be borne by the international community" and the nation benefitting from international assistance shall contribute "a substantial share of the resources" devoted to each program or project, is not a firm, objective standard.[67] Moreover, any limitation on aid or mandate for host nation contribution implicit in Article 25 is overcome by its concluding escape hatch, "unless [the host nation's] resources do not permit this."[68] Very often, of course, the host nations for hotspots are in desperate economic straits, which is a primary reason why their natural resources are imperiled in the first place. Pressures to develop and exploit nature are most acute when there are few if any alternatives for a nation and its people who are struggling in many cases even to maintain a bare subsistence level of income.

In prescient anticipation of a shortfall of available rescue resources and a surplus of pressing and competing needs, the WHC reflects an attempt to set forth a system for setting priorities:

The Committee shall determine an order of priorities for its operations. It shall in so doing bear in mind the respective importance for the world cultural and natural heritage of the property requiring protection, the need to give international assistance to the property most representative of a natural environment or of the genius and the history of the peoples of the world, the urgency of the work to be done, the resources available to the States on whose territory the threatened property is situated and in particular the extent to which they are able to safeguard such property by their own means.[69]

A key feature of the WHC in terms of hotspots preservation centers on the measures it prescribes when sites are imperiled. The World Heritage Committee is supposed to be alerted—by individuals, nongovernmental organizations, or other groups—to possible dangers to a site. If the alert is justified, and the problem serious enough, the site will be placed on the List of World Heritage in Danger, which is provided for by Article 11.4 of the WHC.[70] The List of World Heritage in Danger is reserved for those sites already inscribed on the primary World Heritage List "for the conservation of which major operations are necessary and for which assistance has been requested" under the WHC.[71] The list is to contain an estimate of the costs of any such operations. Furthermore,

The list may include only such property forming part of the cultural and natural heritage as is threatened by serious and specific dangers, such as the threat of disappearance caused by accelerated deterioration, large-scale public or private projects or rapid urban or tourist development projects; destruction caused by changes in the use or ownership of the land; major alterations due to unknown causes; abandonment for any reason whatsoever; the outbreak or the threat of an armed conflict; calamities and cataclysms; serious fires, earthquakes, landslides; volcanic eruptions; changes in water level, floods and tidal waves.[72]

This List of World Heritage in Danger, consisting of imperiled cultural and natural resources, is designed to call the world's attention to natural or human-made conditions which threaten the characteristics for which the site was originally included in the main World Heritage List.[73] In theory, inclusion on the "Danger" list increases the likelihood that funds will be deemed available within the priority-setting triage scheme of Article 13.4 to make a difference in the survival of the resources in question. For this reason, I chose to incorporate the name of the list in the title of this Article. It neatly captures the essence of the hotspots crisis.

The List of World Heritage in Danger included only 33 sites as of September, 2002.[74] Many of the sites on this list are cultural/historical resources rather than natural resources, but it is open to both categories. The United States currently has two sites inscribed on the list, the Everglades and Yellowstone National Parks.[75] Several parks and nature preserves are on the list, including the Srebarna Nature Preserve in Bulgaria; the Manovo-Gounda St. Floris National Park in the Central African Republic; the Mount Nimba Nature Reserve in the Ivory Coast/Guinea; the Virunga, Garamba, Kahuzi-Biega, and Salonga National Parks and Okapi Wildlife Reserve, all in the Democratic Republic of the Congo; the Sangay National Park in Ecuador; the Rio Platano Biosphere Reserve in Honduras; the Manas Wildlife Sanctuary in India; the Air and Tenere Natural Reserves in Niger; the Djoudj National Bird Sanctuary in Senegal; the Ichkeul National Park in Tunisia; and the Rwenzori Mountains National Park in Uganda.

The hotspots should be extensively represented on the List of World Heritage in Danger, on the basis of the confluence of core criteria for inclusion in both categories. If there were broader recognition and comprehension of the hotspots concept worldwide, their representation on the List of World Heritage in Danger would be far more extensive than it is now. By definition, the hotspots are both supremely vital repositories of much of the earth's biodiversity, and, drastically under attack from a variety of destructive/developmental forces. They belong on the List of World Heritage in Danger if anything does.

Unfortunately, the act of inscribing a site on either the World Heritage List[76] or the List of World Heritage in Danger can be very controversial. When Yellowstone National Park was placed on the List of World Heritage in Danger in 1995, there was much political furor arising out of claims that United States sovereignty had been impinged, merely because the WHC had influenced in part President Clinton's decision to issue executive orders providing buffer zones around the park and enhancing its protection against a nearby mining operation.[77] A cynic might be forgiven for opining that this is evidence of the validity of the maxim, "No good deed goes unpunished."

One additional feature of the WHC could be useful under the right circumstances, albeit indirectly. Article 27 focuses on educational and informational initiatives to inform the citizenry as to the importance and fragility of World Heritage sites:

1. The States Parties to this Convention shall endeavor by all appropriate means, and in particular by educational and information programmes, to strengthen appreciation and respect by their peoples of the cultural and natural heritage defined in Articles 1 and 2 of the Convention. 2. They shall undertake to keep the public broadly informed of the dangers threatening this heritage and of the activities carried on in pursuance of this Convention.[78]

The evident intent is to educate the people, at all levels, within the nations that are home to the various World Heritage sites. The drafters of the

WHC recognized the importance, indeed the indispensable nature, of widespread public knowledge and support of conservation efforts, particularly with regard to key natural and cultural treasures. If the people "on the ground" in these nations do not know the value of the sites with which they may interact, and are uninformed as to the dangers threatening the continued existence of the sites, they cannot be expected to hold them in high esteem personally. They cannot be expected to refrain from exploiting and damaging the sites when it is their financial self-interest to do so, let alone voluntarily devote their own time, effort, and money to the preservation of the sites. And absent this type of grass-roots commitment of the citizenry, there is very little real protection that can be imposed on sites from the top down. Thus, the spirit of Article 27 is in tune with a very real and persistent problem that has plagued conservation globally, and, at a minimum, it reflects an attempt to ameliorate the situation by using understanding and information as the best antidotes to apathy and antipathy.

If a signatory fails to fulfill its obligations under the Convention, it risks having its sites deleted from the World Heritage List and, of course, losing any WHC funds it may have been receiving by virtue of having sites on the list. The World Heritage Committee is supposed to be alerted—by individuals, nongovernmental organizations, or other groups—to possible dangers to a site. If the alert is justified, and the problem serious enough, the site will be placed on the List of World Heritage in Danger.[79]

But the biggest flaw in the WHC is that it lacks any true enforcement mechanisms. Despite terms and conditions that purport to obligate parties to refrain from undertaking acts that might directly or indirectly damage a designated resource, the WHC does not address whether sanctions may be taken against countries that violate them.[80] Also, while signatories are required to submit reports regarding domestic measures taken to further WHC aims,[81] there is no provision whereby a party can be penalized or sanctioned for failing to provide requested information or for submitting inaccurate or false information. As a result, reports in many cases have been less than satisfactory.[82] The WHC does not provide a dispute settlement process either.

Philosophically, the WHC is quite compatible with the concept of hotspots preservation and may provide some assistance toward this aim, as it has in other areas.[83] Among the criteria for consideration as a "natural heritage" site is that an area be of "outstanding universal value from the point of view of science or conservation."[84] This definition is tailor made for hotspots. And the factors that determine eligibility for inclusion in the top-priority subsidiary list, World Heritage in Danger, are also entirely consonant with the very definition of a hotspot.

However, this philosophical fit is vitiated by the lack of meaningful "teeth" to enforce its provisions; loss of WHC listing of a nation's resources is the only sanction for noncompliance. This is akin to punishing someone who beats his pet dog by telling him his dog will no longer be allowed to have a license. Moreover, the WHC leaves it up to individual nations to recommend their own resources for inclusion in the World Heritage List in the first place and prohibits inclusion without the consent of the host nation. A nation that is disinclined to preserve its hotspot would be unlikely to nominate it for the list, and would probably veto any attempt by outsiders to inscribe it.

After all, is it true that there are merely 33 places (whether cultural or natural) in the entire world that properly qualify for the List of World Heritage in Danger? If not—if there are many more that deserve that designation—then there must be powerful disincentives at work that have artificially depressed the number of treasures thus inscribed.

There is a great deal of merit in the WHC as it currently exists, even absent any amendments. One key virtue of the WHC is that it can serve as a visible, high-profile vehicle to identify hotspots, one by one, as globally important natural properties. Even if it did nothing more, this would further a laudable purpose by helping to focus public attention on the hotspots in the international community. Heightened public awareness, fostered by what should be widely considered a great honor—recognition as a World Heritage Site—could be a significant step toward more substantive legal measures. Indeed, one of the indirect benefits of listing lies in the potential for increasing tourism; many countries now include their World Heritage listings in their advertising to attract foreign tourists, including eco-tourists.[85] As governments reap the gains in tourism money from their inscribed sites, they will likely develop a greater appreciation for the wisdom of conserving them. At bottom, the plight of the hotspots can be traced to widespread ignorance as to their value and meaning, not only at the level of the citizenry but also at the decision-making levels of government where policy and legal measures are developed.

This ignorance, unfortunately, has manifested itself in a dazzling spectrum of different ways, a veritable rainbow of cluelessness. One outstanding example is the failure to inscribe any of the hotspots even as a World Heritage site, let alone be included on the List of World Heritage in Danger. Not one of the 25 or so primary hotspots has received World Heritage recognition in its entirety, although portions of some have. This is a threshold problem of considerable magnitude, because it proves that much education and persuasion must take place just to get the hotspots listed under the only international legal instrument capable of affording them comprehensive protection. Actually effecting meaningful conservation measures within the WHC context would be a separate, and probably more formidable, challenge, but the threshold must first be crossed.

World Heritage Site designation, once achieved, would generate considerable publicity concerning the merits of any given hotspot, within the host nation and on a global scale. Simply by directing the spotlight on the issue, the WHC could supply a potent antidote to the deadly toxin of epidemic ignorance. Public debate, informed by documented scientific evidence, would educate at least some people as to the primacy of hotspots as well as the nature and magnitude of the local threats to their survival, and that would be all to the good. If enough top-echelon discussion takes place on these points, over a protracted period, the message would become increasingly clear to increasingly sizable numbers of people, even in countries where the local hotspot had traditionally been taken for granted as nothing more than a resource to be freely exploited.

Success in garnering World Heritage site designation for one or more hotspots could tend to breed further success in listing others. It may be that inscribing the first hotspot under the WHC will be the most difficult of all, and that once a precedent is established, more hotspots will be designated in relatively short order. The educational and information-sharing functions of the WHC could alert people in many nations as to the primacy of the hotspots, as the initial debate unfolds and the first one or two hotspots are listed.

Would sufficient numbers of hotspots-cognizant people translate into meaningful conservation action? As the time-hallowed epigram holds, "It couldn't hurt!" Some may remain unpersuaded, albeit better-informed, whether for reasons of overwhelming personal self-interest, philosophical opposition to conservation, or a process of ratiocination that concludes with a judgment call that the host nation would be better served by exploitation than preservation. Anyone who has ever been in a law school classroom understands that unanimity of opinion on an issue—any issue—is the rarest of phenomena, irrespective of the weight of evidence and the clarity of the facts. But knowledge is power, and as some minds change some other things might eventually change too.

In this way, designation as a World Heritage site, and especially placement on the List of World Heritage in Danger, could be helpful irrespective of any direct tangible aid under the Convention. It could facilitate the listing of other hotspots, as both decision-makers and the citizens who might influence them learn more about the significance of the hotspots as the global crown jewels of life. And the private concern generated by such high-profile listings could be used to leverage significant fundraising activities for hotspots preservation by NGOs. This money could be funneled into the WHC system and earmarked for a particular purpose,[86] or used apart from the formal WHC apparatus in purely private conservation initiatives. There is much good that can be achieved by harnessing private sector energy and wealth, and by tapping into the extensive trove of NGO expertise and commitment. NGOs and unaffiliated, dedicated citizens have immense freedom, flexibility, and power to raise money, mobilize workers, organize teams of volunteers, and pressure public officials.

Unfettered by the manifold layers of bureaucracy and institutional inertia that afflict many or all governments, these private sector forces can move in ways that official agencies cannot. The sheer numbers of citizens that could be galvanized into action by the right concatenation of events dwarf the legions of even the largest government's conservation workers, and their collective wealth, drive, and passion can be unrivaled. But it takes a catalyst to make this happen, and the WHC process can provide it. This is an intangible and largely unpredictable advantage of the WHC, but that does not vitiate its power.

An international legal instrument such as the WHC, buttressed by numerous signatories the world over, has the elusive if not unique capability to confer upon particular hotspots the imprimatur of official recognition as a World Heritage resource in danger. Indeed, this is one of the chief virtues of international law—the capacity to apotheosize a previously obscure cause, transforming it into a cause célèbre. It is this aura of official status and legitimacy, coupled with ready access to news media, that vests the WHC with the power to transform the collective will of the people, more so than most books, articles, speeches, paid advertisements, or television programs. And once the engine of private dynamism is started, it can become a veritable juggernaut, unstoppable and indomitable.

Furthermore, once a given site is added to the List of World Heritage resources, Article 27 of the WHC would provide additional impetus to efforts by the host nation's government to educate its people about the site's importance. Of course, absent an effective enforcement mechanism, this and other provisions of the Convention might be ignored with impunity, but at least there would be a formal requirement in effect. This could be the predicate for pressure from other nations, or from conservationist factions within the nation. And at least some signatories would voluntarily comply with the Article 27 strictures, thereby furthering the level of awareness of hotspots issues locally and stoking the fires of private initiative first ignited by World Heritage recognition. Here again the WHC can be a potent stimulus for action by NGOs and private citizens, as well as by government.

A complement to the general education value of the current WHC is its capacity to spur useful research into the hotspots. Article 24's demand of "detailed scientific, economic and technical studies" as a prerequisite for major financial assistance could advance the state of the art as to the contents and significance of each hotspot as well as the optimal means of shepherding these resources. In light of the dismal amount of information available about many of the hotspots, anything that prods further research is welcome. As incremental progress is made as to our knowledge of the biota residing within each hotspot, particularly their present utilitarian value to humankind, there will be a more robust and pragmatic argument for taking steps to protect the habitat. In this way, information can beget further protection. Of course, adequacy of funding for such studies will be a persistent issue; if host nations had the resources and the inclination to conduct these studies, they probably would not need outside assistance to protect their hotspots. Thus, we have sort of a "Catch 22" in Article 24—or perhaps we should call it a "Catch 24."

This highlights another "good news/bad news" aspect of the WHC. The Convention is potentially capable of diverting resources from the haves to the have-nots for purposes of preserving key treasures such as the hotspots. As I have pointed out, this is a phenomenon that must take place much more often, in far greater amounts, and in many more nations than ever before if the hotspots are not to burn out. The WHC has the virtue of actually obligating its signatories, under some set of circumstances, to put their money where their ink is and pay for preservation of global treasures. This is more than any other legal instrument does, at present, and for that reason alone the WHC is worthy of the attention of anyone who cares about the plight of earth's biodiversity. It formalizes the duty of States Parties to bear some of the burden of preserving globally important resources in nations other than their own. What a concept! Global help to save global treasures. This is a vital first step, at least, toward a more enlightened and comprehensive view of what it means—or should mean—to each nation to share the same planet with all other nations.

But we have seen that the Convention's obligations are undermined by caveats, qualifications, ambiguities, reservations, and other legal loopholes. The net result is that the WHC is only as effective in spurring nations to contribute money where it is needed as the nations are willing, voluntarily, to contribute on their own. The WHC might supply some structure to the process, as by identifying areas of special need, but it cannot compel signatories to devote more money than they wish to spend, nor to send it anywhere they would prefer not to send it. Compliance with its terms is essentially voluntary.

Of course, it is also entirely voluntary for nations to become signatories to the WHC or any other international legal instrument in the first place. This is one of the fundamental problems inherent in the international law approach to challenges like the hotspots crisis. It is a variant of the old aphorism, "For those who understand, no explanation is necessary. For those who do not understand, no explanation will suffice." If the leaders and citizens of a nation are inclined to help on any particular issue, and do not believe that the disadvantages of an applicable treaty outweigh the advantages, they will be apt to sign and ratify. Otherwise, they will not. No nation can be forced to commit to any treaty. These international agreements are voluntary affairs, akin to a come-as-you-are party open to anyone who is interested. Guests cannot be dragged in off the street; at most, other partygoers can try to persuade and entice reluctant newcomers with charm, peer pressure, and promises of good times to come. Even nations that may be philosophically sympathetic to a given issue may refuse to sign a treaty that they judge to be fatally flawed, unfair, biased, counterproductive, or otherwise impolitic. You can lead a nation to a treaty, but you cannot make it sign.

For the nations that do not sign the WHC, or that do sign but fail to live up to their commitments thereunder, does the Convention serve any purpose? It still can play the role of an information source, periodically reminding non-signatories of the need to designate additional deserving sites and to provide increased protection for sites already inscribed. Anyone who has ever been nagged by a parent, a spouse, or a significant other (or who has taken the more active role of the nagger) knows that sometimes persistently importuning someone will eventually lead to capitulation. Sometimes it has the opposite effect, of hardening resistance, but at least the recipient of such pleas is kept apprised of recent developments, new discoveries, and other significant news related to the issue. In this manner, WHC reports and news releases can periodically inform non-parties of any progress made in safeguarding listed sites, and notify them of any new areas of concern. Such information might lead a nation's leaders to reconsider their decision not to sign, or motivate them to take other action to help, independent of the Convention.

It would be facile to propose that the WHC be amended to plug its loopholes. Like piles of dirt, accumulated over many years and swept under a carpet, problems continue to pop up elsewhere every time you step on a mound. To amend, the signatories must consent, but they will not consent if they view the changes as contrary to their own interests, and other nonsignatories will not sign on if the requirements are too onerous. As Lerner and Loewe (of Broadway musical fame) might have written in their play "My Fair Lady":

> All is want is a Convention,
> Armed with teeth and no exceptions,
> No more reservations,
> Oh, wouldn't it be loverly?[87]

It would be very nice indeed if one could wave a magic wand and make the WHC (1) applicable to all nations of the world, or at least all that contain hotspots; (2) enforceable with action-provoking levels of sanctions; (3) devoid of ambiguities and discretionary clauses that vitiate the effectiveness of key provisions; and (4) free of crucial reservations and exceptions. While we are wishing upon this star, we might as well also ask that, once the WHC is thus fortified, the crucial decision-makers be moved to nominate and approve each hotspot for designation as a World Heritage site, and then add them to the List of World Heritage in Danger. I would add my personal petition, if I may, to wit that the Chicago Cubs will win a World Series during my lifetime.[88]

There have been some attempts to remedy the lack of teeth in the WHC. For example, in light of massive destruction of important cultural property during the conflict in the former Yugoslavia, the Italian government proposed that U.N. inspectors monitor the world's cultural heritage, and that the international community share responsibility for cultural sites on the World Heritage List.[89] Italy suggested that UNESCO be given powers similar to those of the inspectors of the International Atomic Energy Agency, including the power to enter sovereign territory, so as to monitor compliance with the WHC.[90] However, the Italians withdrew the proposal when it was vigorously opposed by some members of the Executive Board of UNESCO, who indicated that their countries were unwilling to give up authority over their own territory or cultural treasures.[91] This type of non-military, protective international regulatory agency with the internationally recognized right to enter, inspect, recommend, and implement protective action for World Heritage sites would be a partial solution to the WHC's flaws. The failure of the idea to advance beyond the proposal stage is a classic example of the difficulty of making international agreements such as the WHC into truly effective, enforceable legal instruments.

Even if the WHC could be amended to tighten up its internal loopholes and supply it with meaningful enforcement provisions, that would not solve the problem that nations must voluntarily sign on to be bound. In fact, it would exacerbate it. Many current signatories would not agree to such significant amendments, and would not remain if they were effectuated. Nations that are not now States Parties would probably be even less likely to sign on. This, naturally, was a major factor in shaping the way the WHC was written. In order to attract and retain respectable numbers of signatories, the text had to be softened and qualified, with capacious wiggle room for nations to evade onerous provisions. The drafters of treaties and conventions do not inadvertently riddle them with fuzzy language, unknowingly allow many exceptions and reservations, and simply forget to build in real enforcement tools. These are added to the mix during the negotiation process to entice reticent nations to come on board. They are the price of admission, except paid by the ones throwing the party, not by the guests.

Other Global International Agreements

The CBD and WHC are the international agreements that most closely approximate a legal link to the hotspots phenomenon. However, others at least tangentially might touch on the issue. These other international agreements are a very poor fit for the hotspots and definitely do not address the issue on all fours. Nonetheless, for sake of completeness, I include brief mention of some of them here.[92]

Arguably, many additional international agreements could be included in our discussion if we were to take a sufficiently "big picture" view of the hotspots phenomenon. For example, the Kyoto Protocol to the United Nations Framework Convention on Climate Change ultimately may prove to be of great significance to the survival of the hotspots despite its focus on what appears on its face to be an entirely separate issue, global warming. I will not deal with such agreements here in order to maintain some limits on the scope of our analysis, but rather will restrict the discussion to the more directly applicable instruments.

CITES

The Convention on International Trade in Endangered Species of Wild Flora and Fauna (CITES),[93] as the name implies, deals with international trafficking in endangered species. CITES entered into force on July 1, 1975, and now has a membership of 158 countries. These nations act by banning commercial international trade in an agreed list of endangered species and by regulating and monitoring trade in others that might become endangered.[94]

Under CITES, export and import of listed endangered species require a government permit, which can be granted only when trade will not be detrimental to survival of the species, the specimen was not obtained contrary to applicable nature protection laws, and shipment will not result in injury or cruel treatment.[95] Appendices set forth categories of endangered species, with the most vulnerable being most severely regulated.[96] In implementing CITES, the European Community sought to achieve uniform protection within the Community and, for some sensitive species, provided even stricter protection than the Convention required.[97]

CITES provides for some enforcement mechanisms, such as the Article VIII requirement that parties take "appropriate measures" to enforce the CITES provisions, including assessing penalties on violators, confiscating illegal trade, and imposing fines for the costs incurred from the confiscation of illegal trade.[98] Article VIII also requires parties to submit implementation reports to the CITES Secretariat annually.[99] Additionally, Article XIII allows the Secretariat to bring noncompliance matters to the attention of the parties involved when the Secretariat is convinced that treaty provisions have not been "effectively implemented."[100] There is a dispute resolution procedure as well.[101] These enforcement tools have been criticized on multiple grounds as falling "far short of establishing a coherent, uniform system for interpreting and enforcing CITES."[102] One problem is that the use of the word "recommendations" in Article XI indicates that the enforcement mechanisms are not legally binding.

Even on its own terms as a species-specific treaty, CITES has garnered decidedly mixed reviews.[103] In part, this stems from the fact that CITES does not prevent species from harm or even complete elimination domestically within any given nation, but regulates only international events. Significantly, CITES allows parties to take reservations as to any species listed in Appendices I–III or any parts/derivatives specified therein, either at the time the nation becomes a party or upon amendment to an appendix.[104] Such reservations allow reserving parties to be treated as nonparties with regard to trade in the applicable species or its parts/derivatives, unfettered by CITES requirements. Reservations have been used frequently under CITES, to the detriment of listed species.[105]

In terms of hotspots protection, the only utility of CITES would derive from any impact it might have on international trade stemming from poachers and those who profit from poaching. This, of course, does not affect the hotspots as such, nor does it provide overarching protection for the ecosystems or habitats in which endangered species live, although it certainly is a worthy and important provision in its own right. Similar to the ESA and other endangered species laws, CITES operates one species at a time and cannot help until a species approaches its deathbed—a decidedly ineffective approach even to aiding individual species, let alone entire ecosystems or hotspots.[106] Thus, CITES—as with the ESA and similar statutes in many other nations—is best viewed as a supplement to other legal measures directed at hotspots preservation and is not the answer in and of itself, nor was it intended to be.[107]

Bonn Convention

The Convention on the Conservation of Migratory Species of Wild Animals (also known as CMS, or the Bonn Convention)[108] aims to conserve terrestrial, marine, and avian migratory species throughout their range. CMS was intended to promote research relating to migratory species, to protect identified endangered migratory species, and to devise plans to conserve and manage such threatened species. Nations are asked to conserve and, if "possible and appropriate," restore habitats that are crucial for ensuring survival of endangered species and to prohibit the taking of listed endangered animals.[109]

Appendix I lists individual endangered migratory species.[110] For these species, signatories that include part of the range of the species are to "endeavour":

(a) to conserve and, where feasible and appropriate, restore those habitats of the species which are of importance in removing the species from danger of extinction; (b) to prevent, remove, compensate for or minimize, as appropriate, the adverse effects of activities or obstacles that seriously impede or prevent the migration of the species; and (c) to the extent feasible and appropriate, to prevent, reduce or control factors that are endangering or are likely to further endanger the species, including strictly controlling the introduction of, or controlling or eliminating, already introduced exotic species.[111]

There is also language directing range states to prohibit the taking of individual members of Appendix I species, with limited exceptions. These exceptions include, in addition to those for scientific purposes or for the benefit of the species, takings "to accommodate the needs of traditional subsistence users of such species."[112]

Appendix II lists migratory species with "unfavorable" conservation status that require international agreements for their conservation and management, as well as those with a conservation status "which would significantly benefit from the international cooperation that could be achieved by an international agreement."[113] For these species, range states are to "endeavour to conclude Agreements where these should benefit the species and should give priority to those species in an unfavourable conservation status."[114]

Since the Bonn Convention's entry into force on November 1, 1983, its membership has grown to include 79 nations (as of September, 2002) as parties from Africa, Central and South America, Asia, Europe, and Oceania.[115] However, CMS primarily focuses on individual species, one at a time, and only migratory ones at that. Thus, although it may be useful for its intended purpose, it is narrowly focused, as are the ESA-type statutes and CITES, and cannot provide significant protection to hotspots. Furthermore, considerable latitude is built into the language of the Convention, and, although there is a dispute resolution provision,[116] there is no meaningful enforcement mechanism.

Ramsar Convention

The Ramsar Convention on Wetlands of International Importance,[117] signed in Ramsar, Iran, in 1971, is an intergovernmental treaty that provides the framework for national action and international cooperation for the conservation and wise use of wetlands and their resources. One of the first major international treaties designed to protect habitat, the Ramsar Convention formally recognized the significance of wetlands and obligates each signatory to "designate suitable wetlands within its territory for inclusion in a List of Wetlands of International Importance"[118] and to "promote the conservation of wetlands and waterfowl by establishing nature reserves on wetlands, whether they are included in the list or not, and provide adequately for their wardening."[119] There is also a general obligation of parties to formulate and implement their wetland policies "so as to promote the conservation of the wetlands . . . and as far as possible the wise of use of wetlands in their territories."[120]

Additionally, the Ramsar Convention requires its parties to cooperate in the exchange of scientific information relating to wetland management.[121] This requirement is supplemented by an obligation to increase wetland waterfowl populations whenever possible, which requires competent management by appropriately trained wetland personnel.[122] Finally, the parties are directed to take responsibility for the management and conservation of migratory stocks of wetland waterfowl.[123]

There are presently 133 contracting parties to the Ramsar Convention, with 1,180 wetland sites totaling 103.2 million hectares designated for inclusion in the Ramsar List of Wetlands of International Importance.[124] However, the Convention has been the target of criticism because of its enforcement weaknesses.[125]

For example, a party may restrict the boundaries of a designated wetland within its borders or completely delist a wetland from the Ramsar List because of "urgent national interest."[126] This has great potential for abuse because "urgent national interest" is not defined in the agreement, nor are any criteria specified.[127] The Ramsar Convention also lacks a dispute resolution provision, does not set forth guidelines for national legislation on wetland preservation, and fails to set forth specific compatible and incompatible uses for required nature reserves.[128]

These shortcomings limit the efficacy of the Convention even within its own ambit. For purposes of hotspots preservation, there is one other obvious and fatal problem. It is limited to wetlands habitats, and therefore at best can only reach small portions of any of the hotspots. Theoretically, a habitat-based international agreement that focused on tropical forests rather than wetlands might be a useful partial surrogate for hotspots preservation, but thus far there have been only limited and weak forays in this direction.[129]

Regional Conventions

In addition to the aforementioned notable global efforts to address aspects of the biodiversity problem, I should point out that there is an intermediate approach as well that exists somewhere between domestic and worldwide law. International legal agreements for environmental protection also exist on a regional level, including conventions encompassing some of the most vital centers of global biodiversity. Although laudable as a step in the right direction, such regional agreements generally suffer from many of the same defects that render ineffective more global international efforts to preserve the environment.[130] Some major examples of a regional approach to biodiversity law include the following.

ASEAN Agreement

Within Asia there have been several attempts to set down guidelines on biodiversity preservation. There is the South Asian Cooperative Environment Program (SACEP), which is the environmental form of the South Asian Association for Regional Cooperation (SAARC),[131] and the ASEAN Environment Programme with its ASEAN Strategic Plan of Action on the Environment, a product of the Association of South East Asian Nations (ASEAN).[132] The latter has generated the 1985 ASEAN Agreement on the Conservation of Nature and Natural Resources, or ASEAN Agreement.[133]

The ASEAN Agreement has never entered into force, lacking sufficient signatories. After more than 16 years, the Agreement remains of little more than theoretical import. The text of the Agreement includes the "fundamental principle" that the parties, "within the framework of their respective national laws," will "undertake" to adopt, alone or in concert, "measures necessary to maintain essential ecological processes and life-support systems, to preserve genetic diversity, and to ensure the sustainable utilization of harvested natural resources under their jurisdiction in accordance with scientific principles and with a view to attaining the goal of sustainable development."[134] This is to be effected through the development of "national conservation strategies," which would be coordinated within the framework of a conservation strategy for the ASEAN Region.[135]

African Nature Convention

The 1968 African Convention on the Conservation of Nature and Natural Resources, or African Nature Convention,[136] has been in force since 1969. The "fundamental principle" is similar to that of the ASEAN Agreement; parties "shall undertake to adopt the measures to ensure conservation, utilization and development of soil, water, flora and faunal resources in accordance with scientific principles and with due regard to the best interests of the people."[137]

The Convention directs parties to take certain legal actions with regard to a variety of "conservation areas"[138] within their individual borders, as well as flora,[139] "faunal resources,"[140] and protected species.[141] These instructions are not couched in strictly preservationist terms but rather stress notions such as "conservation, wise and development of faunal resources and their environment, within the framework of land-use planning and of economic and social development."[142] Moreover, the Convention is further shackled by the lack of any enforcement mechanisms, which has limited its impact.[143] It is inadequate to preserve Africa's sublime natural treasures.[144]

Western Hemisphere Convention

The 1940 Convention on Nature Protection and Wildlife Preservation in the Western Hemisphere, or Western Hemisphere Convention,[145] entered into force in 1942. The Convention provides that parties "will explore at once the possibility" of establishing within their borders a variety of protected areas, including national parks, national reserves, nature monuments, and strict wilderness reserves, as defined in the Convention,[146] and, "where such establishment is feasible," the creation thereof is to begin as soon as possible.[147] Once established, "the boundaries of national parks shall not be altered, or any portion thereof be capable of alienation, except by the competent legislative authority," and the resources of these reserves "shall not be subject to exploitation for commercial profit."[148] Parties are also "to prohibit hunting, killing and capturing of members of the fauna and destruction or collection of representatives of the flora in national parks except by or under the direction or control of the park authorities, or for duly authorized scientific investigations," and "to provide facilities for public recreation and education in national parks" consistent with the purposes of the Convention.[149]

The Convention also contains provisions for the protection of certain enumerated species[150] as well as restrictions on their importation, exportation, and transport.[151] There are more general guidelines as to other flora and fauna[152] and migratory birds "of economic or aesthetic value or to prevent the threatened extinction of any given species."[153]

The weakness and ambiguity of the Convention's mandates, coupled with the absence of enforcement provisions or any institutions to oversee and ensure implementation, has limited the utility of this agreement.[154] Along with a number of other Latin American accords[155] and the other regional agreements I have mentioned, it may serve some visionary and aspirational purposes, but it lacks the power to preserve hotspots in and of itself.[156]

Apia Convention

Within the crucial South Pacific region, there is the 1976 Convention on the Conservation of Nature in the South Pacific, or the Apia Convention,[157] which finally entered into force in 1990. Each party shall "encourage the creation of protected areas," which, together with preexisting protected areas, "will safeguard representative samples of the natural ecosystems occurring therein (particular attention being given to endangered species)," as well as superlative scenery, striking geological formations, and "regions and objects of aesthetic interest or historic, cultural or scientific value."[158] This last clause could, of course, apply to the hotspots, but little solace can be derived from an edict mandating merely that parties "encourage" the establishment of more protected enclaves.

The Apia Convention attempts to place limits on harm to protected areas in very much the same manner as in the Western Hemisphere Convention. It provides that the "boundaries of national parks shall not be altered so as to reduce their areas, nor shall any portions of such parks be capable of alienation, except after the fullest examination,"[159] nor shall the resources of national parks "be subject to exploitation for commercial profit, except after the fullest examination."[160] Also, there are to be prohibitions on the "hunting, killing, capture or collection of specimens (including eggs and shells) of the fauna and destruction or collection of specimens of the flora in national parks."[161]

As with other regional agreements, the Apia Convention contains provisions for protection of biota generally,[162] and especially of imperiled species.[163] It mentions exotic species, too, and instructs parties to "carefully consider the consequences of the deliberate introduction into ecosystems of species which have not previously occurred therein."[164]

It is readily apparent that the Convention is limited by liberal use of qualifying language as a prelude to adverse actions, such as "except after the fullest examination" and "carefully consider the consequences." And, in a familiar refrain, the Convention is devoid of any enforcement mechanism. Thus, like the other regional agreements we have considered, this is not a satisfactory solution to the hotspots crisis.

Berne Convention

The Convention on the Conservation of European Wildlife and Natural Habitats (Berne Convention) was adopted in Berne on September 19, 1979, at the third European Ministerial Conference on the Environment, and came into force on June 1, 1982. More than 40 European and African nations, plus the European Community, are parties.[165] The Convention is aimed at international cooperation in preserving the natural habitats of wild flora and fauna in Europe generally, with particular emphasis on those whose conservation requires the cooperation of multiple nations and on identified endangered and vulnerable species listed in its Appendices.[166]

The Convention directs parties to take "appropriate and necessary legislative and administrative measures to ensure the conservation of the habitats" of wild species, especially those listed as endangered or vulnerable in the Appendices, and "the conservation of endangered natural habitats."[167] Parties, in their planning and development policies, "shall have regard to the conservation requirements of the areas protected" so as to avoid or minimize "as far as possible any deterioration of such areas."[168] Parties are also to institute specific prohibitions as to the takings of listed species[169] and to make particular efforts to preserve migratory species.[170]

The Berne Convention features a dispute resolution procedure, which includes arbitration.[171] However, there is no enforcement mechanism. The actual text of the Convention contains somewhat fewer opportunities for creative interpretation by parties seeking to skirt its requirements than do most of the other agreements I have mentioned, although there are some potentially inviting ambiguities and loopholes nonetheless.[172] Because of this, and in the absence of substantive teeth, the Berne Convention is not a sufficient solution to the plight of biodiversity within its region.[173]

Problems Inherent in the International Law Approach

In addition to the specific deficiencies I noted with regard to each of the above worldwide and regional international agreements, there are substantial difficulties that inhere in any attempt to protect hotspots through international legal mechanisms.[174] On the most fundamental level, the global family of nations differs from any individual nation in that it does not have a supreme lawmaking legislature capable of enacting laws that bind its people, nor an efficacious means of ensuring compliance. Whereas the citizens of any particular nation can be bound by the duly enacted laws of their own legislature without their specific consent on a law-by-law basis, there is no analog on a global scale. As an alternative, international treaties developed on an ad hoc, piecemeal basis as a means by which consenting—and only consenting—nations may establish mutual legal obligations to achieve a common objective.[175]

Because no nation can be bound by an international legal instrument without its consent, there are great problems both in structuring a substantively meaningful treaty that will attract parties and in enforcing treaty obligations. Treaty terms tend to reflect numerous compromises necessary to garner signatories, and even after lengthy negotiations key nations may refuse to sign and/or ratify; the long struggles over the Law of the Sea and the Kyoto Protocol are two major examples in which the United States played the role of the reluctant party. Treaties may become so weakened with exceptions, qualifiers, reservations, and discretionary provisions that by the time they are acceptable to most nations they are powerless to achieve their stated purpose.[176] International environmental/natural resource agreements are especially prone to the compromise syndrome because they are frequently designed to attract a large number of participants.[177] Nations may sign on to such agreements partially if not solely to gain political approval from other nations, while subsequent compliance is often neglected.[178]

Because of this, sometimes a treaty may actually do more harm than good. This can happen because, in the aftermath of all the publicity highlighting the signing of any treaty by a particular nation, average citizens and political leaders within that nation might falsely assume that the treaty has effectively handled the problem. If there is a widespread belief that a signed treaty equates to a satisfactory solution, people might understandably relax and devote less attention and energy to the relevant issue from that point on. If the treaty itself is actually of little help, this false consciousness can be a serious impediment to further efforts to address the problem in a more meaningful and efficacious way. It is as if a person allows a careless mechanic to inspect her car's tires, and then she embarks on a long trip, confident that all is well, despite the fact that the mechanic failed to correct a slow leak. Misplaced reliance on treaties such as the CBD (after all, the very name of the Convention implies that it has all the bases covered on biodiversity) lets the air out of the tires of positive change, and they go flat.

Additionally, the act of signing a treaty is no guarantee of legal effect. Even after a nation becomes a signatory it is usually not legally bound by the terms of an agreement if its legislature fails to ratify or adopt the treaty.[179] This is the situation that exists with regard to the United States and the CBD; the United States signed it but has never ratified it. Also, under international law, a party has discretion to interpret ambiguous provisions of a treaty provided that the interpretation does not run counter to the enumerated principles of a given treaty.[180]

Another intractable problem is that multilateral agreements often involve reservations, that is, stipulations made at the time a treaty is signed that allow a party, in effect, to excuse itself from certain terms of the treaty.[181] International environmental/natural resource treaties often are riddled with such reservations because of the difficulty of achieving consensus or gathering a sufficient number of signatories without allowing them.[182] As a type of "signing bonus," a given nation can insist on reservations that provide a ready escape hatch from certain key provisions. Thus, the same treaty can have very different legal meanings for its various signatories, with anything but a uniform, universal set of firm requirements.

Perhaps most significant of all is that compliance problems often arise because of the paucity of meaningful enforcement options.[183] Due to complex sovereignty issues that exist in the context of international law in general, a nation cannot normally be compelled to perform its treaty obligations by means involving the use of physical force.[184] Short of force, even certain economic sanctions, such as trade restrictions, may run afoul of the current General Agreement on Tariffs and Trade (GATT).[185] The uneasy nexus between GATT and international environmental protection has been a matter of considerable dispute for years and has brought angry protestors to recent WTO meetings. The crux of the matter is as follows.

When the original GATT[186] was drafted more than 50 years ago, environmental policy was much less developed than it has subsequently become, and for this reason GATT does not refer to environmental measures as such.[187] Rather, the general GATT obligations in furtherance of free trade apply to environmental measures, just as they apply to measures imposed for other policy purposes.[188] As time passed, some formal recognition of environmental concerns was incorporated into the GATT structure. At the meeting held to sign the Final Act Embodying the Results of the Uruguay Round of Multilateral Trade Negotiations in Marrakesh on April 14, 1994, the GATT contracting parties adopted a Ministerial Decision that formally established a new Committee on Trade and Environment (CTE) under the auspices of the newly created World Trade Organization (WTO).[189] The CTE was charged with making appropriate recommendations on "the need for rules to enhance the positive interaction between trade and environment measures for the promotion of sustainable development."[190]

Two GATT/WTO provisions have been interpreted to allow for some measures directed toward environmental protection as limited exceptions to GATT's general preclusion of trade barriers, Article XX(b) and Article XX(g), although the first GATT cases that clearly confronted environmental concerns did not appear until the 1990s. The "chapeau," or preamble, to GATT Article XX states that "adoption or enforcement" of the trade measures listed in (b) and (g) is permitted, "subject to the requirement that such measures are not applied in a manner which would constitute a means of arbitrary or unjustifiable discrimination between countries where the same conditions prevail, or a disguised restriction on international trade." These trade measures must not be a pretext for disguised trade barriers. Additionally, GATT cases usually require that the nation exhaust other reasonable options in adopting the "least restrictive" means.[191]

GATT Article XX(b) would authorize the use of trade measures, including environmental trade measures (ETMs), if "necessary to protect human, animal or plant life or health," and these terms, particularly the word *necessary*, have sometimes been strictly construed against the ETMs.[192] Article XX(g) would permit employment of ETMs "relating to the conservation of exhaustible natural resources if such measures are made effective in conjunction with restrictions on domestic production or consumption." There have been unfavorable decisions regarding ETMs under this provision as well.[193]

Although dolphins, gasoline, and clean air have all been held to be qualified as "exhaustible natural resources"[194] under this provision, there have been controversial and narrow rulings regarding other key parts of Article XX. For example, the WTO/GATT panels have interpreted "relating to" to mean that the ETM must be "primarily aimed at" conservation.[195] Some GATT panel decisions, including the 1991 Report on United States Restrictions on Imports of Tuna (Tuna-Dolphin I), have also held that Article XX(g) applies only to ETMs protecting natural resources within a nation's own boundaries.[196] Attempts to amend GATT provisions such as Article XX to accommodate direct recognition of pro-environmental measures have been unsuccessful.[197]

Some cause for optimism may be found in the WTO Appellate Body Report on Shrimp-Turtles in which it was decided that a U.S. trade measure, which called for restrictions on imports of shrimp and shrimp products from nations failing to take adequate steps to protect endangered sea turtles, met the requirements of Article XX(g).[198] The ETM was deemed a measure "relating to" conservation; turtles, and indeed wildlife generally, were ruled "exhaustible" resources under XX(g); and the ETM was made effective in conjunction with restrictions on domestic harvesting of shrimp. The decision arguably expanded Article XX's scope in a number of ways, perhaps making the GATT/WTO tribunals a more favorable forum for future trade and environment disputes.[199] At least the decision recognized the importance of international environmental protection generally and suggests that ETMs could be consistent with GATT/WTO rules. However, Shrimp-Turtles decision ultimately rejected the ETM on rather narrow grounds, holding that the method of enforcement amounted to an "economic embargo" that required all exporting members to adopt policies identical to U.S. domestic policy and treated nations differently because the period of time to phase in turtle safeguards varied among nations, which did not comport with Article XX's "chapeau."[200]

In December, 1996, the WTO adopted a CTE report in which CTE recognized that the WTO and multilateral environmental agreements are efforts by the international community to pursue shared goals and should be mutually supportive in order to promote sustainable development.[201] Although some important multilateral environmental agreements rely upon trade measures, CTE emphasized that trade measures have been included in a relatively small number of such agreements and that, in its opinion, there is no clear indication as to when and how they may be needed or used in the future.[202]

In addition to GATT, the North American Free Trade Agreement (NAFTA)[203] also places restrictions on trade measures directed at environmental aims within its area of purview.[204] NAFTA subjects environmental standards and regulations to the general principle of nondiscrimination and three legal tests[205] aimed specifically at environmental measures. Trade restrictions may be used to achieve environmental goals only where they are the most effective means of doing so. These binding provisions impose the same obligations on the NAFTA parties as did GATT. Plus, NAFTA Article 104 applies the least-trade-restrictive principle to the relationship between free trade and international environmental agreements.[206] There are numerous other multilateral regional free-trade accords as well, which may have implications for ETMs.

The legal picture remains unclear as to the viability of ETM provisions in some multilateral environmental agreements, such as the explicit trade bans on listed endangered species under CITES and the trade sanctions against nonsignatories to the Montreal Protocol on Substances that Deplete the Ozone Layer.[207] At present, no direct challenge has been mounted under the WTO/GATT to such trade measures. Perhaps the ETM would be held to fit within Article XX(b) or (g) of GATT, although we have seen that WTO decisions along these lines are not entirely encouraging. Also, the Vienna Convention on the Law of Treaties[208] might be interpreted so that the environmental agreement supercedes WTO rules if it is more recent than the WTO rule, or that the rules of the environmental treaty apply because they are more specific. However, it is possible that the WTO, so recently established in 1995, would qualify all WTO-administered trade rules as 1995 rules and thus "later in time" than most multilateral environmental agreements, therefore trumping the ETMs.[209]

In short, free trade and environmental protection have not enjoyed a harmonious coexistence internationally. The perceived obstruction of environmental protection by WTO has famously led to the violent protests at recent WTO meetings.[210] The protestors have reacted to an international legal regime in which profits often appear to take priority over nature, and charismatic creatures such as dolphins are left to the mercy of commercial fishing operations.

Coupled with these GATT/WTO issues and other factors, most international environmental treaties, as we have seen, lack meaningful enforcement provisions in their actual text. Thus, international agreements generally suffer from a "teeth deficit," which renders them largely aspirational, educational, and of limited substantive efficacy absent a commitment from their signatories to engage in a particular course of action independent of any enforceable treaty provisions.[211]

In theory at least, international environmental laws such as those I have discussed can be enforced by litigation in the International Court of Justice (ICJ, or World Court), as well as in ad hoc international tribunals and domestic courts. However, the ICJ hears only cases between nations, and only after the respective nations give their explicit consent to the jurisdiction of the ICJ.[212] There is little likelihood that any nation will attempt to bring a case to the ICJ against another nation claiming that the latter is harming biodiversity or the environment, because most nations fear counterclaims inasmuch as they also have an imperfect record of environmental protection and compliance.[213]

This is not to say that nonbinding international agreements, or "soft law," cannot have some value in influencing behavior. Soft law can create expectations within and among nations, focus public attention on vital issues, help to establish norms and goals, build consensus, shape the political debate, and/or serve as a step toward binding agreements.[214] All of these are worthwhile. But, along with the international agreements discussed herein, they have failed to preserve the hotspots thus far, or even the enumerated species they have earmarked for protection. They are inadequate absent more rigorous substantive requirements and more enforcement-oriented legal mechanisms at either the international or domestic level.

NOTES

1. *See generally*, David E. Bell, *The 1992 Convention on Biological Diversity: The Continuing Significance of U.S. Objections at the Earth Summit*, 26 Geo. Wash. J. Int'l L. & Econ. 479, 492–507 (1993) (providing an overview of international environmental initiatives).

2. Convention on Biological Diversity of the United Nations Conference on the Environment and Development, June 5, 1992, U.N. Doc. DPI/1307, reprinted in 31 I.L.M. 818 (entered into force Dec. 29, 1993).

3. *See* <http://www.biodiv.org/world/parties.asp>.

4. CBD, Art. 1.

5. *See* Francoise Burhenne-Guilmin, and Susan Casey-Lefkowitz, *The Convention on Biological Diversity: A Hard Won Global Achievement*, 3 Y.B. Int'l Envtl. L. 43, 45–46 (1992).

6. CBD, Art. 6.

7. CBD, Art. 7.

8. CBD, Annex I.

9. CBD, Art. 8. Article 8 reads, in its entirety, as follows:

Each Contracting Party shall, as far as possible and as appropriate:

(a) Establish a system of protected areas or areas where special measures need to be taken to conserve biological diversity;

(b) Develop, where necessary, guidelines for the selection, establishment and management of protected areas or areas where special measures need to be taken to conserve biological diversity;

(c) Regulate or manage biological resources important for the conservation of biological diversity whether within or outside protected areas, with a view to ensuring their conservation and sustainable use;

(d) Promote the protection of ecosystems, natural habitats and the maintenance of viable populations of species in natural surroundings;

(e) Promote environmentally sound and sustainable development in areas adjacent to protected areas with a view to furthering protection of these areas;

(f) Rehabilitate and restore degraded ecosystems and promote the recovery of threatened species, inter alia, through the development and implementation of plans or other management strategies;

(g) Establish or maintain means to regulate, manage or control the risks associated with the use and release of living modified organisms resulting from biotechnology which are likely to have adverse environmental impacts that could affect the conservation and sustainable use of biological diversity, taking also into account the risks to human health;

(h) Prevent the introduction of, control or eradicate those alien species which threaten ecosystems, habitats or species;

(i) Endeavour to provide the conditions needed for compatibility between present uses and the conservation of biological diversity and the sustainable use of its components;

(j) Subject to its national legislation, respect, preserve and maintain knowledge, innovations and practices of indigenous and local communities embodying traditional lifestyles relevant for the conservation and sustainable use of biological diversity and promote their wider application with the approval and involvement of the holders of such knowledge, innovations and practices and encourage the equitable sharing of the benefits arising from the utilization of such knowledge, innovations and practices;

(k) Develop or maintain necessary legislation and/or other regulatory provisions for the protection of threatened species and populations;

(l) Where a significant adverse effect on biological diversity has been determined pursuant to Article 7, regulate or manage the relevant processes and categories of activities; and

(m) Cooperate in providing financial and other support for in-situ conservation outlined in subparagraphs (a) to (l) above, particularly to developing countries.

10. CBD, Art. 10.

11. *See* Catherine Tinker, *Responsibility for Biological Diversity Conservation Under International Law*, 28 Vand. J. Transnat'l L. 777, 813 (1995). Principle 21 establishes the duty of nations not to harm the territory of other states or any territory beyond national jurisdiction. *Id.* at 779.

12. CBD, Art. 3.

13. Tinker, *supra* note 11, at 813.

14. This is called for in CBD, Art. 21.

15. CBD, Art. 20.

16. *See* <http://www.biodiv.org/doc/publications/>.

17. *See* Daniel M. Bodansky, *International Law and the Protection of Biological Diversity*, 28 Vand. J. Transnat'l L. 623, 632–34 (1995). *See generally* Timothy M. Swanson, *Economics of a Biodiversity Convention*, 21 Ambio 250 (1992); Jon H. Goldstein, *The Prospects for Using Market Incentives to Conserve Biological Diversity*, 21 Envtl. L. 985 (1991).

18. CBD, Art. 18.

19. CBD, Art.18.3.

20. CBD, Art. 19.2.

21. CBD, Art. 16.3.

22. Philippe Sands, Principles of International Environmental Law I: Frameworks, Standards and Implementation, 385–6 (Manchester, 1995) (discussing the "dismay" of the United States and other developed countries at these provisions of the CBD).

23. *See* <http://www.biodiv.org/doc/publications/>.

24. *See, e.g.*, CBD Arts. 5–11, 14(1), and 20(1).

25. *Id.* Art. 20 (4).

26. *See* Tinker, *supra* note 11, at 802.

27. Benjamin J. Richardson, *Environmental Law in Postcolonial Societies: Straddling the Local-Global Institutional Spectrum*, 11 Colo. J. Int'l Envtl. L. & Pol'y 1, 66 (2000).

28. *Id.*

29. *See generally* Amanda Hubbard, Comment: *The Convention on Biological Diversity's Fifth Anniversary: A General Overview of the Convention—Where Has It Been, and Where Is It Going?*, 10 Tul. Envtl. L.J. 415 (1997) (outlining the spotty results the CBD yielded during its first five years).

30. Convention for the Protection of the World Cultural and Natural Heritage, Nov. 23, 1972, 27 U.S.T. 37, 11 I.L.M. 1358, 1037 U.N.T.S. 151. *See* <http://www.unesco.org/whc/nwhc/pages/doc/main.htm>.

31. WHC, Art. 1.

32. WHC, Preamble.

33. As defined in WHC, Art. 2.

34. As defined in WHC, Art. 1. Article 1 provides for three types of cultural resources: (1) monuments, which are defined as "architectural works, works of monumental sculpture and painting, elements or structures of an archaeological nature, inscriptions, cave dwellings and combinations of features, which are of outstanding universal value from the point of view of history, art or science;" (2) groups of buildings, defined as "groups of separate or connected buildings which, because of their architecture, their homogeneity or their place in the landscape, are of outstanding universal value from the point of view of history, art or science;" and (3) sites, which are "works of man or the combined works of nature and man, and areas including archaeological sites which are of outstanding universal value from the historical, aesthetic, ethnological or anthropological point of view." *Id.*

35. WHC, Art. 2.

36. WHC, Art. 4.

37. *Id.*

38. *Id.*

39. WHC, Art. 6.1.

40. WHC, Art. 6.2.

41. WHC, Art. 6.3.

42. WHC, Art. 5(c).

43. WHC, Art. 5(d).

44. WHC, Art. 7.

45. *See* Daniel L. Gebert, NOTE: *Sovereignty Under the World Heritage Convention: A Questionable Basis for Limiting Federal Land Designation Pursuant to International Agreements*, 7 S. Cal. Interdis. L.J. 427, 436–38 (1998).

46. WHC, Art. 3.

47. WHC, Art. 11.3.

48. Provided for in WHC, Art. 8.

49. WHC, Art. 14.2. The IUCN was initially called the International Union for Conservation of Nature and Natural Resources.

50. *See* <http://www.unesco.org/whc/toc//mainfl1.htm>. For a complete list of sites on the World Heritage List, *See* <http://www.unesco.org/whc/nwhc/pages/doc/main.htm>.

51. *See* <http://www.unesco.org/whc/nwhc/pages/doc/main.htm>.

52. *See* <http://www.unesco.org/whc/toc//mainfl 1.htm>.

53. *See* <http://www.unesco org/whc/nwhc/pages/doc/main.htm>.

54. WHC, Art. 15.3.

55. WHC, Art. 22.

56. WHC, Art. 15.3.

57. *Id.*

58. WHC, Art. 17.

59. WHC, Art. 15.4.

60. *Id.*

61. WHC, Art. 16.1.

62. WHC, Art. 16.4.

63. WHC, Art: 16.5.

64. WHC, Art. 22.

65. WHC, Art. 22 a–f.

66. WHC, Art. 24.

67. WHC, Art. 25.

68. *Id.*

69. WHC, Art. 13.4.

70. WHC, Art. 11.4.

71. *Id.*

72. *Id.*

73. *See* <http://www.unesco.org/whc/nwhc/pages/doc/main.htm>.

74. *See* <http://www.unesco.org/whc/toc//mainfl 1.htm>.

75. For a list of all sites on the List of World Heritage in Danger, *see* <http://www.unesco.org/whc/nwhc/pages/doc/main.htm>.

76. *See* Ben Boer, *World Heritage Disputes in Australia*, 7 J. Envtl. L. & Litig. 247, 258–76 (1992) (describing several disputes arising out of World Heritage listing proposals in Australia).

77. *See* Matthew Machado, *Mounting Opposition to Biosphere Reserves and World Heritage Sites in the United States Sparked by Claims of Interference with National Sovereignty*, 1997 COLO. J. INT'L ENVTL. Y.B. 120.

78. WHC, Art. 27.1–2. Similarly, Article 28 requires nations which receive international assistance for a World Heritage site to "take appropriate measures to make known the importance of the property for which assistance has been received and the role played by such assistance."

79. WHC, Art. 11.4.

80. *See* SIMON LYSTER, INTERNATIONAL WILDLIFE LAW: AN ANALYSIS OF INTERNATIONAL TREATIES CONCERNED WITH THE CONSERVATION OF WILDLIFE at 301–02 (1985) (criticizing the WHC as having "proved relatively ineffectual" because, inter alia, it failed to establish "a system of administration to monitor and oversee" enforcement).

81. WHC, Art. 29.1 (providing that upon the request of a specified United Nations committee, a party "shall . . . give information on the legislative and administrative provisions which they have adopted and other action which they have taken").

82. *See* Edith Brown Weiss, *The Five International Treaties: A Living History,* in ENGAGING COUNTRIES: STRENGTHENING COMPLIANCE WITH INTERNATIONAL

ENVIRONMENTAL ACCORDS, at 104 (Edith Brown Weiss and Harold K. Jacobsen, eds. 1998).

83. *Id.* at 93–105, 125–35.

84. WHC, Art. 2.

85. *See* Ben Boer, *World Heritage Disputes in Australia*, 7 J. Envtl. L. & Litig. 247, 258–76 (1992) (describing several disputes arising out of World Heritage listing proposals in Australia).

86. WHC, Art. 15.4.

87. With apologies to Alan Jay Lerner and Frederick Loewe, the authors of the immortal musical play "My Fair Lady," and the song therein, "Wouldn't It Be Loverly."

88. As I mentioned in Chapter 1, the Chicago National League Baseball club most recently won a World Series in 1908, although the Cubs have been to a World Series as recently as 1945. Enough is enough.

89. *See* M. Catherine Vernon, NOTE: *Common Cultural Property: The Search for Rights of Protective Intervention*, 26 Case W. Res. J. Int'l L. 435, 444 (1994).

90. *Id.*

91. *Id.*

92. A table showing the nations that are parties to each of these conventions may be found at <http://www.wcmc.org.uk/convent/treaties_iv.htm>.

93. Convention on International Trade in Endangered Species of Wild Flora and Fauna, Mar. 3, 1973, 993 U.N.T.S. 243 (1976) (entered into force July 1, 1975).

94. *See* <http://www.cites.org/>.

95. CITES, Arts. III–V.

96. Appendix I lists species "threatened with extinction." It includes all apes, lemurs, the giant panda, many South American monkeys, the great whales, cheetahs, leopards, tigers, Asian and African elephants, all rhinoceroses, any birds of prey, cranes and pheasants, all sea turtles, some crocodile and lizards, giant salamanders, some mussels, orchids, and cacti. Appendix II lists species and specimens that are not yet threatened with extinction but which "may become" so if trade in them is not controlled. Appendix II includes primates, cats, otters, smaller whales, dolphins and porpoises, some birds of prey, tortoises, crocodiles, fur seals, the black stork, birds of paradise, the coelacanth, some snails, birdwing butterflies, and black coral. Appendix III contains species listed by nations that have stricter legislation than CITES requirements, restricting import and export of species not listed in Appendices I or II. Nations can list such species in Appendix III, after which the other parties must regulate trade in those species. *See* Patricia Birnie, *The Case of the Convention on Trade in Endangered Species*, in ENFORCING ENVIRONMENTAL STANDARDS: ECONOMIC MECHANISMS AS VIABLE MEANS? 233 (Jochen Abr. Frowein et al., eds., 1996); Michelle Ann Peters, *The Convention on International Trade in Endangered Species: An Answer to the Call of the Wild?* 10 Conn. J. Int'l L. 169, 176 (1994).

97. Margaret Rosso Grossman, *Habitat and Species Conservation in the European Union and the United States*, 45 Drake L. Rev. 19, 20–21 (1997).

98. CITES, Art. VIII(1)(a), 1(b), and (2). Under Article VIII, all parties "shall" take appropriate measures to enforce the provisions of CITES and to prohibit trade in specimens taken in violation thereof. These shall include measures to penalize trade in, or possession of, such specimens or both, and measures to provide for the confiscation or return to the state of export of such specimens. The measures

mentioned in Article VIII(1) must include, inter alia, appropriate penalties for trading in prohibited specimens and the power to confiscate species and provide for their return to the state of export. Failure to enact penalties constitutes a violation of CITES. The provisions of Article VIII indicate that each party has the obligation to implement CITES through its own domestic legislation, as the United States has done with the Endangered Species Act (ESA).

99. *Id.*, Art. VIII(7). The report is to consist of information on the number and type of permits allocated with respect to species protected by CITES.

100. *Id.*, Art. XIII(1).

101. *Id.*, Art. XVIII(1) and (2). There is a provision for voluntary referral of a dispute to arbitration, with specific mention of the Permanent Court of Arbitration at The Hague.

102. *See* Carlo A. Balistrieri, *CITES: The ESA and International Trade*, 8 Nat. Resources & Envtl L. 33, 54 (1993).

103. *See, e.g.*, Michael Glennon, *Has International Law Failed the Elephant?*, 84 Am. J. Int'l. L. 1, 20 (1990) (stating that it "seems fair to conclude that throughout the 1980s, the trade boomed despite the CITES protective regime for a fairly obvious reason: CITES did not sufficiently diminish the incentives of producers, middlemen or consumers"); Julie Cheung, *Implementation and Enforcement of CITES: An Assessment of Tiger and Rhinoceros Conservation Policy in Asia*, 5 Pac. Rim L. & Pol'y J. 125, 125–26 (1995) (questioning whether CITES has been successful in protecting tigers and rhinos); Joonmoo Lee, *Poachers, Tigers and Bears . . . Oh My! Asia's Illegal Wildlife Trade*, 16 Nw. J. Int'l L. & Bus. 497, 503–04 (1996) (critiquing CITES as "being largely powerless to enforce its resolutions" while noting some success stories as well); Kevin D. Hill, *The Convention on International Trade in Endangered Species: Fifteen Years Later*, 13 Loy. L.A. Int'l & Comp. L.J. 231, 277 (1990) (noting that some developing countries do not want to shut down the international trade in endangered species because to do so would eliminate an important source of income for their economies).

104. CITES, Art. XV(3); Art. XVI(2).

105. Sands, *supra* note 22, at 378–9.

106. *See* John C. Kunich, *The Fallacy of Deathbed Conservation Under The Endangered Species Act*, 24 Envt'l L. 501, 5022–28 (1994).

107. Numerous other international agreements are aimed at the preservation of particular types of living things, whether plants, birds, marine species, or particular subsets thereof. These can be helpful within their limited ambit, but they generally suffer from the same problems inherent in the ESA approach and are not appropriate for broader hotspots preservation. *See, e.g.*, the 1950 International Convention for the Protection of Birds, 638 U.N.T.S. 185, October 18, 1950, entered into force January 17, 1963; 1951 International Convention for the Establishment of the European and Mediterranean Plant Protection Organization, April 18, 1951, entered into force November 1, 1953, U.K.T.S. 44 (1956).

108. Convention on the Conservation of Migratory Species of Wild Animals, June 23, 1979, entered into force November 1, 1983, 19 I.L.M. 15 (1979).

109. *Id.* Arts. II–III.

110. Listings are to be determined by the Conference of the Parties, aided by the input of the Scientific Council. The Scientific Council may make recommendations to the Conference of the Parties as to the migratory species to be included in Appendices I

and II, together with an indication of the range of such migratory species, as well as specific conservation and management measures to be included in agreements on migratory species. *Id.*, Art. VIII.5.c–d.

111. *Id.* Art. III.4.

112. *Id.* Art. III.5.

113. *Id.* Art. IV.1.

114. *Id.* Art. IV.3.

115. *See* <http://www.wcmc.org.uk/cms/>.

116. CMS, Art. XIII.

117. Convention on Wetlands of International Importance, Especially as Waterfowl Habitat, Feb. 2, 1971, TIAS No. 11,084, 996 U.N.T.S. 245 (entered into force Dec. 21, 1975).

118. *Id.* Art. 2(1). In the case of "urgent national interest," a party can delete or restrict the boundaries of a wetland on the list, but it is then supposed to compensate for loss of wetland resources, creating additional nature reserves for waterfowl and to protect their habitat. *Id.* Art. 4(2).

119. *Id.* Art. 4(1). The Ramsar Convention encourages consultation among signatories and periodic conferences dealing with the conservation of wetlands. *Id.* Arts. 5, 6.

120. *Id.* Art. 3(1).

121. *Id.* Art. 4(4).

122. Art. 4(4) instructs parties to "endeavor through management to increase waterfowl populations on appropriate wetlands." Art. 4(5) provides that parties "shall promote the training of personnel competent in the fields of wetland research, management and wardening."

123. *Id.* Art. 4(2) (requiring parties to "compensate for any loss of wetland resources" and create additional reserves of an "adequate portion of the original habitat" when they delete or restrict the boundaries of a wetland on the list).

124. *See* <http://www.ramsar.org/>. One hectare, often abbreviated "ha," equals 2.47 acres.

125. Cherly Jamieson, *An Analysis of Municipal Wetlands Laws and Their Relationship to the Convention on Wetlands of International Importance Especially As Waterfowl Habitat (Ramsar)*, 4 Pace Envtl. L. Rev. 177, 210–16 (1986).

126. Ramsar Convention, Art. 4(2).

127. Jamieson, *supra* note 84, at 211.

128. *Id.* at 215.

129. *See* 1983 International Tropical Timber Agreement, November 18, 1983, entered into force April 1, 1985, which includes the objectives of developing industrial tropical timber reforestation and forest management activities, encouraging national policies aimed at sustainable use and conservation of tropical forests and their genetic resources, and maintaining the ecological balance in the regions concerned. Unfortunately, other objectives include the expansion and diversification of international trade in tropical timber and promotion of the industrialization of tropical timber-producing member nations. *See also* nonbinding instruments such as the 1992 Forest Principles, June 13, 1992, 31 I.L.M. (1992), 881. Sands, *supra* note 22, at 407–8.

130. *See generally* Kathleen Rogers and James A. Moore, *Revitalizing the Convention on Nature Protection and Wild Life Preservation in the Western Hemisphere: Might*

Awakening a Visionary but "Sleeping" Treaty be the Key to Preserving Biodiversity and Threatened Natural Areas in the Americas?, 36 Harv. Int'l L.J. 465 (1995).

131. SAARC consists of Afghanistan, Bhutan, Bangladesh, Maldives, Nepal, Pakistan, India, and Sri Lanka. *See* Ben Boer, *The Rise of Environmental Law in the Asian Region*, 32 U. Rich. L. Rev. 1503, 1514–22 (1999).

132. *Id.* at 1524–34. ASEAN includes Brunei, Indonesia, Malaysia, Myanmar, the Philippines, Singapore, Thailand, Vietnam, and Laos.

133. ASEAN Agreement, 15 E.P.L. (1985), June 9, 1985 (not in force).

134. *Id.* Art. 1.1.

135. *Id.* Art. 1.2.

136. African Nature Convention, 1001 U.N.T.S. 3, September 15, 1968, entered into force June 16, 1969.

137. *Id.* Art. II.

138. *Id.* Art. X. This Article provides:

1. The Contracting States shall maintain and extend where appropriate, within their territory and where applicable in their territorial waters, the Conservation areas existing at the time of entry into force of the present Convention and, preferably within the framework of land-use planning programmes, assess the necessity of establishing additional conservation areas in order to: (1) protect those ecosystems which are most representative of and particularly those which are in any respect peculiar to their territories, (2) ensure the conservation of all species and more particularly of those listed or which may be listed in the annex to this Convention; 2. The Contracting States shall establish, where necessary, around the borders of conservation areas, zones within which the competent authorities shall control activities detrimental to the protected natural resources.

139. *Id.* Art. VI.

140. *Id.* Art. VII.

141. *Id.* Art. VIII.

142. *Id.* Art. VII.

143. Sands, *supra* note 22, at 389. There is a provision for dispute resolution in Article XVIII, SETTLEMENT OF DISPUTES: "Any dispute between the Contracting States relating to the interpretation or application of this Convention which cannot be settled by negotiation, shall at the request of any party be submitted to the Commission of Mediation, Conciliation and Arbitration of the Organization of African Unity."

144. The 1985 Protocol Concerning Protected Areas and Wild Fauna and Flora in the Eastern Africa Region (1985 Nairobi SPA Protocol), I.E.L.M.T. 985:47, is a similar regional agreement with applicability in Eastern Africa.

145. Western Hemisphere Convention, 161 U.N.T.S. 193, entered into force May 1, 1942.

146. *Id.* Art. I.

147. *Id.* Art. II.1. The next section provides:

If in any country the establishment of national parks, national reserves, nature monuments, or strict wilderness reserves is found to be impractical at present, suitable areas, objects or living species of fauna or flora, as the case may be, shall be selected as early as possible to be transformed into national parks, national reserves, nature monuments or strict wilderness reserves as soon as, in the opinion of the authorities concerned, circumstances will permit.

Id. Art. II.2.

148. *Id.* Art. III.

149. *Id.*

150. *Id.* Art. VIII.

151. *Id.* Art. IX.

152. *Id.* Art. V. Parties are to "adopt, or to propose such adoption to their respective appropriate law-making bodies, suitable laws and regulations for the protection and preservation of flora and fauna within their national boundaries," and "laws which will assure the protection and preservation of the natural scenery, striking geological formations, and regions and natural objects of aesthetic interest or historic or scientific value." *Id.*

153. *Id.* Art. VII.

154. Sands, *supra* note 22, at 391.

155. *See, e.g.*, 1978 Treaty for Amazonian Cooperation (Amazonian Treaty), 17 I.L.M. (1978), 1045, July 3, 1978, in force February 2, 1980 (mainly devoted to economic development and the right of each sovereign nation to use its natural resources, with the secondary purpose of preserving the environment); 1989 Amazon Declaration, 28 I.L.M. (1989), 1303, May 6, 1989 (linking environmental protection with economic development and objecting to conditionalities imposed in the allocation of international resources/emphasizing the need for financial support and assistance from developed nations); Agreement for the Conservation of the Biodiversity and Protection of Priority Uncultivated Areas of Central America [Convenio para la conservación de la biodiversidad y protección de areas silvestres prioritarias en America Central], opened for signature June 1992, 17 Integración Latino Americana 78 (Jul. 1992); Regional Convention for the Management and Conservation of Natural Forest Ecosystems and the Development of Forest Plantations; Convention for the Protection and Development of the Marine Environment of the Wider Caribbean Region, Mar. 24, 1983, 22 I.L.M. 227.

156. *See generally* Michael Holley, *Sustainable Development in Central America: Translating Regional Environmental Accords into Domestic Enforcement Action*, 25 Ecology L.Q. 89 (1998); Rogers and Moore, *supra* note 89.

157. Apia Convention, I.E.L.M.T. 976:45, June 12, 1976, entered into force June 28, 1990.

158. *Id.* Art. II.1.

159. *Id.* Art. III.1.

160. *Id.* Art. III.2.

161. *Id.* Art. III.3. Provision shall also be made for "visitors to enter and use national parks, under appropriate conditions, for inspirational, educative, cultural and recreative purposes." *Id.* Art. III.4.

162. *Id.* Art. V.1.

163. *Id.* Art. V.2–3.

164. *Id.* Art. V.4.

165. *See* <http://www.nature.coe.int/english/cadres/berne.htm> (listing all parties and the dates of signature and ratification).

166. Berne Convention, Art. 1, Sept. 19, 1979, entered into force June 1, 1982.

167. *Id.* Art. 4.1. "Specially protected" flora species are listed in Appendix I, "specially protected" fauna species in Appendix II, and "protected" fauna species, the harvesting of which is authorized but must be regulated, in Appendix III; Appendix IV lists prohibited means and methods of killing, capture, and other forms of exploitation.

168. *Id.* Art. 4.2. However, Article 2 introduces a potentially important caveat. Parties are to take "requisite measures to maintain the population of wild flora and fauna at, or adapt it to, a level which corresponds in particular to ecological, scientific and cultural requirements, *while taking account of economic and recreational requirements* and the needs of sub-species, varieties or forms at risk locally" (emphasis added). There could be room within the ambit of "taking account of economic and recreational requirements" to allow parties to pursue their other responsibilities less than aggressively.

169. *Id.* Arts. 5–8. Exceptions to the prohibitions on takings are provided for in Article. 9.

170. *Id.* Art. 10. Parties are required to coordinate their efforts with regard to migratory species and to ensure that their procedures are adequate to protect such species.

171. *Id.* Art. 18.

172. Sands, *supra* note 22, at 396.

173. European biodiversity is also governed by the 1982 Benelux Convention on Nature Conservation and Natural Resources, June 8, 1982, in force October 1, 1983, 2 S.M.T.E. 163, which requires the harmonization of policy principles, instruments, laws and regulations, information exchange, education campaigns, and coordinated implementation of other agreements. Additionally, the 1992 EC Directive on the Conservation of Natural Habitats and of Wild Fauna and Flora, Council Directive 92/43/EEC of May 21, 1992, is directed at conservation of natural/species habitats and species protection. It provides a basis for taking into account ecological conditions and needs of all territories of the EC member states, and recognizes the common responsibility to promote conservation of habitats and species. *See* Sands, *supra* note 22, at 398–401. The Habitats Directive is discussed in more depth in Chapter 4.

174. *See generally* Edith Brown Weiss, *Understanding Compliance with International Environmental Agreements: The Baker's Dozen Myths*, 32 U. Rich. L. Rev. 1555 (1999); Edith Brown Weiss, *International Environmental Law: Contemporary Issues and the Emergence of a New World Order*, 81 Geo. L.J. 675 (1993); David G. Victor, *Enforcing International Law: Implications for an Effective Global Warming Regime*, 10 Duke Env. L. & Pol'y J. 147 (1999).

175. *See* Sands, *supra* note 22, at 136–7.

176. *See* Sands, *supra* note 22, at 450–2.

177. *See* Lyster, *supra* note 46, at 4.

178. Weiss, *supra* note 133 at 1556, 1559.

179. However, the Vienna Convention on the Law of Treaties establishes that merely signing a treaty creates a legal obligation not to defeat the object and purpose of the treaty. *See* Vienna Convention of the Law of Treaties, May 23, 1969, Art. 18(a), U.N. Doc. A/CONF.39/27 (entered into force Jan. 27, 1990). The provisions of the Vienna Convention of the Law of Treaties are recognized as a codification of the customary international law of treaties, and therefore any given nation's failure to ratify a treaty does not necessarily vitiate that treaty's applicability to that nation. *See* LASSA OPPENHEIM, OPPENHEIM'S INTERNATIONAL LAW 1199 (Robert Jennings and Arthur Watts, eds., 9th ed. 1992).

180. Lyster, *supra* note 46, at 5–6.

181. *Id.* at 9.

182. Eric J. Pan, *Authoritative Interpretation of Agreements: Developing More Responsive International Administrative Regimes*, 38 Harv. Int'l L.J. 503, 509 (1997) (criticizing the reservation phenomenon as undermining the goal of regulatory uniformity and resulting in different parties having different legal obligations under the same treaty).

183. George W. Downs, *Enforcement and the Evolution of Cooperation*, 19 Mich. J. Int'l L. 319, 321 (1998); Sands, *supra* note 22, at 141–3.

184. Brad L. Bacon, Note, *Enforcement Mechanisms in International Wildlife Agreements and the United States: Wading Through the Murk*, 12 Geo. Int'l Envtl. L. Rev. 331, 336 (1999).

185. General Agreement on Tariffs and Trade 1994, Apr. 15, 1994, 33 I.L.M. 1125. *See* Weiss, *supra* note 133 at 1585–86. *See generally* Chris Wold, *Multilateral Environmental Agreements and the GATT: Conflict and Resolution?*, 26 Envtl. L. 841 (1996); Christine Crawford, *Conflicts Between the Convention on International Trade in Endangered Species and the GATT in Light of Actions to Halt the Rhinoceros and Tiger Trade*, 7 Geo. Int'l Envt'l L. Rev. 555 (1995).

186. General Agreement on Tariffs and Trade, opened for signature October 30, 1947, 61 Stat. A-3, 55 U.N.T.S. 187 [hereinafter GATT].

187. *See generally* ERNST-ULRICH PETERSMANN, THE GATT/WTO DISPUTE SETTLEMENT SYSTEM: INTERNATIONAL LAW, INTERNATIONAL ORGANIZATIONS AND DISPUTE SETTLEMENT (1997) (summarizing the history of GATT and the WTO and their dispute settlement methods).

188. GATT includes three core obligations intended to liberalize trade and eliminate discrimination between parties: (1) Article I requires parties to treat products from all other GATT parties the same (most-favored-nation principle); (2) Article III requires parties to treat foreign and domestic products alike (national treatment principle); and (3) Article XI limits the use of quantitative restrictions. *See* Annick Emmenegger Brunner, *Conflicts Between International Trade and Multilateral Environmental Agreements*, 4 Ann. Surv. Int'l & Comp. L. 74, 79–80 (1997).

189. The World Trade Organization (WTO) was created in 1994 to be the institutional body that governs GATT and several other trade agreements that have been negotiated under the auspices of GATT. *See* Final Act Embodying the Results of the Uruguay Round of Multilateral Trade Negotiations, Apr. 15, 1994, LEGAL INSTRUMENTS—RESULTS OF THE URUGUAY ROUND vol. 1 (1994), 33 I.L.M. 1125 (1994); *see also* JOHN H. JACKSON, THE WORLD TRADE ORGANIZATION: CONSTITUTION AND JURISPRUDENCE 1 (1998).

190. Trade and Environment, GATT Ministerial Decision of April 14, 1994, 33 I.L.M. 1267 (1994).

191. *See, e.g.*, GATT Dispute Panel Report on United States—Restrictions on Imports of Tuna, 30 I.L.M. 1598, para. 5.28 (Sept. 3, 1991) (Tuna-Dolphin I) (declaring illegal a U.S. embargo on tuna caught by fishing methods causing high rates of dolphin mortality). *But see* the broader interpretation in GATT Dispute Settlement Panel Report on U.S. Restrictions on Imports of Tuna, 33 I.L.M. 839, (June 16, 1994) (Tuna-Dolphin II) (but nonetheless noting that the "long-standing practice of panels has . . . been to interpret [Article XX] narrowly," because of concerns that a broader reading would undermine GATT).

192. Panels interpreting Article XX(b) commonly employ a three-step analysis: (1) Is the substance of the policy of the measure in question the protection of

human, animal, or plant life or health? (2) Is the measure for which the exception is being invoked necessary to protect human, animal, or plant life or health? and (3) Is the measure applied consistently with the chapeau, avoiding arbitrary or unjustifiable discrimination and/or a disguised restriction on international trade? *See* Thomas J. Schoenbaum, *International Trade and Protection of the Environment: The Continuing Search for Reconciliation*, 91 A.J.I.L. 268, 276-7 (1997). In one case, Thailand restricted the importation of cigarettes because of their negative health effects. Because Thailand did not use the "least restrictive" or the "least GATT-inconsistent" measure available, the GATT panel refused to recognize an Article XX(b) exception for this ETM, even though significant human health risks were at issue. Report of the GATT Panel on Thailand—Restrictions on Importation of and Internal Taxes on Cigarettes, Nov. 7, 1990, reprinted in 30 I.L.M. 1122, 1127, 1138–39 (1991). *See* Lakshman Guruswamy, *The Promise of the United Nations Convention on the Law of the Sea: Justice in Trade and Environment Disputes*, 25 Ecology L.Q. 189, 201–02 (1998).

193. WTO/GATT panels analyze Article XX(g) in terms of four requirements: (1) that the policy of the measures for which the provision is invoked falls within the range of policies relating to the conservation of exhaustible natural resources; (2) that the measures for which the exception is being invoked—that is, the particular trade measures inconsistent with the General Agreement—are related to the conservation of exhaustible natural resources; (3) that the measures for which the exception are being invoked are made effective in conjunction with restrictions on domestic production or consumption; and (4) that the measures are applied in conformity with the requirements of the introductory clause of Article XX. *See* Schoenbaum, *supra* note 151, at 277–9. For example, in 1988, Canada tried for an Article XX(g) exception, claiming its ETM was justified to preserve an "exhaustible resource" in herring and salmon. The effect of Canada's ban on the export of unprocessed herring and salmon prevented U.S. fishing vessels from returning to the United States with their harvests. In the opinion of the GATT panel the ETM was a disguised protectionist measure, and the panel refused to grant an ETM exception, holding that the measure was not "primarily aimed at conservation" because there was no domestic ban on consumption of salmon or herring. Report of the GATT Panel on Canada—Measures Affecting Exports of Unprocessed Herring and Salmon, Mar. 22, 1988.

194. Tuna-Dolphin I, para. 5.26 and Tuna-Dolphin II, para. 5.13 (dolphins); United States—Taxes on Automobiles, 33 I.L.M. 1937, paras. 5.57 (1994) (gasoline); United States—Standards for Reformulated and Conventional Gasoline, 35 I.L.M. 274, para. 6.37 (1996) (clean air).

195. *See, e.g.*, Canada—Measures Affecting Exports of Unprocessed Herring and Salmon, Mar. 22, 1988, GATT B.I.S.D. (35th Supp.) 98 (1988); United States—Standards for Reformulated and Conventional Gasoline, Appellate Body Report, 35 I.L.M. 603 (1996).

196. *See* Kazumochi Kometani, *Trade and Environment: How Should WTO Panels Review Environmental Regulations Under GATT Articles III and XX?*, 16 NW. J. Int'l L. & Bus. 441, 443 (1996) (discussing the right of the U.S. dolphin protection policy to have extraterritorial effect in light of the conflicting GATT panel decisions in Tuna-Dolphin I and Tuna-Dolphin II).

197. *See* Jill Nissen, *Achieving a Balance Between Trade and the Environment: The Need to Amend the WTO/GATT to Include Multilateral Environmental Agreements*, 28 L. & Pol'y Int'l Bus. 901, 920–23 (1997) (noting that opposition from developing

nations to any formal recognition of environmental standards has prevented adoption of measures to formally recognize ETMs within the GATT framework); Gregory C. Shaffer, *The World Trade Organization Under Challenge: Democracy and the Law and Politics of the WTO's Treatment of Trade and Environment Matters*, 25 Harv. Envtl. L. Rev. 1, 19–23 (2001).

198. Report of the Appellate Body in United States—Import Prohibition of Certain Shrimp and Shrimp Products, Oct. 12, 1998, 33 I.L.M. 121 (Shrimp-Turtles Appellate Body). The U.S. ETMs were provided for by the Marine Mammals Protection Act of 1972, 16 U.S.C. 1361-1421h (1994), as were the ETMs at issue in both of the Tuna-Dolphin cases.

199. *See generally* Susan L. Sakmar, *Free Trade and Sea Turtles: The International and Domestic Implications of the Shrimp-Turtles Case*, 10 Colo. J. Int'l Envtl. L. & Pol'y 345 (1999); Howard F. Chang, *Toward a Greener GATT: Environmental Trade Measures and the Shrimp-Turtle Case*, 74 S. Cal. L. Rev. 31 (2000).

200. Shrimp-Turtles Appellate Body, paras. 161–77.

201. Report of the WTO Committee on Trade and Environment, Nov. 14, 1996, PRESS/TE 014 (1996), adopted by the WTO Ministerial Conference in Singapore in December 1996.

202. *Id.*, para. 174. *See* Steve Charnovitz, *A Critical Guide to the WTO's Report on Trade and Environment*, 14 Ariz. J. Int'l & Comp. L. 341, 342 (1997) (criticizing the lack of progress reflected in the report after years of discussions); James Cameron, *Dispute Settlement and Conflicting Trade and Environment Regimes*, in TRADE AND THE ENVIRONMENT: BRIDGING THE GAP (Agata Fijalkowski and James Cameron, eds., 1998) (decrying the failure of the CTE to produce more environmentally favorable solutions to the trade versus environment dilemma under WTO/GATT law).

203. North American Free Trade Agreement, January 1, 1994.

204. *See generally* Beatriz Bugeda, *Is NAFTA Up to Its Green Expectations? Effective Law Enforcement Under the North American Agreement on Environmental Cooperation*, 32 U. Rich. L. Rev. 1591 (1999).

205. *Id.* Art. 904(1), (4); Art. 2101(1). (1) Does the standard relate to environmental protection? That is, is the trade restrictive standard directly connected with an environmental program and primarily aimed at achieving an integral aspect of that program? (2) If so, does the standard create an unnecessary obstacle to trade? That is, is a trade restriction necessary to achieve the environmental goal? (3) If a trade restriction is necessary, has the least-trade-restrictive measure been chosen? That is, is the degree to which trade is impeded essential to achieve the environmental goal in question? *See* Bradly J. Condon, *Reconciling Trade and Environment: A Legal Analysis of European and North American Approaches*, 8 Cardozo J. Int'l & Comp. L. 1, 12–18 (2000).

206. Unlike the WTO, NAFTA does formally recognize the legitimacy of specified multilateral environmental agreements and permits the use of ETMs, such as sanctions, bans, or restrictions, under these agreements as an exception to NAFTA rules.

207. Montreal Protocol on Substances That Deplete the Ozone Layer, Sept. 16, 1987, 26 I.L.M. 1541. The Montreal Protocol was amended on June 29, 1990; Nov. 25, 1992; Dec. 7, 1995; Sept. 17, 1997; and Dec. 3, 1999.

208. Vienna Convention on the Law of Treaties, May 23, 1969, Art. 30(3), 1155 U.N.T.S. 331.

209. *See* Nathalie Chalifour, *Global Trade Rules and the World's Forests: Taking Stock of the World Trade Organization's Implications for Forests*, 12 Geo. Int'l Envtl. L. Rev. 575, 591–2 (2000).

210. *See, e.g.*, R.C. Longworth, *Globalization Foes Consider Joining Forces Against WTO*, Chicago Tribune, August 20, 2001, p. 1.

211. *See* Johanna Rinceanu, *Enforcement Mechanisms in International Environmental Law: Quo Vadunt?*, 15 J. Envtl. L. & Litig. 147, 148–9 (2000).

212. *See* Article 34, Statute of the International Court of Justice, 59 Stat. 1055, T.S. No. 993. According to Article 96(1) of the U.N. Charter, the International Court of Justice also has an advisory jurisdiction, enabling it to provide an advisory opinion on any legal question raised by the General Assembly or the Security Council. Article 96(2) of the U.N. Charter states that other organs of the United Nations and specialized agencies, which may at any time be so authorized by the General Assembly, may also request advisory opinions of the ICJ on legal questions falling within the scope of their activities.

213. *See* Mary Ellen O'Connell, *Enforcing the New International Law of the Environment*, 35 German Y. B. Int'l L. 293, 311–4 (1992).

214. Weiss, *supra* note 133 at 1567–8. *See* Harold K Jacobsen and Edith Brown Weiss, *Assessing the Record and Designing Strategies to Engage Countries*, in ENGAGING COUNTRIES: STRENGTHENING COMPLIANCE WITH INTERNATIONAL ENVIRONMENTAL ACCORDS, at 511, 545 (Edith Brown Weiss and Harold K. Jacobsen, eds., 1998).

• 4 •

Biodiversity Preservation, Nation by Nation

INDIVIDUAL NATIONS' LEGAL EFFORTS TO PRESERVE BIODIVERSITY

We will now proceed seriatim through the generally accepted list of hotspots, as set forth in Chapter 2, and examine the internal laws of each nation as applicable to hotspots preservation. There can certainly be reasoned debate as to the regions denominated as hotspots, both as to their identity and their boundaries, but the areas discussed here are probably a good approximation of the most significant ones and are the hotspots usually featured in the relevant scientific literature. I have also added two of the most significant Major Tropical Wilderness Areas, which, although not within the usual hotspots definition because they are as yet relatively pristine and not at immediate risk, are undoubtedly among the world's greatest centers of endemism. We will consider the major conservation measures provided for by domestic law, nation by nation, and the extent to which these measures are affording adequate protection to each hotspot. Certain recurring themes will quickly become apparent.

Honesty and a spirit of full disclosure compel me to warn you that this chapter is long, detailed, and repetitive, as well as depressing. For the average reader, it may be both merciful and sufficient to skim this chapter, or to read only a few of the sections. Because this book is intended to be a comprehensive treatment of the law on biodiversity preservation, I have included a great deal of information, nation by nation, for those specialists and others who may have a particular interest in any given country. For most "normal" readers, feel free to tread lightly over the troubled waters of this chapter and quickly move on. I promise you, I will not be offended. In fact, unless I happen to be reading over your shoulder right now (don't look!), I will not even know.

Madagascar

New legislation was passed in 1990 in order to outline and give effect to Madagascar's national environmental policy.[1] This law, Number 90,033, establishes a long-term Environmental Action Plan in phases to be executed over at least 15 years. Phase One, which began in 1990, was designed to address the most urgent environmental issues.

The particularly relevant specified goals of Phase One are:

1. management and protection of biodiversity;
2. conservation of the soils and reforestation; and
3. environmental research concerning the diverse ecosystems.[2]

Each of the specified goals are to be achieved by particular agencies, with the preservation of biodiversity component to be implemented by the Department of Waters and Forests (DEF) with the support of the National Association for the Management of the Protected Areas (ANGAP). The principal objectives of this component are: to establish a reserve of 50 protected areas covering about 1.4 million hectares; ameliorate the living conditions of the 70,000 families living in the peripheral zones; develop agriculture with about 0.3 million hectares; and create 1,100 jobs in the public and private sector, with 39 percent of them to be in conservation.[3]

Madagascar has established some conservation areas of varying degrees of protection. There are six national parks (open to the public) covering 175,340 hectares, 11 strict nature reserves covering 569,542 hectares, and 23 special reserves covering about 376,000 hectares, the latter two categories providing only limited public access. Together, all of these protected areas encompass a total of 1,121,482 hectares, or 1.9 percent of the hotspot.[4] For a hotspot as hot as Madagascar, this is an abysmal level of legal protection.

There is a network of about 267 "classified forests" and forest reserves that comprise an additional 4,000,000 or so hectares, or 7 percent of the country, but the government of Madagascar intends to use these for "sustainable" timber harvesting, which may render their level of protection questionable.[5] It is not apparent how effective forest protection has been. Indeed, there is evidence of continuing and widespread devastation to these irreplaceable habitats.[6] However, in light of the fact that reforestation is one of the objectives outlined in the new legislation, and that the government has created a comprehensive, detailed scheme specifically giving priority to biodiversity, most of these areas will at least theoretically be protected. It should be a matter of the highest priority to ensure that they have actual and not merely paper protection.

Atlantic Coast Brazil/Atlantic Forest Region

Brazil has taken some meaningful steps to protect this phenomenal hotspot. There are 14 national parks, 14 federal biological reserves, and six federal ecological stations within this hotspot, totaling 756,977 hectares.[7] There are also many state and municipal parks and reserves that supplement the federal protection and bring the overall protected area to 35.8 percent of the hotspot region.[8] Additionally, the Private Natural Heritage Reserve Program offers landowners tax incentives for the protection of natural habitats on their property. However, there are numerous practical problems that threaten even the protected areas, including unresolved land claims, inadequate staffing, illegal human encroachment, and a variety of developmental activities.[9]

The Brazilian Constitution provides:

Everyone has the right to an ecologically balanced environment. . . . This imposes upon the Public Authorities and the community the obligation to defend and preserve it for present and future generations. . . . It is incumbent upon the Public Authorities . . . to preserve and restore essential ecological processes and to provide for the ecological management of species and ecosystems.[10]

Brazil has adopted a comprehensive environmental scheme with a "National Environmental Policy" setting forth several objectives, which include measures designed for the protection of animals and plants as well as the control of pollution. Definitions of "environmental crimes" have been promulgated along with penalties to enforce environmental violations of both a criminal and administrative nature. Under Brazil's governmental scheme, states are authorized to promulgate their own environmental legislation and regulations so long as they are not inconsistent with the federal regulations, and municipalities can likewise supplement these state regulations.[11] Only one state, São Paulo, has thus far promulgated such environmental regulations setting out state environmental policy.[12]

In 1981, Law No. 6,938 was promulgated by the president which outlined the "National Environmental Policy as well as objectives, development and procedures."[13] This act is mainly a policy statute, but it establishes a comprehensive scheme by creating agencies of different levels and outlines in detail the responsibilities they will have. Under Article 2, its broad objective is for the "preservation, enhancement and restoration of environmental quality essential to life aiming at insuring socio-economic development conditions." Some of the relevant means that will be used to accomplish this goal are: using government action to "maintain ecologic equilibrium considering the environment as public property to be necessarily guaranteed and protected, taking account of its beneficial use to the public"; protection of ecosystems including the preservation of representative areas; reclamation of areas of degradation; and protection of areas threatened with degradation.[14] Here, the government is clearly taking responsibility as protector of public property, but is also giving recognition to the fact that Brazil's economy must be allowed to grow through the use of its natural resources. This is a theme that is echoed throughout its environmental protection scheme.

Recognition of the necessity for growth is also apparent in the composition of the distinct bodies that are created under this law as part of the "National Environmental System" (SISNAMA). The "Superior Agency," the National Environmental Council (CONAMA), is to assist the president in developing the directives of the National Environmental Policy as an advisory body. It is composed of representatives of the state governments, the presidents of the National Confederations of Industry, Agriculture, and Commerce, and includes the presidents of unions representing the workers of the above associations.[15]

There is a second agency, the Special Environmental Agency (SEMA) under the Ministry of the Interior, who is to "promote, discipline and evaluate execution" of the policy.[16] Among SEMA's responsibilities are to propose rules and criteria for licensing of potentially polluting activities to CONAMA, which licenses will be issued by the states and supervised by SEMA. SEMA is also responsible for the imposition of fines and penalties.[17] Failure to comply with regulations and conditions of licensing can result in the ordered suspension of activities, and the polluter may be required "irrespective of the existence of fault" to repair damage to the environment and to any affected third parties.[18]

Law No. 6,938, Article 18, specifically creates "Ecological Reserves or Stations" to be overseen by SEMA for forests and other forms of natural plant life of "permanent preservation listed in Article 2 of the 9-15-65 Forestry Code," where those forests are home to bird species protected by the treaties and international agreements signed by Brazil. This provision is significant because the forests are to receive additional protections based on being habitats for species, and because it gives effect to treaties that have been signed.

This environmental scheme was further developed under Decree No. 99.274, enacted on June 6, 1990. This legislation is significant because it provided for CONAMA to create subcouncils consisting of the "Plenary Assembly" and "Technical Councils."[19] Notably, members to be included in CONAMA's Plenary Assembly are two representatives from associations whose primary focus is the defense of natural resources as well as one representative of a legally recognized (as found in the National Register) nongovernmental environmental organization from each region. These representatives are to be chosen by each organization and then appointed by the president for renewable two-year terms.[20]

Though these representatives are subject to the approval of the president, it is an idea unique to Brazil formally to include nongovernmental organizations in deliberations for the proposal of legislation. There are currently 700 active Brazilian NGOs.[21] It is, however, unclear whether this participation is limited to Brazilian NGOs or whether international NGOs can also be listed in the National Register. The Technical Councils are referred to only in Article 8. This short section simply provides that each council is to be composed of seven members with CONAMA deciding what their responsibility should be, but the concept of parceling out a portion of the diverse areas that need environmental protection to a smaller group with particular expertise is a positive one.

This Plenary Assembly is to meet every three months in open session with at least half the members present.[22] Other responsibilities of the Plenary Assembly, in addition to the proposal of policy directives through the Secretary of the Environment, include issuing standards necessary to execute and implement National Environmental Policy and to establish general standards relative to the "Conservation Units" and activities that may be permitted in areas surrounding the units. These "surrounding areas" are defined as a 10 kilometer radius around the Conservation Units, and any activity that "might affect the biota" is to be subject to standards published by CONAMA. Therefore, these representatives have a real chance to directly be involved in and create guidelines for conservation.

What is also of interest is the intended scope of the legislation's reach. It is intended to cover not only public but private property.[23] The government is affirmatively responsible through its "supervisory and investigatory" agencies to "guide and assist" landowners in attaining compliance with the environmental objectives. Such attainment is encouraged and fostered by the specific directive to "give priority" to applications to federal financing and credit agencies for improvement of "rational use of the soil and sanitary and living conditions of properties" in areas that are subject to environmental protection.[24] Such incentives theoretically supply the impetus for local compliance and acceptance, which is lacking in so many other endangered areas. Not only does the Brazilian government realize that socioeconomic development is integral to an understanding of the importance of environmental protection, but it is approaching the problem of funding and execution by providing federal funding to better living conditions contingent upon compliance with environmental regulations.

This legislation also has teeth in the form of fines. The law provides that fines shall be imposed in proportion to the "environmental degradation"caused, a ten-for-one penalty.[25] Some of the relevant "infractions" are: causing pollution that leads to the destruction of cultivated or wild plants; harming, killing, or capturing within Conservation Units by any means "species considered rare among regional biota"; and "causing environmental damage of any type which causes the destruction or has undesirable effects on the natural biota."[26] This legislation is very broadly drafted, but the emphasis on the primary importance of rare species and conservation areas is apparent.

Legislation passed in January 1997 provides specific protection for tropical forests and was intended to establish a model for "sustainable development of Brazilian tropical forests" to be implemented by all levels of government "with the technical and financial support of the international community."[27] This law provides for the "1st Phase" of this "pilot program" with the strengthening of state environmental agencies, the establishment of logging reserves and indigenous lands, and the establishment of "centers of scientific excellence."[28]

Under Article 3, a "Coordination Committee" is created to control the investment of funds on an annual basis, to analyze the results of annual technical studies, to implement the phases of the program, and to monitor project performance.[29] The composition of this committee, along with representatives from each of the major federal agencies, also provides for two state representatives from the environmental organizations of the states of the Legal Amazon, two representatives from NGOs "with activities" in the Legal Amazon, and one representative from an operating NGO in the Atlantic Forest region.[30] This clearly opens participation to national as well as international NGOs and environmentalists, allowing them to be involved from the beginning in the analysis of the information received from technical experts and in the creation of policies. What is also interesting is the acknowledgment and acceptance of international funds with the simultaneous provision for participation. This is a remarkable opening of a national government to international involvement. The representation is only a few members, but the concept is novel and surprising.

Another intriguing approach taken by the Brazilian government is the designation of "environmental crimes." This concept seemed to first appear in the new Constitution adopted in 1988 in Article 26, where destruction of the rainforests of the Amazon and the Atlantic Forests was deemed a crime under the penal code.[31] A law promulgated by the president in 1998 provides for both "Crimes Against Animals" and "Crimes Against Plants."[32] "Any party who in any way participates" in the practice of the covered crimes, with the specific provision for personal liability of corporate actors, is liable.[33] The law contains mitigating and aggravating circumstances and provides for minimum terms of imprisonment for many violations.

The following are some of the particularly relevant provisions. Under Article 29, it is a crime to kill, pursue, hunt, capture or use "specimens of wild animals, native or on a migratory route" without a proper license or authorization. This crime carries a penalty of detention of six months to one year and a fine. There is provision for an increase of the penalty by one-half when the above actions occur at night, in a Conservation Unit, or by the use of methods that are capable of mass destruction.[34] Article 33 is aimed at polluters causing environmental damage whereby the "disappearance of aquatic fauna" is caused by effluent or the transporting of materials, with a penalty of detention for one to three years or a fine or both. This may be particularly directed towards mining operations, which are a recognized problem in the Amazon because mercury, used in extracting gold, has caused severe environmental damage to much of the Amazon River. The government also has inserted an exclusionary provision for those who take animals to satisfy hunger for themselves or for their families.[35]

"Crimes against plants" include the destruction or harming of plants under permanent protection and the cutting of forests under permanent protection, carrying penalties of imprisonment for one to three years or a fine or both.[36] It is also a crime to cause direct or indirect harm to "Conservation Units," which are defined as including all designated areas at every level of government and "areas which may be created by Public Authorities."[37] Under Article 53, the penalty will be increased by one-third to one-sixth for various reasons, including under Part II, subsection (c), "against rare species or those threatened with extinction even if the threat occurs only at the location of the violation."

Section V is entitled, "Crimes Against Environmental Authorities." Here, it is made criminal to issue false or misleading statements to public officials, omit the truth, or withhold technical or scientific data.[38] There is also a provision and penalty for public officials who issue licenses in violation of environmental regulations.[39] These two articles carry a penalty of imprisonment for one to three years and a fine. Under Article 70, any party finding evidence of a violation can notify authorities. The above provisions begin to address what has been recognized as a major problem in Brazil, where much of the responsibility for enforcement lies with state and local authorities and powerful interests are in opposition. Some public officials have been killed and many are in fear.[40]

The Minister of the Environment and Legal Amazon issued a decree in 1999 that provides for administrative fines supplemental to the above penalties.[41] What is particularly notable about these regulations is that they incorporate and give effect to the lists of threatened species of Annexes I and II of the 1975 Convention on International Trade in Endangered Species (CITES). There is a designation of crimes consisting of killing, trapping, or capturing species of wild fauna, whether native or migratory, and for the "bulk export of skins and bodies of amphibians and reptiles without authorization" with an increase in fines for threatened species listed on both the Brazilian Official List of Threatened Species and the Annexes of CITES.[42] These fines are imposed per "unit" of species taken. This decree also provides supplemental penalties for activities not in conformance with a license, destruction or harming of protected forests, and the cutting of trees.[43] Thus, Brazil has at least defined both criminal and civil violations with definite penalties.

Although the states are permitted to promulgate supplementary regulations, São Paulo appears to be the only one that has. This is positive because São Paulo is the industrial center of the region, but in a system whereby the federal government promulgates laws of broad, general objectives and guidelines, all the states need to develop specific environmental regulations before they can be effectively enforced.

Western Ecuador/Chocó-Darien-Western Ecuador

Within the broader Chocó-Darien-Western Ecuador hotspot, 6.3 percent (16,471 square kilometers) is protected in a system of national parks, science centers, forest reserves, ecological reserves, military reserves, and indigenous reserves.[44] Some of the protection derives from enclaves such as the Awa Indian Reserve (straddling the border with Colombia), which, although not primarily devoted to biodiversity, still serve to provide some safeguards against development. There are also private initiatives, including the 3,000-hectare Bilsa Biological Reserve.[45]

Designation of parks or reserves does not guarantee protection, however. The Machalilla National Park has suffered considerable degradation since its establishment in 1979.[46]

Ecuador, like Brazil, has a sectoral approach to its environmental legislation. The relevant legislation includes The Forests and Natural Areas and Wildlife Conservation Act of 1981.[47] Furthermore, the Constitution guarantees the right of its citizens to live in an environment free of contamination. However, when one NGO, the Corporación de Defensa de la Vida (CORDAVI), filed a suit with the Tribunal of Constitutional Guarantees (the equivalent of the U.S. Supreme Court) to stop the exploration of oil within the national parks system because the constant spills were damaging the environment, the court initially ordered the government to cease from granting any additional development permits in protected natural areas, but reversed its ruling one week later.[48] This suggests that political pressures to support economic growth may trump biodiversity protection.

Ecuadorian law and government policy have contributed to the rate of deforestation. In 1964, there existed a law, the Unoccupied Lands and Colonization Law of 1964, that essentially encouraged the development of land.[49] Under this law, indigenous people could not qualify as legal holders of land until they had complied with one of the various "productive uses" specified.[50] In most instances, "productive use" became synonymous with the conversion of forests into cropland or pastures for cattle.[51] Recent guidelines promulgated under the law by IERAC (the group created under this law in 1964 to implement it) evaluate the soil and terrain capacities in determining what satisfies "use" for adjudication of a plot in question.[52] Nevertheless, many of the IERAC agents have been employed for their entire careers by the IERAC, and they often still look to the traditional requirements that the land be sufficiently "worked," meaning it has been clear-cut and is suitable for grazing.[53] Furthermore, because of the lengthy delays in the IERAC's adjudication process, many settlers feel compelled to clear their parcels because of the potential that one who comes along may gain superior rights over them. Once again, the limited resources available to developing countries create obstacles to the shift to a more protected environment.

The forestry policy of the government and the recurring failure to enforce the forestry laws has created perhaps the most deforestation. It was not until 1981 that passage of the Forestry, Natural Areas, and Wildlife Law (Forestry Law) came about.[54] Prior to this, no legal structure existed with regard to the harvesting of timber. Interestingly, a program of sustained management was created with the assistance of the United Nations Food and Agricultural Organization specifically for the northwestern area of Ecuadorian forest.[55] In short, based on the assurances of sustainable management assistance from the UN, the government continued awarding timber contracts to companies but without an existing reforestation process. This inevitably led to increased deforestation and increased colonization in those areas cleared.[56] The 1981 Forestry Law provided for timber companies' regulation, but the regulations have not been implemented.

Finally, there is a lack of government coordination. Ecuadorian law separates federal lands into three categories:

1. national parks and reserves, which are protected;
2. areas considered part of the National Forest System, which can be colonized pursuant to certain limitations; and
3. lands open to colonization, known as *tierras baldías*.

The reality is that the boundaries between these areas are, at best, "imprecise."[57]

Moreover, the agencies responsible for these areas are divided. Specifically, the national parks and national forest system are within the authority of the Ecuadorian Forestry and Natural Areas Institute (INEFAN), while the lands open to colonization fall under the authority of the IERAC. Often there are agency conflicts; the IERAC has often "rubber-stamped" colonist settlements that have advanced into protected areas.[58] One can reasonably infer that the IERAC chooses to ignore the legal restrictions under the forestry law for its own self-preservation. The IERAC has elevated its "apparent" workload by publishing data on the quantities of agricultural land it has distributed to landless settlers when in fact, "it does no more than issue land titles to spontaneous colonists who settled their lands without any help from IERAC."[59] Additionally, the INEFAN is so lacking in financial and manpower resources that it cannot effectively control unlawful occupation of land.[60]

As for Colombia, it was one of the first Latin American countries to adopt federal environmental legislation.[61] The Inderena (the Development Authority for Renewable Resources and the Environment) was created in the 1960s and was part of the Ministry of Agriculture. In 1993, a new law, Law No. 99, created the Ministry of the Environment and a regional system of environmental organizations, known as Regional Autonomous Corporations (RACs).[62] These entities assumed the Inderena's responsibilities, which were ultimately absorbed into the Ministry of the Environment.[63] The Ministry of the Environment creates national environmental policies and issues regulations, which are then implemented by the various states and municipalities, the constitutional authority of which is contained in Article 3 of Law 99.[64]

In Decree 1753 of 1994, a new law comparable to the NEPA procedural structure was implemented. This law requires an EIS for any activity "significantly affecting" the environment, which is to be submitted to an RAC.[65] Alternatives may be proposed and public participation allowed. Any individual, without having to show standing, may participate in administrative hearings specifically directed to the permitting or licensing of activities that may affect the environment.[66]

Colombia was the first Latin American country to implement federal legislation regarding forestry.[67] Under the 1974 Civil Code on Renewable Resources and Environmental Protection, general definitions, protective measures, and instructions as to how the statutes would be implemented were outlined. However, oil and gas interests are quite important to the proposed economic growth of the country, especially since the discovery of oil in 1991 at Cusiana. Oil is in fact now Colombia's primary export.[68] Obviously, oil and gas projects have raised significant environmental concerns. Thus, even though Colombia has encouraged the petroleum companies to reforest areas they have intruded upon[69] (which indicates a growing environmental awareness), Colombia cannot yet be labeled environmentally progressive. Specifically, Colombia has the highest per-capita use of agrochemicals in Latin America.

There are mechanisms for enforcement as well, such as criminal and civil penalties, but they have been used sparingly and leniently. By way of example, after perhaps the worst environmental incident in Colombia's history (a pesticide spill in the Bay of Cartagena), those responsible were assessed a fine of only $1,000.[70]

Western Amazonia Uplands/Tropical Andes

The broader Tropical Andes hotspot contains all or part of 77 governmentally protected areas that, combined, include 79,687 square kilometers, or 6.3 percent of the hotspot territory.[71] Perhaps the most significant biodiversity enclaves in the world are found in the large Madidi National Park in Bolivia, the adjacent Bahuaja-Sonene Park in Peru, and adjoining portions of Peru's Tambopata Candamo Reserved Zone.[72] Much more can and should be done to create and vigilantly safeguard such havens here, given the importance of this hotspot and the existence of large amounts of relatively undisturbed natural habitat.

Tragically, this area is under siege from a menace usually associated with damage to humans, not ecosystems—the illegal drug trade. The impact that coca cultivation and refining for cocaine production has had on the environment in Colombia, Peru, and Bolivia includes severe tropical deforestation and soil erosion as drug growers clear new land in fragile ecosystems.[73] A recent report states that the expansion of coca cultivation, production, and trafficking in these three countries has led to the destruction of "at an absolute minimum, 2.4 million hectares of fragile tropical forest in the Andean region over the last 20 years."[74] In addition to direct deforestation, the massive and indiscriminate dumping of the various chemicals used to turn raw coca leaves into cocaine also causes extensive land and water pollution.[75]

Although its 1979 Constitution established the right of its citizens to live in an appropriate environment,[76] Peru has often displayed a lack of willingness to impede economic growth with environmental limitations and the attendant costs. Prior to 1994, the National Office for Natural Resource Evaluation was the authority responsible for the environment.[77] However, due to extreme dissatisfaction by the citizenry, Peru finally enacted the Environment and Natural Resources Code.[78] Now, environmental regulation is headed by a national environmental agency known as CONAMA, created in 1994.[79] Essentially, CONAMA has great autonomy in resolving environmental disputes and assessing the effects of new environmental laws. This is established in the Environment and Natural Resources Code, Article 12, which states that CONAMA takes precedence over legislation that runs counter to protection of the environment and natural resources. Moreover, the agency establishes criteria and has an ongoing duty to oversee Peru's environmental impact system.[80]

Unfortunately, even with CONAMA established as an autonomous environmental protection council, it does not have clear enforcement powers.[81] Moreover, there is reasonable doubt as to whether the Peruvian government will even enforce any environmentally protective laws in that it recently modified the 1990 Environment and Natural Resources Code after businesses complained of the high costs.[82]

Even though Peru's protected areas cover some of the most biologically diverse locations, they are often subjected to industrial pollution from oil production and mining.[83] Indeed, more than half of Peru's protected areas are without any real protection whatsoever.[84]

This would be a good time to perform a sanity check on yourself. You have made it through the first four of the hotspots. The road ahead is much longer than the road behind you. If you are finding the narrative thus far to be, as Mark Twain once said (not about my book!), "chloroform in print," congratulations! You are still rooted in reality. Be of good cheer, for the next umpteen pages of this chapter will basically repeat the lamentable refrain you have probably already memorized. Here is a tip: If you are already angry, sad, and determined to take action, skip to the next chapter unless you are either a legal scholar, a conservation biologist with a particular interest in the remaining hotspots, a masochist, or an insomniac. For everyone other than those four categories of people (which are not mutually exclusive and may in fact overlap considerably), the primary purpose of this chapter is to generate an appropriately energized emotional response in you, dear reader. Once that happens for you, you have my official permission to skip ahead.

Eastern Himalayas/Mountains of South-Central China

The 1982 Constitution of the People's Republic of China mandates the protection and improvement of the living environment and ecosystems, prevention of pollution, proper utilization of natural resources, and protection of important animals and plants.[85] The Forest Law of 1979 enhanced forest preservation and imposed new regulations on logging to require sustainable practices.[86] In addition, there is the Law of Wild Animals' Protection[87] and a variety of statutory instruments and orders.

China has no special national laws devoted exclusively to nature reserves or other protected areas. The relevant provisions are scattered in other laws, such as the Environmental Protection Law, Grasslands Law, Forest Law, Administrative Measures for Forest and Wild Animal Natural Reserves, Circular on Strengthening Protection of the Natural Environment, and others.[88] For example, the Forest Law provides that all forms of exploitation and utilization of nature reserves that may cause damage, such as lumbering, hunting, fishing, grazing, and mining, are prohibited.[89]

Within this hotspot, a total of 16,562 square kilometers, or 2.1 percent of the area, are within parks and reserves. Some of the most important are the famous Wolong Nature Reserve, the Lu Gu Hu Nature Reserve, the Gao Li Nature Reserve, the Nu Jiang Nature Reserve, the Bai Ma Xue Shan Reserve, and the Luo Shan Nature Reserve.[90] But nature reserves face many problems in China. There is a fairly small number of reserves for such a large country; the structure and distribution of reserves is not very rational; there is incomplete legal protection; managers are few and often unqualified; there is lax enforcement of applicable laws and regulations; scientific research and knowledge are inadequate; and established reserves are experiencing constant damage.[91]

China is still facing a degradation of forest coverage and quality, which is due to excessive deforestation. According to the State Forestry Administration, China has strengthened the protection of forests and curbed the occupation of woodlands. Official statistics from 2000 show that local administrations at all levels have effectively supervised 85 percent of the country's woodlands occupied by construction works. These local administrations reportedly have also punished an incredible 2.2 million cases involved in destroying forests, saving the country a direct economic loss of 1.7 billion yuan ($204 million in U.S. dollars).[92] The sheer volume of enforcement actions is both encouraging and also a sign that there is a huge challenge facing the Chinese conservation officials.

Biodiversity in this hotspot has also been threatened by illegal poaching and trade in endangered animals and plants.[93] In recognition of this, making sustainable use of biology resources has topped the environmental protection agenda in western areas during China's 10th Five Year Plan period (2001–05), according to the deputy director of the Department of Nature and Ecology Conservation of the State Environmental Protection Administration.[94] Environmental officials have vowed to take more steps to protect endangered local biological resources in China's western regions.

For example, China has announced plans to increase its nature reserves to 1,880 with a total area of 155 million hectares, or 16.14 percent of the nation's land area, in the coming 10 years.[95] China had 1,276 natural reserves at the end of 2000, with a total area of 123 million hectares, or 12.44 percent of China's land area, including 909 natural reserves established by the forestry administration. Of course, not all of the current or planned protected areas fall within this hotspot, but nonetheless they should help preserve biodiversity in this key area.

Peninsular Malaysia/Northern Borneo/Sundaland

Indonesia's legal regime includes the Act Concerning the Conservation of Living Natural Resources and their Ecosystems,[96] which establishes the basic principles and general rules for the management, conservation, and use of biological resources, natural habitats, and protected areas. Indonesia has set up an extensive array of parks and reserves, with some much better protected than others. Vital enclaves such as Gunung Leuser National Park in northern Sumatra have a history of inadequate safeguards.[97] There is also a Regulation on the Protection of the Forest,[98] but illegal logging still continues at an alarming rate, and the government has not taken effective steps to halt it, despite promises that it would.[99]

Many types of ecosystems within Indonesia are not yet represented in protected areas.[100] Illegal trading in endangered species is flourishing as well, despite an array of legal protections on the federal, provincial, and district level.[101]

Environmentalists and government officials alike have acknowledged that forest destruction in Indonesia is among the worst in the world and that sustainable forest management should be implemented as soon as possible.[102] The rate of deforestation reached some 1.6 million hectares (3.9 million acres) annually from 1985 to 1998, according to a report by Indonesia's Junior Ministry for Forestry.[103] The Indonesian forest industry, however, generates some \$3.4 billion per year, which pits profits against preservation.[104] In addition, mining takes a major toll on the forests due to a presidential declaration that gives mining activities priority over all other land uses.[105] Intense international pressure has had only limited success in moving the government to safeguard the Indonesian forests, including those within supposedly protected national parks.[106]

Borneo has instituted a series of "peace parks" contiguous to other protected areas. The Lanjak-Entimau Wildlife Sanctuary in Sarawak is contiguous to Batang Ai National Park and the Gunung Bentuang and Karimun reserves in Kalimantan. This system can enhance the effectiveness of conservation efforts.[107] Tragically, Borneo is also experiencing an immense increase in deforestation, even in protected areas, as greed, corruption, lawlessness, and violence overcome whatever legal protections exist.[108]

Malaysia has enacted biodiversity-oriented legislation as well. The most significant are the Protection of Wildlife Act of 1972,[109] which has been amended on multiple occasions and supplemented by various official orders, and the National Parks Act of 1980.[110]

Throughout the Sundaland hotspot, commercial logging and rapidly increasing human population are major threats to biodiversity.[111] The logging and clear-cutting also have heightened the risk of devastating forest fires.[112] All of this has proceeded without effective legal restraint.

Philippines

Republic Act 7586, passed in 1992, established a National Integrated Protected Areas System (NIPAS) throughout the Philippines. This has targeted several areas for increased protection, in recognition of the problems plaguing the country's preservation efforts.[113] It requires formulation and approval of management plans, safeguards, and allowable activities within the protected areas, and is designed to involve local people in protected area management as well as encourage the participation of indigenous and local communities in the management scheme.[114] The Department of Environment and Natural Resources (DENR) is the main entity responsible for NIPAS implementation.[115] But as of 1995, only 1.3 percent of the total land area of the Philippines was in any type of protected area, and many key pockets of biodiversity enjoyed no legal protection at all. Most of the parks even contained human settlements and had poorly demarcated boundaries.[116] This is despite the fact that ever since 1932, the Philippines has had a national legal regime providing for a system of protected parks and preserves.[117]

Republic Act 7586 (the National Integrated and Protected Areas System Act of 1992) imposes a ban on hunting activities in the Philippines.[118] RA 7586 allows hunting on a limited scale, but individuals must first secure a permit from the Protected Area Management Board of the concerned area where they intend to hunt.[119] Additionally, Presidential Decree 1559 requires the Philippine government to conserve wildlife and regulate hunting activities.[120] This nation has been regulating hunting since 1916 when Republic Act 2590 was enacted, making it unlawful to hunt, take or kill, possess, transport, or export any living or dead protected bird or mammal.[121] Indeed, the Philippine Constitution states that all wildlife and other natural resources belong to the state.[122] And the Game and Fish Protection Act, as amended, aims to protect three categories of fauna during the "closed season"— protected birds, mammals, and other species recommended by DENR—and prohibits taking, possessing, purchasing, shipping, selling, and so forth.[123] Specific pieces of legislation prohibit the killing and hunting of several individual species as well.[124]

The reality is less impressive than the paper protections. The Philippines loses 3,000 hectares of forest each year because of clearing activities for the establishment of shrimp farms alone.[125] There is also a vast amount of totally unprotected coral reefs.[126] Approximately 80 percent of the country's reef area is already damaged.[127]

There has also been deforestation on a colossal scale, with only 3 to 6 percent of the original vegetation remaining.[128] The Philippines' once sprawling 16 million hectares (39.5 million acres) of virgin forests dominated by hardwoods is now down to only 700,000 hectares (1.7 million acres), and the blame falls on Philippine governments that over the years have passed laws favorable to logging concessions and implemented forest protection poorly.[129] With a deforestation rate of 1,900 hectares (4,695 acres) a day, the situation is critical; unchecked illegal logging remains the main culprit, aided by governmental negligence that has allowed commercial loggers to invade much of the remaining forests.[130]

The government has failed to provide adequate security provisions for putatively protected forests; there is only one forest guard for every 3,000 hectares (7,413 acres) of forests.[131] Reportedly, much of the nation's forests were open season to any logging company, particularly on the islands of Mindanao and Northern Luzon, where logging firms circumvented government forestry laws and corrupt local officials enriched themselves.[132] A common practice has been for firms to apply for a Timber Licensing Agreement on areas exceeding those required by law and have these areas subcontracted by smaller loggers, including those operating illegally.[133]

Overall, habitat destruction, population pressure, and harmful governmental policies have combined to inflict the Philippines with among the largest numbers and highest percentage of threatened mammals in the world.[134] In 1996, the Philippines ranked second only to Madagascar in the list of countries with the largest proportion of threatened mammals, according to the Red List of Threatened Animals released by the World Conservation Union (IUCN).[135] The wildlife protection laws are not fully implemented due to lack of public knowledge and appreciation of the value of wildlife protection, as well as the difficulty of apprehending illegal hunters and other violators; there are few enforcement officers and even fewer where they need to be to catch poachers.[136] The result is apparent.

By this point, if you are still reading, I hope you have begun to see a definite recurring pattern of paper protection, lack of comprehensive planning, and inadequate enforcement. If you have not discerned this pattern, perhaps you should turn down the loud music in the background and turn off the television; you are not paying attention. Hello? All right. Let me say it again, in case you were in hyperscan mode the first time a few pages ago. My primary goal in relentlessly setting forth this somber story again and again, country after country, is to arouse in you three emotions: sorrow, anger, and determination. When you reach the last two chapters of this book, I want you to be ready to take action, and I will present an idea that could make a huge difference. And after you finish those chapters, I want you to add one more emotion to your list: hopefulness. But before we get there, it is necessary to set the stage and prove that whatever we, the people of the world, are doing now to save biodiversity, it clearly is not working. The status quo is broken. And so we charge on to the next sad story. If you are leaving us now for the greener pastures of Chapter 5, have a nice trip. It certainly has been my pleasure depressing you today.

New Caledonia

This territory currently has a network of 25 reserves consisting of 52,654 hectares, roughly 2.8 percent of New Caledonia's land area.[137] Unfortunately, even these protected areas are often available for mining; 46 percent of the reserves are vulnerable to this threat. There is generally inadequate on-the-ground management and enforcement of the legal protections that do exist. And the reserves do not coincide very well with the most vital pockets of biodiversity, and some key regions are not protected at all.[138]

Fires, mining, and poaching are causing terrible damage to natural sites of exceptional value in New Caledonia. Fires are a persistent problem, whether caused by carelessness, slash-and-burn cultivation, deliberate setting to flush out game animals or exterminate rats and other vermin, the burning of rubbish, or arson, and their results are impoverishment of the soil, the acceleration of erosion, shrinkage of natural forests, the disappearance of unique plants, and the destruction of the nests of rare birds and insects.[139]

Mining has also taken a huge toll on New Caledonia's soil, which is extremely rich in nickel, chromium, cobalt, manganese, and lead, all of which are toxic for plants.[140] Nickel (probably the world's biggest deposit) is so abundant that New Caledonia is one of the world's largest producers, and early mine owners practiced strip mining on a massive scale.[141] Moreover, until the 1970s, spoil from the mines was shoved down the mountainsides, taking with it the thin layer of fertile soil. Also, the metallic oxides leached out by the rains pollute first the rivers, then the coral lagoons, causing great harm to biodiversity.[142]

Small areas have been declared land-based or marine reserves, but the record of actual preservation is troubling. For example, the 1980 delisting of the Oro Peninsula nature reserve on the Île des Pins was pushed through to make room for a hotel complex.[143] And in the botanical reserve of the Chutes de la Madeleine, the local authorities have set up a recreation area with shelters, barbecues, and toilets, and felled thousand-year-old trees belonging to a rare species with a distinctive twisted shape, for their perfumed essential oils.[144]

Southwestern Ivory Coast/Guinean Forests of West Africa

Both the Ivory Coast and the larger Guinean Forest hotspot suffer from very poor protection, on paper and in actuality. Lack of enforcement of the forest reserves that do exist only exacerbates the problem of too little action to establish reserves in the first place.[145] Key enclaves such as the Tai National Park in the Ivory Coast, the Bia National Park in Ghana, and the Sapo National Park in Liberia are under increasing threat from loggers and rural farmers and have been badly damaged. Others, including the Cross River National Park in Nigeria and the Korup National Park in Cameroon, may also be decimated without greatly improved protection.[146]

In the Ivory Coast, official governmental figures supplied by the environment and forestry ministry indicate that deforestation is occurring at a rate of 6.5 percent each year, with 300,000 hectares of forest land being destroyed annually while only 10,000 hectares are replanted.[147] The size of the forests has shrunk from 11 million hectares in 1956 to 2.5 million hectares today. Much of the damage is done by numerous "charcoal-makers, fire-burners, tree-fellers and wood-gatherers."[148] In an attempt to limit the destruction, since 1995 the Ivory Coast government has allowed only finished and semifinished wooden products to be exported, apart from logs of teak. The Ivory Coast has also set up a system of 170 "classified forests," although these are not well protected, as well as some national parks and nature reserves.[149]

In Cameroon, the government recently decided that it will have to use helicopters and even planes to supplement existing measures to stop illegal forestry exploitation and poaching.[150] There has been an intractable problem with logging companies operating illegally in Cameroon's dense jungle forests.[151] The Cameroon government had increasingly come under pressure from the international community to slow the exploitation of forest resources, which brought the country's deforestation rate to 0.9 percent annually.[152] The enforcement challenge includes severe budgetary constraints, such that the Cameroon government allocates about $8 per square kilometer per year, with one field ranger per 100 square kilometers.[153] This degree of enforcement has proved insufficient to conserve and protect key habitats and endangered animals such as the western black rhinoceros.[154]

Ghana has also found it difficult to convince its growing population, still mired in poverty, of the urgent need to preserve the environment on which they and their ancestors have long relied for crops, building materials, and the "bushmeat" of wild animals.[155] With the economy still struggling to maintain consistent growth, Ghana's portion of this hotspot is threatened by deforestation, desertification, and pollution.

Ghana's forests, which once covered much of the south and center of the country with mahogany and other valuable trees, have been drastically reduced. In 1900, Ghana had 8.2 million hectares of forest, which was cut to half that amount by 1950 and, according to official statistics, 1.4 million hectares today, although environmentalists say the true figure is much lower.[156]

Although Ghana has laws on the books to protect its forests, enforcement has been a nightmare. Loggers and other raiders go deep into the forest in the night, and sometimes exchange gunfire with the forest rangers.[157] Environmental groups have declared that there is no effective monitoring and that bribery of state officials, local leaders, and other people makes the devastation possible.[158]

Eastern Arc Mountains and Coastal Forests of Tanzania/Kenya

Tanzania has struggled desperately with intractable poverty, which has undoubtedly caused biodiversity preservation to take a backseat. Nonetheless, there are some important national parks and other reserves that are intended specifically for such preservation and are in fact well protected, including Udzungwa National Park, the Amani Nature Reserve, the University Forest Reserve at Mazumbai, and Malundwe Hill in Mikumi National Park.[159] Unfortunately, a large percentage of the putatively protected forests elsewhere in Tanzania is in "forest reserves," which are managed primarily for forestry, not biodiversity.[160]

Tanzania attempts to protect portions of its biodiversity primarily through a cluster of laws, including the National Parks Ordinance Act Number 27 of 1974, the Wildlife Conservation Act Number 12 of 1974, the Forest Ordinance of 1957, the Forest Resources Management and Conservation Act Number 10 of 1996, and the National Environment Management Act Number 19 of 1993.[161] The Wildlife Conservation Act is a type of endangered species act, and the other laws set standards for the management of natural resources of various types. On paper at least, Tanzania has made progress toward protection of its natural resources, but political exigencies have made full implementation and enforcement impracticable.

In Kenya, which is home to part of the larger hotspot, there is more bad news, despite legal protections on the books. The Forests Act empowers the Minister of Environment and Natural Resources to "declare any unalienated Government land to be a forest area" and declare it or part thereof a "nature reserve" such that "no cutting, grazing, removal of forest produce or disturbance of the flora shall be allowed except with the permission of the Chief Conservator, and permission shall only be given with the object of conserving the natural flora and amenities of the reserve."[162] National parks, national reserves, local sanctuaries and protection areas are governed by the Wildlife [Conservation and Management] [Amendment] Act, which provides penalties including fines and imprisonment for violations.[163] But protection of wildlife through these reserves and parks has come up against major challenges, including encroachment by the rapidly growing population.[164]

The government of Kenya recently announced its intention to excise, that is, deforest, over 67,000 hectares, in spite of the already critically low forest cover (less than 2 percent of Kenya's total land area).[165] The government proposes to excise 35,301 hectares of the Eastern Mau Forest (54 percent of the forest reserve) and 22,797 hectares of Southwestern Mau (27 percent of the forest reserve), among others.[166] Critics have charged that the excisions will lead to a significant loss of Kenya's biodiversity because the few remaining forests harbor 50 percent of the nation's plant species, 40 percent of the mammal species, 35 percent of the butterfly species, and 30 percent of the bird species.[167] All told, the area to be sacrificed amounts to about 10 percent of Kenya's remaining forests.[168]

Such actions demonstrate the vulnerability of some systems of "protected areas."[169] Given the delicate ecological balance in Kenya, there is a risk that this portion of the hotspot may be turned into a vast desert.[170] Additionally, squatters have been able to invade theoretically protected forests and cause damage due to cutting, poaching, burning, and farming; the few guards assigned to the forests have been overwhelmed.[171]

Western Ghats of India and Sri Lanka

India has a long history of biodiversity protection laws, much longer than most other nations. For more than a century India has had a national protected area system, but it was significantly enhanced with the passage of the National Wildlife Action Plan of 1982[172] and the Wildlife Protection Act of 1972.[173] The Indian Constitution, in its 42nd Amendment of 1976, made protection of the environment, forests, and wildlife a directive for national and state policies. India also has several other applicable statutes, including the Wild Bird Protection Act of 1887, the Indian Forest Act of 1927,[174] and the Wild Bird and Animals Act of 1912.[175]

The Western Ghats has 14,000 square kilometers (9 percent) of its area under some form of protection. This consists of eight national parks and

39 sanctuaries, with national parks receiving the more stringent level of safeguards.[176]

Soaring human population has, of course, placed intense pressure on this hotspot. Habitat destruction and indiscriminate overexploitation of resources have caused the extinction of 33 known plant species and the diversion of over 4,300 million hectares of forest land to developmental purposes.[177]

Sri Lanka has a system of national parks, strict nature reserves, jungle corridors, and sanctuaries administered by the Department of Wildlife Conservation. Together, these areas constitute about 12 percent (7,840 square kilometers) of the entire national land area and 21.1 percent (4,750 square kilometers) of the hotspots (Wet Zone) region.[178] The most important protected areas include the Sinharaja Forest Reserve, Peak Wilderness Sanctuary, Kanneliya Forest Reserve, Victoria-Rantambe Sanctuary, Kunckles Range Forest Reserve, and Horton Plains Biosphere Reserve. These enclaves are particularly vital given the developmental pressures brought about by the rapidly growing population; deforestation is a major threat in Sri Lanka.[179]

Cape Floristic Province of South Africa

About 14,060 square kilometers (19 percent) of this hotspot are conserved within 244 nature reserves and national parks.[180] However, much of the protected area is in the mountains, where the developmental threat is lowest. Some of the most significant enclaves are the Cape Peninsula National Park, the Cape Agulhas National Park, and the West Coast Biosphere Reserve. But even the areas theoretically protected are threatened by poor enforcement and insufficient funds for routine management operations.[181]

This hotspot is threatened by massive invasion of alien species of trees and shrubs brought in from other parts of the world, which are outcompeting native species and the fauna dependent on them.[182] Additionally, agriculture and grazing have claimed huge amounts of land, and other human activities related to urban and industrial activities have also taken a heavy toll.[183]

The Forest Act of 1984[184] was intended to supplement the system of protected areas within South Africa by, inter alia, providing an organized scheme for use of the forest resource. This was complemented in 1998 by the National Forest Act, which allows the minister concerned to declare land as specially protected areas in forest nature reserves, forest wilderness areas, or other types of protected areas.[185] The National Parks Act of 1976[186] has set up a system of some 18 national parks, with some parks included in a schedule to the act. Such parks may only be alienated, excluded, or detached from a park by Parliament. Other parks, however, are merely included in a register and enjoy less protection.

More broadly, the Environment Conservation Act of 1989[187] set up a system of multiple categories of protected areas: Category I consists of scientific reserves and wilderness areas; Category II is national parks and equivalent reserves; Category III is natural monuments and areas of cultural significance; Category IV is habitat and wildlife management areas; Category V is protected land/seascapes; and Category VI is sustainable use areas.[188] Additionally, the Cape Nature and Environmental Conservation Ordinance 19 of 1974[189] allows for establishment of local nature reserves by local authorities,[190] as well as private nature reserves.[191]

This rather extensive legal regime has not been sufficient to safeguard adequately the natural resources of this hotspot. The areas currently under legal protection do not adequately reflect all of the ecosystem/habitat types.[192] There is a need for a systematic and scientifically sound plan of action and a comprehensive statute governing all protected areas.[193]

At this point, gentle reader, you deserve a break. Stand up and stretch your stiff muscles. Eat some chocolate. Hug someone you love. Pet a warm, fuzzy animal (but be careful that it isn't someone else's spouse). The long, painful nightmare of Chapter 4 is more than half over now. I renew my offer to you. Feel free to lightly skim the rest of this chapter, if only to reinforce your assumption that the recurring theme of failure will continue to recur with mind-numbing dependability. Then break through to the other side. The remainder of the book will offer hope, not just despair.

Southwestern Australia

Australia has an extensive phalanx of environmental laws relevant to biodiversity protection. Some of the most significant are the Endangered Species Ordinances of 1980,[194] the Endangered Species Protection Act of 1992,[195] the Wildlife Protection (Regulation of Exports and Imports) Act of 1982,[196] the National Parks and Wildlife Conservation Act of 1975 as implemented by the National Parks and Wildlife Regulations of 1977,[197] and the Migratory Bird Ordinances of 1980.[198]

The State Department of Conservation and Land Management maintains a series of protected areas on the national and state levels. About 10.8 percent of the Southwest Botanical Province is in some type of federal governmental reserve, with another 5.9 percent in state forests or timber reserves, for a total of 16.6 percent (51,462 square kilometers) under some form of government protection.[199] Much of the remaining land is too dry for agriculture and too densely covered with bush for grazing, and thus is unlikely to be exploited. These factors combine to make this one of the least threatened and best protected of all the hotspots.[200]

California Floristic Province

This area contains several national parks, including Yosemite, Sequoia, Redwood, and Channel Islands, plus approximately 50 wilderness areas and 16 national wildlife refuges.[201] There are also 107 state parks and partially protected military installations. All together, about 31,443 square kilometers (9.7 percent) of this hotspot is officially protected at some level. Some of these areas are open for public recreation.[202]

Some types of habitat within the hotspot, such as subalpine conifer forest, receive generous amounts of protection, while others (like riparian forests and perennial grasslands) need much more attention.[203] The location of this hotspot within the United States has caused several preservationist organizations based here to focus attention and money on it, resulting in a relatively positive overall threat assessment.[204] However, this is also a very heavily populated area, and the pressures from myriad human activities are intense as people encroach ever further into the natural regions.[205]

The portion of this hotspot located within the United States is within the ambit of the Endangered Species Act (ESA).[206] This controversial statute, along with its analogs in many other nations, focuses on already imperiled species, which must be individually identified and listed to come within its protections.[207] There are rather strict prohibitions on "taking" any individual representative of listed threatened or endangered species, whether by private individuals or governmental actions, and *taking* has been broadly defined by both the statute[208] and the implementing regulations.[209] The act also makes it unlawful for any person to "possess, sell, deliver, carry, transport, or ship" any species that has been "taken."[210] Additionally, for any listed species, whether or not it has been "taken," it is unlawful to "deliver, receive, carry, transport, or ship in interstate or foreign commerce, by any means whatsoever and in the course of a commercial activity"[211] or to "sell or offer for sale in interstate or foreign commerce"[212] any such species. In this way, the ESA implements CITES[213] for the United States.

With regard to the actions of federal agencies, the ESA also requires consultations with the applicable regulatory agency (either Fish and Wildlife Service, under the Department of the Interior, for terrestrial and freshwater species, or National Marine Fisheries Service, under the Department of Commerce, for marine species) to gauge the extent of "jeopardy" to listed species or their critical habitat from any given federal action.[214] Jeopardy, in this context, refers to a specieswide impact on both the survival and recovery of a listed species as a whole,[215] not merely the taking of one or more individual members of a listed species.

The ESA has been widely criticized on multiple grounds, including the perverse incentives it creates, its "deathbed conservation" approach, and its emphasis on individual species rather than ecosystems, among many other flaws.[216] And, in practice, the ESA has long been plagued by delays and/or outright failures in the slow, cumbersome listing process and in the follow-on actions of designating critical habitat[217] and development of recovery plans for listed species.[218] The result is a statute that has been less than a resounding success in preserving threatened and endangered species within the United States.[219]

Central Chile

Chile has a system of national parks, national reserves, nature sanctuaries, and national monuments managed within its National Protected Area System (SNASPE).[220] Although 19 percent of continental Chile as a whole is protected, the hotspot area itself does not fare as well. The two components of the hotspots, the Winter Rainfall Desert area and the Mediterranean area, have only 1.8 percent and 4.2 percent, respectively, of their total expanse protected.[221]

The Chilean Environmental Law, Decreto 24 of 1997, would allow the acquisition of additional privately owned land for conservation or the establishment of private reserves, but the former is expensive and the latter has yet to be aggressively implemented.[222] At present, the situation is unsatisfactory.

There are multiple, serious threats to this hotspot. Smog is a major problem in Chile.[223] In addition, water pollution, widespread use of pesticides, and deforestation plague the country, the results of extensive mining, fruit farming, fishing, and paper making, all of which are part of Chile's traditional economic base.[224]

Hawaii/Polynesia/Micronesia

The broader Polynesia/Micronesia hotspot has 221 terrestrial protected areas of one type or another, covering a total of 4,913 square kilometers, or 10.7 percent of the hotspot.[225] Hawaii itself has 107 protected areas and 58 percent of all the safeguarded land within the hotspot.[226]

Because of the smallness of many of the Pacific island nations, much of the conservation work proceeds on a regional level. The South Pacific Commission established the South Pacific Regional Environmental Program (SPREP) in 1978 to handle environmental issues.[227] Since then, the South Pacific Biodiversity Conservation Program (SPBCP) was created and funded to establish and manage a series of large conservation areas for the protection of ecological functions.[228]

The myriad islands and atolls of the South Pacific face a widespread loss of forests, which threatens not only biodiversity but also the livelihood and unique culture of the area; a recent report by the Manila-based Asian Development Bank (ADB) cites "agro-deforestation" as a major threat to some 17 nations and territories scattered across the South Pacific from the Marianas to French Polynesia.[229] According to the report, forests are being cleared to make way for farms and expanding towns, and deforestation is particularly serious in the smaller Pacific islands and atolls, where population pressures mean that very little native forest still remains.[230] Large-scale plantations of cash crops like coconuts, bananas, and sugarcane are among the primary threats to these vital forests.[231]

Mesoamerica

A total of 138,437 square kilometers, or 12 percent, of this huge hotspot is within a protected area of some type.[232] Of the nations that are home to this hotspot, some have been much more diligent in preserving it than others. For example, the following percentages of the total land area within each nation enjoy some form of legal protection: Costa Rica, 24.1; Guatemala, 22.6; Nicaragua, 16.8; Panama, 16.8 (but 27.8 percent of the hotspot area); Belize, 10.4; Mexico, 8.4 percent of the Neotropical region; Honduras, 7.7; and El Salvador, 0.25.[233]

These nations, in conjunction with major international conservation groups,[234] have determined that the creation and maintenance of a Mesoamerican Biological Corridor is a top priority. The corridor is dedicated to maintenance of currently protected areas, establishment of new ones, and connection of the myriad individual conservation enclaves through a system of forests and other suitable habitats.[235] The bridgelike aspect of the corridor is crucially important, both within this hotspot and as a link between the biodiversity in North and South America. This initiative is in response to the problem that, despite the fact that the region's countries have generally set aside important areas as reserves, more than half of Mesoamerica's approximately 461 protected areas are considered too small to play a significant role in protecting biodiversity, and legal protection of even those areas is notoriously lacking.[236]

There is a mixed record within Mesoamerica in terms of individual nations' commitment to legal protection for this hotspot, with most of the news well within the "bad" range.[237] The beef industry is probably the most important cause of deforestation from Mexico to Panama, but there are other significant threats as well.[238] We will examine a few examples.

Even Costa Rica, which has a history of taking the lead in preservation, has had difficulty effectively safeguarding its legal enclaves because of inadequate enforcement resources; poachers have been able to circumvent the protective measures to a significant extent.[239] And Costa Rica's system of "sustainable management plans" through which logging is permitted has been faulted for making it possible to fell 500-year-old trees, which sell for as little as $100 apiece, and for allowing legalized deforestation.[240]

The current laws in Costa Rica stipulate that any logging on privately owned land must be carried out within the framework of a previously approved sustainable management plan, but these plans are drawn up only by forestry experts rather than multidisciplinary teams that could best determine what areas of forest should be left untouched.[241] Moreover, logging companies regularly exceed the established ceiling of five trees felled per hectare due to the lack of adequate mechanisms to enforce the legal limit.[242] And there is a convenient escape hatch from the existing legal strictures in that any investment project, whether involving tourism or infrastructure development, can be declared a "project of national interest" by the Costa Rican government, thus granting the authorization to fell trees and build whatever is necessary.[243]

Panama experienced precipitous declines in its forests for much of the 20th century, and deforestation continues at an alarming rate, even in national parks and in the Panama Canal watershed.[244] About 80 percent of Panama's coral reefs have been destroyed.[245] Soil erosion is becoming a serious problem in many areas, and Panama's desert in the province of Los Santos is expanding as a result of slash-and-burn ranching activities. Illegal gold mining is also contaminating rivers and local water supplies in the Darien and Portobello National Parks.[246]

In Nicaragua, the important Bosawas Biosphere Reserve near the Nicaragua-Honduras border has recently become a focal point of Central America's deforestation struggles.[247] The Nicaraguan government has little presence in the region, giving Bosawas a Wild West atmosphere, according to some experts; among the problems in the reserve listed by Nicaragua's environmental agency, MARENA, are the invasion of agriculture, illegal logging, poverty, land-tenancy disputes, and roving armed bands. Land mines remain from the armed conflicts that plagued Nicaragua, but the native people have come back, including nonindigenous Nicaraguans who are pushing in from the southwest, destroying the forest as they establish farms and ranches.[248] The national government is under pressure to allow commercial logging by foreign corporations.[249] Poaching of jaguars, scarlet macaws, and other endangered species is another major problem in and around the Bosawas Reserve.[250]

El Salvador has barely 2 percent of its original forest cover, 80 percent of its soils suffer from serious erosion, and 90 percent of the rivers are polluted, according to ecologists.[251] Extremely weak enforcement of existing environmental laws, including grossly inadequate fines for noncompliance, make it profitable to violate the law.[252]

Mexico's nature reserves have come under increasing pressure from various factors, including population growth, deficient development policies, the search for short-term economic benefits, and extensive poverty in rural areas.[253] Many forests have been converted for agriculture and cattle ranching; the total forested area has dropped from 60 percent of the country to less than 33 percent, and only 25 percent of the forest land is considered biologically undisturbed.[254] In an effort to protect valuable habitats, the Mexican government has created 96 "Natural Protected Areas," covering nearly 11.2 million hectares, but protective actions in several of these areas have been hampered by budget constraints.[255] And some key areas do not even have paper protection, including Los Chimalapas, one of Mexico's greatest areas of biodiversity, which is in danger of destruction.[256]

Mexico's first official attempt to address environmental concerns was made in 1972, with the establishment of the Under-Ministry of Environmental Improvement, but it was not until 1982 that the first institution to have environmental protection as one of its main purposes was created, that is, the Ministry of Urban Development and Ecology, and even this agency gave higher priority to urban development than to environmental protection.[257] Finally, in 1995, the Ministry of Environment, Natural Resources, and Fisheries (SEMARNAP) was established, representing Mexico's first comprehensive attempt to bring together the control of environmental protection and the management of key natural resources (such as water, forests, and fishes) under one agency; SEMARNAP also controls Mexico's National Water Commission, the National Institute of Ecology, and the Federal Attorney for Environmental Protection (PROFEPA).[258]

In 1982 Mexico enacted its first federal Law of Environmental Protection, but it had many gaps, leading to the passage of the General Law of Ecological Balance and Environmental Protection in 1988.[259] In 1997, this was amended to incorporate economic incentives, self-regulation, environmental auditing, research, ecological education, and "right-to-know" principles.[260] Today, all 31 of Mexico's states and the Federal District (Mexico City) have established their own environmental agencies and promulgated their own laws, and many municipalities have incorporated environmental provisions in their operations.[261]

Unfortunately, enforcement remains a substantial problem due to insufficient resources in terms of trained personnel, material, and equipment. Enforcement capabilities have been hampered by Mexico's financial crises and subsequent budget cuts on the federal, state, and local levels.[262]

Throughout Mesoamerica, deforestation has been a factor in exacerbating the destructive effects of natural disasters. Population growth has led people to settle in flood-prone valleys and unstable hillsides, where deforestation and climate change have increased the vulnerability to disasters such as Hurricane Mitch, which produced economic losses of $8.5 billion in Central America in 1998—equal to the combined gross national products of Honduras and Nicaragua, both of which were hit by the hurricane.[263]

Caribbean

Approximately 41,000 square kilometers, or 15.6 percent, of this hotspot has some legal protection, but enforcement of these protections is a problem.[264] For example, although Jamaica has about 40 parks and reserves, including the recently established Blue Mountain and John Crow National Parks, they are poorly protected, unmanaged, and are mostly vulnerable to habitat encroachment, hunting, and other threats.[265]

Similarly, the Dominican Republic has set aside 44 protected areas (down from 52 in 1996) encompassing 18 percent of its land area, but its parks are mostly small and fail to represent some key ecosystems, and only 10 of the parks have management plans.[266] The government of the Dominican Republic has recognized the threat to its biota and went so far as to enact a decree in 1992 prohibiting any activity causing capture, death, mutilation, or captivity of any wild animals or their eggs, nests, or feathers within a period of 10 years in the whole territory of the country.[267]

The Bahamas have also enacted applicable legal measures. Among these are the Wild Birds (Protection) Act of 1952[268] and the Wild Animals (Protection) Act of 1968,[269] as well as the Bahamas National Trust Act of 1959,[270] under which the Inagua Park and the Exuma Land/Sea Parks have been established.[271]

Cuba has approximately 200 conservation units, but logging is permitted in some of them, and many are too small to be effective in preserving biodiversity.[272] Even Everglades National Park in Florida has been considerably damaged despite an array of legal protections.[273]

For more than three decades, the Caribbean Conservation Association (CCA) has brought together governmental and private institutions to address the problem.[274] A regional approach may help to ameliorate some of the imbalances in terms of available funding, manpower, and other conservation resources.

All right. Let us be perfectly honest. This chapter is not going to be made into a major motion picture. We have no Frodo, no Strider, no Legolas, only lots of orcs. But this long, sad story is one that needs to be documented, if only as a prelude to our call for dramatically new action in the last two chapters of the book. If we did not suffer through this agonizing recitation of the status quo, we would not be so ready to break out of the box we are in. The endlessly recurring refrain of incomplete statutory coverage, suboptimal preservation choices, and lax enforcement grates on us like a Wagnerian leitmotif from an eternally boring tragic opera or the chorus from an interminably repetitious disco song. The monotony is only exceeded by the tragedy. Gradually, painfully, the message bores into our brain, even as it bores us, and perhaps spurs us to resolve to do something to help. And so, once more unto the breach, dear friends, once more!

Brazilian Cerrado

I have already discussed the legal regime in Brazil in the section on the Atlantic Coast Brazil/Atlantic Forest Region hotspot. The Brazilian Cerrado hotspot, although of immense importance, is very poorly protected. Only 1.2 percent (2.2 million hectares) of its area is safeguarded within 12 national parks, one national forest, three ecological stations, one biological reserve, and two environmental protected areas.[275] Some of these are threatened as well, including the large Emas National Park, which is being surrounded by expanding agricultural areas. Moreover, the Cerrado was not recognized as a National Heritage Site in the 1988 Brazilian Constitution, reflecting the view within Brazil that this is a major potential agricultural resource.[276]

Mediterranean Basin

There are more than 200 parks, reserves, and other protected areas within this expansively defined hotspot, totaling 42,123 square kilometers, or 1.8 percent of the terrestrial territory.[277] This is obviously a long-developed region, with few remaining pristine enclaves after thousands of years of civilization. The various nations involved have made serious attempts to improve conservation, including many local and regional programs.[278]

One of the most significant legal initiatives relevant to this hotspot is the European Union's 1992 "Habitats Directive."[279] This legislation is directed at the identification, ranking, and conservation of natural/species habitats as well as individual species protection. It provides a basis for taking into account ecological conditions and the needs of all territories of the EU member states and recognizes the common responsibility to promote conservation of habitats and species. Annex I of the Habitats Directive provides for listing, usually upon nomination by the member state(s) within which they are situated, of "natural habitats of community interest,"[280] and "priority habitat types."[281] Similarly, individual species of community interest and priority species are to be listed in Annex II, with species of community interest "in need of strict protection" listed in Annex IV. A coherent European ecological network of special areas of conservation is to be set up under the title Natura 2000. This network, composed of sites hosting the natural habitat types listed in Annex I and habitats of the species listed in Annex II, is intended to enable the natural habitat types and the species' habitats concerned to be maintained or, where appropriate, restored.[282] These listings are to be based on scientific information and on the criteria set forth in Annex III.[283]

For special areas of conservation, EU members are to establish the "necessary conservation measures involving, if need be, appropriate management plans specifically designed for the sites or integrated into other development plans, and appropriate statutory, administrative or contractual measures that correspond to the ecological requirements of the natural habitat types in Annex I and the species in Annex II present on the sites."[284] Members are to take "appropriate steps to avoid, in the special areas of conservation, the deterioration of natural habitats and the habitats of species as well as disturbance of the species for which the areas have been designated, in so far as such disturbance could be significant" in relation to the objectives of the Habitats Directive.[285]

In addition, the directive has a NEPA-like provision. Any plan or project not directly connected with or necessary to the management of a listed habitat, but "likely to have a significant effect thereon, either individually or in combination with other plans or projects," is to be subjected to "appropriate assessment of its implications for the site in view of the site's conservation objectives."[286] After such assessment, the competent national authorities "shall agree to the plan or project only after having ascertained that it will not adversely affect the integrity of the site concerned and, if appropriate, after having obtained the opinion of the general public."[287]

The Habitats Directive is a step forward in the legal protection of biodiversity. It recognizes the need to identify, in a methodical and scientifically informed manner, and to protect key habitats as well as individual endangered species. Importantly, it also reflects an understanding of the need for international funding of the often expensive conservation measures it calls for.

These efforts are coming not a moment too soon—this may be the most endangered of all the hotspots. The areas of relatively untouched natural vegetation are, as one would expect, quite small and badly fragmented, bearing the impact of thousands of years of human settlement.[288] Any further expansion of agriculture, grazing, urbanization, or other encroachment could have a devastating effect on the roughly 13,000 remaining endemic species that cling to the narrow pockets of nature; it is likely that more species already have been driven into extinction in this hotspot than in any other.[289]

Caucasus

There are 36 strict nature reserves (in which only scientific research is legally permissible), two biosphere reserves, and one national park in this hotspot.[290] Together, these amount to 10,650 square kilometers, or 2.1 percent of the hotspot.[291] Unfortunately, the political and economic exigencies have combined to enervate enforcement and management efforts, and illegal poaching, grazing, forest cutting, and other harmful activities threaten even the protected areas.[292] Passage of a new protected area system law by the Georgian Parliament in 1996[293] holds out the promise of new enclaves and enhanced protection of existing ones, but implementation and enforcement remain serious obstacles.[294]

One problem is that the Caucasus hotspot is spread over the territories of multiple nations. Russia's North Caucasian region, plus the nations of Georgia, Azerbaijan[295] and Armenia, and part of Turkey, are all involved. This creates predictable obstacles in terms of intergovernmental cooperation and coordination, although there have been some limited success stories in this regard, such as the agreement between Turkey and Georgia.[296]

New Zealand

Several statutes provide protection for New Zealand's biodiversity, including the Wildlife Act of 1953, the Native Plant Protection Act of 1934, the Reserves Act of 1977,[297] the National Parks Act of 1980, the Environment Act of 1986, the Resource Management Act of 1991, the Forests Act of 1943 (amended in 1993), the Fisheries Act of 1908 (amended in 1996), the

Conservation Act of 1987,[298] and the Marine Reserves Act of 1971.[299] The Department of Conservation is primarily responsible for the protection and sustainable use of biodiversity.

A large amount of New Zealand's land area (79,764 square kilometers, or 29.5 percent) is within some form of park, reserve, sanctuary, wilderness area, or other specially protected area, although a considerable amount is available for a wide range of developmental activities such as grazing, agriculture, mining, and recreation.[300] There are 13 national parks and about 4,000 reserves, but some habitats are not as well represented as they should be. Overall, however, New Zealand is one of the better examples of hotspots preservation.[301]

However, an official 1997 report indicates that decline in biodiversity is New Zealand's most worrying environmental problem.[302] At least 800 species are threatened with extinction, and the main causes appear to be the destruction and fragmentation of habitats, along with pests and weeds. In a familiar vein with an unusual twist, more than 1.7 million hectares of the "conservation estate" protected area is at risk of major changes, including canopy loss, through destruction by possums and other pests.[303]

Succulent Karoo of South Africa

The Republic of South Africa enacted the National Park Act in 1976, which provides for a system of protected areas.[304] The act has been amended on numerous occasions from 1979 to 1998.

Approximately 2,352 square kilometers (2.1 percent) of this hotspot are protected in a system of seven statutory reserves, including the large Richtersveld National Park.[305] This is clearly inadequate, but there are initiatives to expand the reserve system, both by adding to existing reserves and setting aside new ones.[306]

Although overgrazing is a problem in some areas, much of the territory is used for "natural grazing," which may be able to coexist with the endemic species.[307] Agriculture and diamond mining are also serious threats. About 27 percent of the hotspot is still in a relatively pristine condition.[308]

Wallacea

This hotspot is made up of many islands, all of them entirely within the boundaries of the nation of Indonesia, and some of these islands are very seriously threatened. Overall, 20,415 square kilometers, or 5.9 percent, of the hotspot are legally protected.[309] The most important enclaves are the large Bogani Nani Wartabone National Park in North Sulawesi, which has had to endure illegal encroachment by miners, farmers, loggers, and hunters,[310] and the Lore Lindu National Park, which is also threatened by agriculture and road building.[311]

Commercial logging has greatly reduced Wallacea's forested areas and in the process has made the region more vulnerable to fires.[312] Additionally, the human population has soared, partially as a result of Indonesia's transmigration program that relocated hundreds of thousands of people to less densely populated areas.[313]

Papua New Guinea

This remarkable region is not usually listed as a hotspot because it has thus far escaped the extensive devastation that has decimated the other hotspots. CI considers it a Major Tropical Wilderness Area rather than a hotspot, in recognition of its outstanding importance, and it is for this reason that I include an analysis of its legal protections here. Moreover, although it has not suffered on the massive scale that the usual hotspots have, the area is by no means untouched. In my opinion, it is better to classify it as at least worthy of heightened attention, so we can proactively intervene and prevent it from experiencing the same decimation that has claimed so many other once pristine centers of biodiversity.

Tribal land rights are stringently protected in Papua New Guinea and serve as an inherent source of control over deforestation and the loss of natural resources and species. These rights are constitutionally recognized in that the government cannot change a use of the land without unanimous consent from the tribe.[314] About 97 percent of the territory of Papua New Guinea is owned communally by the tribes.[315]

Environmental legislation has been enacted specifically for the protection of the tropical forests. Under the Forestry Act of 1973, the government is permitted to buy certain rights from the clans, and when the government sells these rights to timber companies, the clan receives 75 percent of the royalties.[316] This act also imposes environmental criteria for the issuance of logging licenses.[317]

In 1992, the Forestry Act was amended and the Papua New Guinea Forest Authority was created mainly in response to the large amount of raw timber being exported. There had been an increase in demand as a result of the depletion of the great forests of Indonesia and Malaysia to the west. The purpose of the amendment was to create an agency under which forest policy would be effected through a uniform agency instead of the prior system under which the provincial governments were left to enforce the laws themselves. Under this amendment, procedures were also put in place to limit the discretion of government officials with respect to the giving of timber permits.[318]

In 1996, the Code of Logging Practice was enacted primarily to provide specific protection for the "mangrove forests," which are that part of the tropical forest that grows in intertidal areas and is subject to daily flooding. Under this code logging is lawfully permitted to occur within 50 meters from any water body, high tide mark, or edge of the mangroves only if permission is obtained from the Forest Authority. In 2000, however, an amendment was enacted whereby an exclusion was made for local communities where villagers could cut timber for local use and logging operations of less than 500 cubic meters did not require permission.[319] The 2000 amendments were spurred by the National Executive Council's concern that a 1999 moratorium against any new logging concessions was not being followed.[320] The moratorium had been imposed as a condition for further aid from the World Bank and Australia.[321]

Significantly, environmental conservation is a priority under this act, imposing mitigation measures to lessen and control the environmental effects of logging. It also is a further indication of Papua New Guinea's protection of its peoples by ensuring that tribal rights are respected and that a large percentage of the profits are returned to them. Unfortunately, the financial incentives encourage the tribes to give up their rights, resulting in diminished protection of the natural forests.

There are indications that these national forest laws are not achieving their purpose and that illegal, and therefore uncontrolled, logging is continuing. The Minister of the Environment has been accused of deceiving the public by stating in public speeches that there is little evidence of corruption and circumvention of law in that logging has proceeded in accordance with the Forestry Act. These speeches have apparently been an effort to convince the World Bank and Australia that the moratorium has been maintained. These allegations were based on a finding that the results prepared by an independent review committee instituted by the World Bank were not consistent with the Minister's statements.[322]

Another effort at conservation has taken the form of "farming programs." Under these programs, farms for the harvesting of certain species—which had been severely threatened because of their export value—have been created to meet the demand and protect both the wild species and their habitats. This has most notably benefitted crocodiles and butterflies.

By the middle 1960s, many of Papua New Guinea's famous "birdwing" butterfly species were severely decimated as a result of commercial collecting.[323] These farms are locally operated as well but overseen by the Insect Farming and Trading Agency (IFTA).[324] Local villagers plant flowers to attract the large, beautiful butterflies, and after the female lays her eggs on the leaves, they are collected, packaged, and shipped to facilities run by the IFTA. This program has been successful in relieving the pressures on the butterflies in the wild, and much income has been generated and returned to the tribes. IFTA retains only 25 percent of the profits, with the rest being distributed among the tribes. As of 1991, tribes were annually receiving the equivalent of $300,000 U.S. dollars.[325] Success has been attributed in part to the remoteness of butterfly habitats and to moderate development pressure.[326]

These farming programs have successfully intertwined local involvement spurred by financial incentives with the goal and result of habitat preservation.

For such a relatively undeveloped country where so much of the land is communally owned, such programs may be appropriate. It is difficult to determine how successful they will be when population increases demand more land and more timber companies. It is also, of course, too limited where only a few species are protected and how they are chosen is based on their commercial value.

Two major pieces of environmental legislation were passed in 1978. The Environmental Planning Act, No. 45/1978, empowered the Minister of the Environment to require a project proponent to prepare and submit an environmental plan if the project is determined to have "specific environmental implications." Under the Conservation Areas Act of 1978, No. 52/1978, a National Conservation Council was established to make recommendations for the creation of conservation areas and established a national register of such areas with a provision for control and management. It is unclear how effective this has been.[327]

Congo River Basin/Democratic Republic of the Congo

As with Papua New Guinea, this area is denominated a Major Tropical Wilderness Area, not a hotspot, by CI. Nonetheless, it is worthwhile to outline the risks encountered by even the few comparatively intact centers of endemism of the world to illustrate the urgent need for greater conservation efforts. Where the situation is still comparatively good, we have a rare opportunity to be proactive in conservation and prevent harm before it happens rather than attempt to practice damage control after the harm has been done.

This key region does have a system of protected areas,[328] but enforcement is a persistent problem. Important enclaves such as the large Salonga National Park are the only habitats for some unique species.[329] Threats from logging, gold mining, hunting, and other activities[330] may turn this from a "good news" story to one more in our long list of imperiled hotspots.

For centuries "bushmeat" has been an important source of protein for indigenous African populations in this nation and elsewhere, and it usually did not seriously threaten biodiversity.[331] However, beginning in the 1980s, logging access roads began transforming once sustainable hunting practices into an unsustainable commercial venture. Heavily armed, law-defying commercial hunters now plunder the previously impenetrable forests of equatorial Africa, not only in the Democratic Republic of Congo, but also in Guinea, Liberia, Ivory Coast, Ghana, Cameroon, Equatorial Guinea, and Gabon.[332] Logging trucks transport the illegally taken meat across borders to distant capital cities, where attractively high levels of profits await the outlaw hunters.[333]

This recent intensification of the poaching threat has caused some scientists who once focused mostly on preserving rainforests to devote increased attention to "defaunation." An estimated 1.1 million pounds a year of illegal bushmeat is a major drain on the biodiversity of these hotspots.[334]

Indo-Burma

This is one of the most imperiled hotspots, with extensive logging and cultivation of once vast forests. Widespread deforestation and intentional burning, as well as other impacts from the rapidly growing human population, are threatening the region's rich biodiversity.[335] Overall, about 7.8 percent of the original extent of natural vegetation is currently under some form of legal protection.[336] In addition to the impact on biodiversity, massive deforestation in Indochina has caused the annual flooding of the Mekong River, which passes through each of the countries, as millions of acres of forest have been destroyed in the region to make way for agriculture and for the timber industry.[337] Huge hydroelectric dams, built by China and other nations, also threaten much of the biodiversity in and near the Mekong.[338]

Thailand has a relatively extensive system of protected areas, with national parks covering 39,285 square kilometers, or 7.7 percent, of the nation's total land area, and wildlife sanctuaries covering an additional 27,866 square kilometers (5.4 percent) of the land. The most important is the Western Forest Complex, a combination of 10 adjoining parks and sanctuaries centered on the Thung Yai-Huai Khaeng World Heritage Site.[339] However, some habitat types are not sufficiently included in the protected system, and conservation/enforcement is inadequately funded, resulting in vulnerability to illegal poaching, encroachment, and logging.[340] As in other nations in this region, rampant deforestation has greatly exacerbated the dangers from flooding.[341]

Vietnam has 87 conservation areas that together encompass 9,566 square kilometers (2.9 percent) of the land area, but this is not enough to protect the great biodiversity present. There are several important reserves, including Cat Ba Island National Park, Cuc Phuong National Park, Bach Ma National Park, Cat Tien Reserve, and Yok Don National Park.[342] But Vietnam has experienced intense deforestation during the past few decades, as natural vegetation succumbed to war, logging, and the cultivation of coffee, pepper, and rubber, as well as the forced relocation of thousands of people.[343] As of 1995, the last year for which data are available, only some 8 million hectares of natural forest remained, covering less than a quarter of Vietnam's land area, compared to the 14.3 million hectares that covered over two-fifths of the country in 1945.[344] In addition to deforestation, other environmental stressors have also caused much damage to Vietnam's natural resources.[345]

Cambodia declared a National Protected Areas System in 1993 and has established seven national parks, 10 wildlife sanctuaries, three protected landscapes, and three multiple-use areas.[346] Together, these encompass 32,033 square kilometers, or 17.6 percent of the nation's land area, but there is much more forested area that could be added.[347]

Myanmar/Burma has a growing system of protected areas, although most of the original 18 enclaves were of rather small size and covered an aggregate of only 1.1 percent of the nation's land area.[348] There are plans to protect about 5 percent of the territory eventually.[349] In the interim, there has been substantial devastation, particularly in the forests of northern Burma, where for the last several years a massive, unregulated, and largely unnoticed timber trade with neighboring China has stripped bare hundreds of square kilometers of ancient tropical forests.

Ironically, the deforestation in Myanmar is directly linked to strengthened protections for the forests within China. In 1998, China issued a ban on logging to protect its fast-disappearing forests and to halt massive soil erosion that had contributed to deadly floods.[350] From 12 provinces in 1998, the logging ban was extended to 18 in 2000, with no logging allowed in the upper reaches of the Yangtze or Yellow Rivers, and reduced levels of logging in Manchuria, Inner Mongolia, the northwestern Xinjiang territory and elsewhere.[351] Meanwhile, China's imports of logs skyrocketed from less than 5 million cubic meters (175 million cubic feet) in 1998 to more than 10 million in 1999 and between 14 million and 15 million in 2000, with much of this wood coming from Burma's tropical forests, where the trees are often centuries old.[352] In Burma, forest cover has dropped from 21 percent in 1949 to less than 7 percent today.[353] As evidence of the rapidity of the deforestation, as of 1997 Chinese loggers had cleared 35 miles into Burma, and have now reached 60 miles.[354]

Laos has a system of some 17 protected areas. Combined, these cover about 30,000 square kilometers, or 12.6 percent of the country.[355] Laos has had only limited success in stemming deforestation and slash-and-burn cultivation; indeed, forestry industry sources claim that the past three years have brought wholesale "rape" of Laos's forest reserves, especially by its neighbor, Vietnam.[356]

China and India have established some protected areas within the Indo-Burma hotspot. India has set aside several enclaves here, including the important Namdapha National Park, five small national parks, and three sanctuaries, while China has carved out numerous small reserves and protected areas.[357]

NONGOVERNMENTAL ORGANIZATIONS

The foregoing discussion has concentrated on domestic and international law and on the role of governments in protecting the hotspots. However, nongovernmental organizations (NGOs) can also provide useful assistance at times in the area of international environmental law.[358]

NGOs can serve as watchdogs, monitoring compliance with various legal mechanisms, gathering and disseminating information at multiple levels, and applying pressure on governments for enhanced compliance.[359] A persistent, dedicated, well-organized, vocal NGO can be effective in heightening public and governmental awareness of key issues and problem areas and may help build consensus for meaningful action.[360]

One advantage of NGOs is that they are often free of direct governmental control and may be less encrusted with the bureaucratic barnacles that plague governmental entities. They are usually populated with people committed to a cause and inspired by a vision, and thus may be capable of generating significant energy and money. As private-sector actors, NGOs can be more efficient and more flexible and may be a useful supplement to more official agents of change. They can direct funds and workers where they see the greatest possible cost-benefit return on investment, relatively free from the ancillary political concerns that can hamstring governments.

Conservation International has certainly taken the lead in the hotspots realm. CI's books and Web site[361] have helped to get the hotspots idea known internationally and to identify places where intervention is most needed. CI, like the World Wildlife Fund, BirdLife International, and many other NGOs, has raised and disbursed substantial amounts of private money for specific projects in furtherance of its particular preservationist vision.

Of course, NGOs are not a panacea for the hotspots problem or any other international legal situation. Some NGOs can lose their credibility if they are seen as too dogmatic and fanatical in their single-minded devotion to a particular cause; it can be difficult to verify their claims, and the public may become skeptical of an NGO that reflexively takes a predictable stance on issue after issue. Also, their very independence may be a weakness of some NGOs if their internal agenda moves them to take and/or advocate certain actions that run counter to the purpose of a given domestic or international law. In their zeal to advance their cause and free from the restraining hand of official political accountability, NGOs may fail to consider all relevant factors and may bring about unintended adverse effects.[362]

All good things must come to an end, and all painful things as well, thankfully. If you have read this long, sad chapter in its entirety, you deserve a medal. I will not be giving you one, so don't bother asking me, but you deserve it nonetheless. Congratulations. And now that we have clearly established that there is a problem, we can begin developing a solution.

NOTES

1. "Rapport sur l'Etat de l'Environnement a Madagascar" (Report on the State of the Environment in Madagascar), Web site of the government of Madagascar summarizing environmental legislation, <http://www.refer.mg/cop/nature/fr/reem/index.htm> (visited April 23, 2001). Chapter 15, "La Politique Nationale de L'Environnement" (National Environmental Policy), 15.1.

2. *Id.* at 15.2.

3. *Id.* at 15.4.1.

4. Russell A. Mittermeier, Norman Myers, and Cristina Goettsch Mittermeier, Hotspots: Earth's Biologically Richest and Most Endangered Terrestrial Ecoregions at 199 (2000) (hereinafter Hotspots).

5. *Id.*

6. *See A Treasure-Island Tragedy,* Toronto Star, March 3, 2001 (noting that forest fires in Madagascar have done enormous damage to biodiversity and key habitats in recent decades, due to a rapidly increasing human population, now growing at a rate of 2.8 per cent a year—sufficient to cause a doubling of population every 25 years.)

7. Hotspots, *supra* note 4, at 142.

8. *Id.*

9. *Id.*

10. English Translation of Brazilian Constitution (Constituicao Federal capitulo VI, art. 225).

11. Robert M. Hardaway, Karen D. Dacres, and Judy Swearingen, *Tropical Forest Conservation Legislation and Policy: A Global Perspective* 15 Whittier L. Rev. 919, 927 (1994).

12. *See* Law No. 9.509 of March 20, 1997, establishing State Environmental Policy and Law No. 10.019 of July 3, 1998, establishing the State Coastal Management Plan, both issued by the governor of São Paulo (Brazil).

13. Section Law No. 6.938 of August 31, 1981.

14. *Id.* at Article 2, Sections I, IV, VIII and IX.

15. *Id.* Articles 6 and 7.

16. *Id.* Article 6.

17. *Id.* Article 8.

18. *Id.* Article 14.

19. Decree No. 99.274 of 6 June 1990, Ch. II, Article 4. (Brazil).

20. *Id.*

21. Hotspots, *supra* note 4, at 141.

22. Brazilian Constitution *supra* note 10, Article 6.

23. Law No. 6.938, Article 5.

24. Brazilian Constitution *supra* note 10, Articles 30 and 32.

25. *Id.* Title III, Article 34.

26. *Id.* Sections VI, VII and XI, respectively.

27. Decree No. 2.119 of 1-13-97, Article 2 (Brazil).

28. *Id.*

29. *Id.* Articles 3 and 6.

30. *Id.* Article 3.

31. Emilio F. Moran, *The Law, Politics, and Economics of Amazonian Deforestation,* <http://www.law.indiana.edu/glsj/vol.1/.html> (visited April 30, 2001).

32. Law No. 9.605 of February 1998, "Regulates Criminal and Administrative Penalties Relating to Behavior and Activities Harmful to the Environment," Sections I and II respectively. (Brazil).

33. *Id.* Articles 2 and 3.

34. *Id.* Article 29, paragraph 4.

35. *Id.* Article 37.

36. *Id.* Articles 38 and 39, respectively.

37. *Id.* Article 40, paragraph 1.

38. *Id.* Article 66.

39. *Id.* Article 67.

40. Roger W. Findley, *Legal and Economic Incentives for the Sustainable Use of Rainforests*, 32 Tex. Int'l L.J. 17, 18–19 (Winter, 1997).

41. Section Decree No. 3.179 of September 21, 1999, "Defines the Penalties Applying to Behavior and Activities Harmful to the Environment" (Brazil).

42. *Id.* Articles 11 and 13 respectively.

43. *Id.* Articles 18, 25, and 26 respectively.

44. HOTSPOTS, *supra* note 4, at 130.

45. *Id.*

46. *Id.*

47. Hardaway et al., *supra* note 11, at 928.

48. *See* Judith Kimerling, *Disregarding Environmental Law: Petroleum Development in Protected Natural Areas and Indigenous Homelands in the Ecuadorian Amazon*, 14 Hastings Int'l & Comp. L. Rev. 849, 895 (1991).

49. Corporación de Estudios y Publicaciónes, Ley de Tierras Baldias y Colonización (1964), as cited and translated in Andrew Jones, *The Global Environment Facility's Failure to Promote Sustainable Forestry in Ecuador: The Case Of Ecoforest 2000*, 14 Va. Envtl. L.J. 507 (Spring 1995).

50. *Id.* at 512.

51. *Id.*

52. *Id.* at 513.

53. *Id.*

54. *Id.*

55. *See* Alvaro Umana, Ecuador ENDESA/BOTROSA Reforestation Project: Independent Review of Biodiversity and Social Impact Issues 6, (1993) (citing Gonzalo Oviedo, Biodiversity Protection of Conservation Units, Support of Protected Areas Systems [Appendix 5 of Ecuador GEF Project], 1991).

56. *See* Jones, *supra* note 49, at 514.

57. *Id.* at 515.

58. *Id.* at 516.

59. *See generally*, THOMAS RUDEL, TROPICAL DEFORESTATION: SMALL FARMERS AND LAND CLEARING IN THE ECUADORIAN AMAZON (1993).

60. *See* Jones, *supra* note 49, at 516.

61. *See* Eduardo Zuleta and Juan Manuel Garrido D., *Colombia Environmental Regulations*, Latin Am. Legal Dev. Bull. (Baker and McKenzie, New York, N.Y.), October 1994, at 2.

62. *Id.* at 19.

63. *Id.*

64. *Id.*

65. *Id.* at 23.

66. *Id.* at 25.

67. Hardaway et al., *supra* note 11, at 927.

68. *See* Republic of Colombia, Economic Guide For Investors, <http://www.coinvertir.org.com>.

69. *See* Rocio Cuellar Rocha, Petroleras, A Expandir Su Campo, EL ESPECTADOR, Oct. 9, 1996 <http://www.elespectador.com/9610/05/opindice.htm>, as cited in Rosencranz, Campell, and O'Neill, *Rio Plus Five: Environmental Protection and Free Trade in Latin America*, 9 Geo. Int'l Envtl. L. Rev. 527, at 528.

70. German Palacio, *Constitutional Mechanisms for Environmental Protection in Colombia*, J. Envtl. Pol'y and Law 113, 114 (1994).

71. HOTSPOTS, *supra* note 4, at 80.

72. *Id.* at 81.

73. *Illegal Drug Crops Cause Massive Environmental Damage*, Environment News Service, April 19, 2001.

74. *Id.* (Citing the State Department report, "The Andes Under Siege: Environmental Consequences of the Drug Trade," available at <http://www.usinfo.state.gov/products/pubs/andes/homepage.htm>)

75. *Id.*

76. Frederick Anderson, *Environmental Aspects to Foreign Investment in Latin America*, 643 PLI/Comm 151 at 162 (1992).

77. Hardaway et al., *supra* note 11, at 931.

78. *Id.*

79. *See* Peru to Launch National Environmental System and Create Environmental Protection Agency, Env't Watch Latin Am., Nov. 1, 1992, available in 1992 WL 2653476 (Westlaw).

80. *See* Jorge Caillaux, *Peru, Country/Region Reports*, 1995 Y.B. Int'l Envt'l. L. 405.

81. *See Selected Environmental Events in the Western Hemisphere*, 7 Colo. J. Int'l Envtl. L. & Pol'y 225, 236 (Winter 1996).

82. *Id.*

83. *Id.*

84. *See* Parks Authority Presents Plan to Protect Threatened Reserves, Int'l Envtl Rep. (BNA), July 12, 1995, available in LEXIS, Envirn. Library, NEWS File.

85. HOTSPOTS, *supra* note 4, at 347.

86. *Id.* at 348.

87. The Wild Animals Protection Law, adopted November 8, 1988. This act, inter alia, provides for the conservation of rare or endangered terrestrial and aquatic animals; lays down the principle that wild animal resources belong to the nation; sets down the obligation for the state to protect such resources; provides that rare or endangered wild animals shall be under "national key protection"; species so protected shall be listed by administrative decisions in either of two categories; and establishes a system of penalties. Hunting or killing of animals on the national priority list is forbidden, as is selling and buying them or derivative products. *See* INTERNATIONAL ENCYCLOPAEDIA OF LAWS, ENVIRONMENTAL LAW, Vol. 2, 80–82 (R. Blanpain, general editor, Kluwer, 2000) (hereinafter INTERNATIONAL ENCYCLOPAEDIA).

88. *Id.* at 77.

89. *Id.* at 78.

90. *Id.*

91. *Id.* at 76.

92. *China Makes Stable Progress in Forest Protection*, Business Daily Update, May 21, 2001.

93. *China: Environment Crucial to West*, China Daily, May 17, 2001. (Noting some of China's planned conservation initiatives.)

94. *Id.*

95. *China to Build Nature Reserve Network*, Daily China News, April 25, 2001.

96. No. 5 (1990). This act provides a broad framework for the conservation of life support systems, species and ecosystems, and for the sustainable utilization of

living natural resources, based on the principles of the World Conservation Strategy; provides for the establishment of protected areas and for the protection of endangered and rare species; prohibits the collection, destruction, possession, transport, sale, and export of protected plants and parts thereof and the killing, capture, injuring, possession, rearing, transport, sale, processing, and export of protected animals or parts thereof, and of goods made of such parts; exceptions to these prohibitions may be granted only for the purpose of research, for the safeguarding of the species concerned, or when an animal endangers human life; and provides for enforcement measures and penalties. Most of the provisions of the act are to be developed through the adoption of regulations. Indonesia has long had some protected area laws in effect, including the Nature Protection Ordinance of 1941 (Stbl. 1941, No. 167), complemented by the Wildlife Protection Ordinance of 1931 (Stbl. 1930, No. 134) and a list of implementing regulations promulgated by the Minister of Agriculture and supplemented by regulations from provincial and district administrations. INTERNATIONAL ENCYCLOPAEDIA, *supra* note 87, Vol. 3, 120–23.

97. HOTSPOTS, *supra* note 4, at 288.

98. Statutory Instrument, of 1985. *See also* Nature Protection Ordinance of 1941, No. 167.

99. Kanis Dursin, *Indonesia: Donors Urged to Tie Aid to Logging Ban*, Inter Press Service, May 4, 2001. (Discussing efforts by environmentalists to force the government to take appropriate measures against illegal logging by asking donors, who give the country billions of dollars in loans for various programs and for budgetary support, to make the moratorium on industrial logging a prerequisite for fresh borrowing by the Indonesian government.)

100. INTERNATIONAL ENCYCLOPAEDIA, *supra* note 87, Vol. 3, 119.

101. *Id.* at 123.

102. Praginanto, *Eco-labels Undercut Wood Exports*, The Nikkei Weekly, May 21, 2001.

103. *Id.*

104. *Id.* An eco-label is a form of certification that was implemented to ensure that wood used in manufacturing comes from sustainable forest resources. To obtain the certificate can be costly, and many Indonesian makers may have to withdraw from major foreign markets because they cannot afford the initial outlay to gain certification. The world's major environmentalist groups say that eco-labeling is necessary to gain some control over deforestation. *Id.*

105. *Indonesia Says Cannot Carry Out Significant Reforms Yet*, Japan Policy & Politics, April 30, 2001.

106. *Id.*

107. HOTSPOTS, *supra* note 4, at 288.

108. Joe Cochrane, *Greed, Corruption Killing Indonesian Forests, Wildlife*, Deutsche Presse-Agentur, April 29, 2001. (Charging that illegal activities plunder the forests with the help of bribes, which begin with local police and park rangers, and move through the armed forces, all the way up to the Ministry of Forestry in Jakarta.) *See also* Richard L. Hill, *Pressures Push Wild Orangutans Closer to Extinction*, The Oregonian, March 21, 2001, at D13. (Describing the corruption and bribery that facilitate illegal destruction of protected habitat and have brought orangutans to the edge of extinction in Borneo and throughout Indonesia.)

109. An Act to consolidate the laws relating to and to further provide the protection of wildlife and for purposes connected therewith, No.76 (1972), as amended. The act provides for the establishment of wildlife reserves and sanctuaries; lists "totally protected species" of wild animals and "protected species" of wild animals; prohibits the killing, taking, or possession by any person of "totally protected" animals, or of their eggs or nests except under a permit, for scientific research, or for zoological gardens; prohibits the shooting, killing, or taking of "protected" animals and the taking of their nests and eggs except under a license; prohibits the keeping in captivity and captive breeding of "protected" species, the keeping of any trophy and the import or export of any such species, except under a license; regulates trade in wildlife and taxidermy; requires the licensing of wildlife dealers and taxidermists; prohibits dealers from acquiring protected wild animals or parts thereof from persons other than licensed hunters; prohibits taxidermists from acquiring such animals or parts thereof from any other person than licensed hunters or dealers; prohibits any person from selling protected wild animals or parts thereof to persons other than licensed dealers or taxidermists; provides for enforcement measures and penalties. The schedules list indigenous protected and game species and CITES Appendix I and II species. Where CITES appendices list taxa higher than the species, this law lists all the species included in these taxa; there are, however, some omissions.

110. An Act to provide for the Establishment and Control of National Parks and for Matters connected therewith, No. 226 (1980).

111. HOTSPOTS, *supra* note 4, at 286.

112. *Id.* at 286–7.

113. HOTSPOTS, *supra* note 4, at 314.

114. INTERNATIONAL ENCYCLOPAEDIA, *supra* note 87, Vol. 5, 69–70. There is provision for penalties as well, including fines, imprisonment, or both. *Id.* at 71.

115. *Id.* at 70.

116. HOTSPOTS, *supra* note 4, at 314.

117. Act No. 3915 (1932), an act providing for the establishment of national parks, declaring such parks as game refuges, and other purposes. Numerous parks and refuges have been set aside under this act, at least in theory.

118. Earl Warren B. Castillo, *Environment Department Rejects Unregulated Hunting*, BusinessWorld, October 19, 2000, at 21. (Discussing the Department of Environment and Natural Resources rejection of the request of a hunters group to allow unregulated hunting activities in the Philippines.)

119. *Id.*

120. *Id.*

121. *Id.*

122. Art. 12, Sect. 2.

123. INTERNATIONAL ENCYCLOPAEDIA, *supra* note 87, Vol. 5, 72.

124. *Id.* at 72–73.

125. Earl Warren B. Castillo, *Experts Urge Greater Stress on Environmental Impact of Trade, Economic Policies*, BusinessWorld, April 13, 2000, at 19.

126. *Id.*

127. *Philippines: Hottest Hot Spot*, BusinessWorld, December 2, 1999, at 21.

128. *Id.*

129. Michael Bengwayan, *Illegal Logging Wipes Out Philippine Forests*, Environment News Service, October 11, 1999.

130. *Id*. Deforestation in the Philippines has been identified as the major reason behind flooding, acute water shortages, rapid soil erosion, siltation, and mudslides that have proved costly not only to the environment and properties but also in human lives. *Id*.

131. *Id*.

132. *Id*.

133. *Id*. Since the 1950s, many Philippine politicians have been in the logging business, and they have prevented forestry officials from implementing forestry laws. *Id*.

134. Johanna Son, *Philippines-Environment: Red Flag Up over Threatened Species*, Inter Press Service, October 15, 1996.

135. *Id*.

136. INTERNATIONAL ENCYCLOPAEDIA, *supra* note 87, Vol. 5, 145.

137. HOTSPOTS, *supra* note 4, at 373.

138. *Id*.

139. Bequette, *New Caledonia: Threats to Biodiversity*, UNESCO Courier, October, 1997.

140. *Id*.

141. *Id*.

142. *Id*.

143. *Id*.

144. *Id*.

145. HOTSPOTS, *supra* note 4, at 248.

146. *Id*. at 249.

147. Isabelle Ligner, *Ivory Coast Forests Being Denuded by Charcoal-Makers, Fire-Burners*, Agence France Presse, January 29, 2001.

148. *Id*.

149. *Id*. Decree providing for rules and procedures for the establishment and deestablishment of strict or partial nature reserves and of national parks, No.66-432 (1966), which establishes procedures for the creation of protected areas and regulates human activities within such areas in the Ivory Coast. Under this law, by separate decrees, national parks have been established: Como, Marahone, and Mount Peko. *See also* Loi-Cadre No. 96-766 of October 3, 1996, the Ivory Coast's general environmental protection statute. Available in French at <http://faolex.fao.org/faolex/index.htm>.

150. *Cameroon to Check Forest Exploitation with Helicopters*, Panafrican News Agency (PANA) Daily Newswire, January 5, 2001.

151. *Id*.

152. *Id*. Cameroon also recently levied heavy fines against four logging companies for violating its forestry law. The order threatened the four companies with the withdrawal of their exploitation licenses if they fail to pay their fines. *Id*.

153. Tansa Musa, *Cameroon: Last Chance for Western Black Rhino*, Inter Press Service, November 27, 2000.

154. *Id*.

155. Victor Mallet, *Ghana: Nature Is Taking a Hammering from the Law Breakers*, Financial Times (London), November 29, 2000.

156. *Id.*

157. *Id.*

158. *Id.*

159. HOTSPOTS, *supra* note 4, at 213.

160. *Id.*

161. Each of these is available online at <http://faolex.fao.org/faolex/index.htm>.

162. Chapter 385, Sections 5(1)(a) and 6(1)–(3). *See* INTERNATIONAL ENCYCLOPAEDIA, *supra* note 87, Vol. 4, 83.

163. Chapter 376. The Wildlife [Conservation and Management] [Amendment] Act, No. 16, of 1989. Available online at <http://faolex.fao.org/faolex/index.htm>. *See* INTERNATIONAL ENCYCLOPAEDIA, *supra* note 87, Vol. 4, 83–84.

164. INTERNATIONAL ENCYCLOPAEDIA, *supra* note 87, Vol. 4, 93.

165. *Kenya; Government Plans to Give Away 5% of Its Forests,* Africa News, May 9, 2001.

166. *Id.*

167. *Id.*

168. Danna Harman, *Forest of Controversy Grows in Kenya,* The Christian Science Monitor, March 23, 2001. (Noting that Kenya's Environment Minister, Francis Nyenze, defends the plan, saying it redefines forest boundaries in areas already occupied by squatters, prevents further encroachment, and gives land to the needy, while opponents of the plan say that prime forest land is being handed over by the government to supporters as a way of currying favor before next year's expected elections.)

169. *See* Sudarsan Raghavan, *Kenyan Tribes Fight High-Tech Battle for Land Rights and Forest Conservation,* Knight Ridder Washington Bureau, April 28, 2001; *Kenya: State Challenged on Conservation,* Africa News, April 19, 2001.

170. *See* Ann M. Simmons, *Kenya's Forest Allocation Plan Unsettles Environmentalists,* Los Angeles Times, April 15, 2001, Part A; Part 1; Page 3. (Noting that several Kenyan nongovernmental organizations have filed suit in the Kenyan high court to block the planned deforestation and forestall changes in woodland boundaries, citing a breach of Kenyan laws, environmental policies, and international conventions against forest destruction to which Kenya is a signatory.)

171. *Id.*

172. HOTSPOTS, *supra* note 4, at 362.

173. An Act to provide for the protection of wild animals and birds and for matters connected therewith or ancillary or incidental thereto, No. 53 (1972). Inter alia, this act provides for the appointment of a Central Government Director of Wildlife and of a State Chief Wildlife Warden in each state; provides for the establishment of a Wildlife Advisory Board; provides for the establishment of national parks, sanctuaries, and areas closed to hunting; lists protected animal species and a small number of protected plant species; prohibits dealing in trophies and articles made from any animal listed in Schedule I or part II of Schedule II, including articles or objects in which the whole or any part of such animal has been used; specifies that animals and protected plants taken in a sanctuary or national park declared by the central government, and any parts thereof or articles made therefrom, shall be the property of the central government; and provides for enforcement measures and penalties.

174. No. 16 (1927). *See also* The Forest (Conservation) Rules of 1981.

175. HOTSPOTS, *supra* note 4, at 362.

176. *Id.*

177. *India: In Search of Biological Hotspots*, Business Line, September 13, 2000.

178. HOTSPOTS, *supra* note 4, at 363.

179. *Id.*

180. *Id.* at 226. *See* National Parks Act of 1976. *See also* John Yeld, *South Africa; At Last We Have a Peninsula National Park*, Africa News, May 29, 1998.

181. *Id.*

182. *Id.* at 225.

183. *Id.*

184. An Act to provide for the protection, management and utilization of forests; the protection of certain plant and animal life; the regulation of the trade in forest produce; the prevention and combating of veld, forest and mountain fires; the control and management of a national hiking way system and national botanic gardens; and matters connected therewith.

185. National Forest Act 84 of 1998. *See* INTERNATIONAL ENCYCLOPAEDIA, *supra* note 87, Vol. 5, 234–35. This act provides criminal penalties for violations, in Sect. 10(1).

186. National Parks Act 57 of 1976. *See* INTERNATIONAL ENCYCLOPAEDIA, *supra* note 87, Vol. 5, 232.

187. Environment Conservation Act 73 of 1989 (GN 449, May 9, 1994). *See* IN-TERNATIONAL ENCYCLOPAEDIA, *supra* note 87, Vol. 5, 229.

188. INTERNATIONAL ENCYCLOPAEDIA, *supra* note 87, Vol. 5, 229–30.

189. *Id.* at 238–39.

190. Section 7.

191. Section 12(1).

192. *See* INTERNATIONAL ENCYCLOPAEDIA, *supra* note 87, Vol. 4, 231.

193. *Id.* at 246–47.

194. An Ordinance relating to the Protection of endangered Species of wild Fauna and Flora, Nos. 2 and 5 (1980). This act implements the CITES Convention for certain portions of Australia; establishes the requirement of an import permit for the importation of Appendix II specimens; provides that the minister shall not grant an import permit or a certificate for the introduction from the sea of any specimen of species listed on Appendices I or II of CITES when such specimen would be likely to affect adversely the survival of any other species included in Appendix I or Appendix II; provides that the exportation of specimens of Appendix I or Appendix II species shall not be authorized if the specimen was obtained in contravention of any law of the Commonwealth or a state or territory relating to the protection of fauna and flora; and provides that the re-exportation of a specimen shall not be authorized unless the importation of that specimen was in accordance with the provisions of CITES.

195. An Act providing for the conservation and management of species, No. 194 (1992).

196. An Act to further the protection and conservation of wildlife by regulating the export and import of certain animals, plants and goods, and for related purposes, No. 149 (1982). This act, inter alia, regulates the export of specimens that are, or are derived from, native Australian animals or native Australian plants; regulates the export and import of specimens that are, or are derived from, animals that are threatened with extinction and, in particular, of species listed in Appendix I to the CITES Convention; regulates the export and import of specimens that are, or are derived from, animals and plants of a kind that might become threatened with extinction, in

particular, of species listed on Appendix II to CITES, if international trade in such specimens were not regulated; regulates the export and import of specimens that are or are derived from animals or plants of a kind that require or might require that form of special protection; and regulates the import of animals and plants of a kind the establishment of which in Australia or an external territory could have an adverse effect on, or the habitats of, native Australian animals or plants.

197. Statutory Instrument No. 217 (1977). This regulates activities by visitors in national parks and provides for penalties for violations of these regulations; regulates the use of chemicals, scientific research, and construction in such national parks; empowers the Director of National Parks and Wildlife to regulate certain activities carried out by Aboriginals in National Parks; and prohibits the taking and possession of and trade in, except under a license, of certain species of animals and plants on the continental shelf of Australia, in the superjacent waters beyond the adjacent coastal sea, on the sea bed and in the subsoil beneath those waters, and in the airspace above those waters.

198. An Ordinance relating to the protection of migratory birds, Nos. 1 and 4 (1980).

199. *Id.* at 414.

200. *Id.*

201. *Id.* at 184.

202. *Id.* at 183–4.

203. *Id.*

204. *Id.* at 184.

205. *Id.* at 182–3.

206. 16 U.S.C. § 1531 et seq.

207. 16 U.S.C. § 1533.

208. 16 U.S.C. § 1532(19). The ESA defines "taking" of listed species expansively to mean "harass, harm, pursue, hunt, shoot, wound, kill, capture or collect, or to attempt to engage in any such conduct."

209. 50 C.F.R. § 17.3. "Harm" is defined as "an act which actually kills or injures wildlife . . . [to] include significant habitat modification or degradation where it actually kills or injures wildlife by significantly impairing essential behavioral patterns, including breeding, feeding, or sheltering." "Harass" is defined as "an intentional or negligent act or omission which creates the likelihood of injury to wildlife by annoying it to such an extent as to significantly disrupt normal behavioral patterns which include, but are not limited to, breeding, feeding or sheltering."

210. 16 U.S.C. § 1538(a)(1)(D).

211. 16 U.S.C. § 1538(a)(1)(E).

212. 16 U.S.C. § 1538(a)(1)(F).

213. Convention on International Trade in Endangered Species of Wild Flora and Fauna, Mar. 3, 1973, 993 U.N.T.S. 243 (1976) (entered into force July 1, 1975).

214. 16 U.S.C. § 1536(a)(1)–(2).

215. 50 C.F.R. § 402.02; 51 Fed. Reg. at 19,933–34, 19,935.

216. Among the more comprehensive broad-based critiques of the ESA are: James C. Kilbourne, *The Endangered Species Act Under the Microscope: A Closeup Look from a Litigator's Perspective*, 21 Envtl. L. 499 (1991); John C. Kunich, *The Fallacy of Deathbed Conservation Under The Endangered Species Act*, 24 Envt'l L. 501 (1994); Oliver A. Houck, *The Endangered Species Act and Its Implementation by the U.S. Departments of Interior and Commerce*, 64 U. Colo. L. Rev. 277 (1993);

Edwin M. Smith, *The Endangered Species Act and Biological Conservation*, 57 S. Cal. L. Rev. 361 (1984); Jacqueline Lesley Brown, *Preserving Species: The Endangered Species Act Versus Ecosystem Management Regime, Ecological and Political Considerations, and Recommendations for Reform*, 12 J. Envtl. L. & Litig. 151 (1997); Holly D. Doremus, *Patching the Ark: Improving Legal Protection of Biological Diversity*, 18 Ecology Law Quarterly 265 (1991); Patrick Parenteau, *Rearranging the Deck Chairs: Endangered Species Act Reforms in an Era of Mass Extinction*, 22 Wm. & Mary Envtl. L. & Pol'y Rev. 227 (1998); and John Copeland Nagle, *Playing Noah*, 82 Minn. L. Rev. 1171 (1998).

217. *See* Houck, *supra* note 215, at 303, 307. (Arguing that, by expanding the "not prudent" and "no additional benefit" exceptions into a general rule, and making a routine practice of not designating critical habitat, DOI has transformed a mandatory duty of the ESA into a "discretionary and minimally-observed act"). One study of FWS listings during the 1980–1988 period found that FWS failed to designate critical habitat on 320 occasions. For 317 of these, the reason given was that designation was not prudent, in that it would lead to increased vandalism, takings, and/or intrusion by collectors. Similarly, for the December 1988 through May 1992 period, critical habitat was not designated in 174 out of nearly 200 listings. In 159 of these 174 instances, lack of prudency was given as the reason FWS declined to designate critical habitat. *Id. See also* James Saltzman, *Evolution and the Application of Critical Habitat Under the Endangered Species Act*, 14 Harv. Envtl. L. Rev. 311, 332–33 (1990).

218. *See, e.g.*, Kunich, *supra* note 215, at 533–39.

219. *See* Brown, *supra* note 215, at 171–77. (Arguing that, as of 1997, during the entire history of the ESA, "[o]nly ten, possibly eleven, species have been delisted because they actually recovered to levels that warranted removal from the lists," and not even all of those could be credited to the influence of the ESA. Similarly, "only a few (probably five) . . . reclassifications [from endangered to threatened] can be directly attributed to the ESA").

220. *Id.* at 171.

221. *Id.*

222. *Id.*

223. Sharmila Devi, *Chile Chokes on Its Economic Growth: Environmentalists Expect Their Ranks to Swell As the Cost of Pollution Becomes More Apparent*, Financial Times (London), August 21, 2000, London Edition 1.

224. *Id.*

225. HOTSPOTS, *supra* note 4, at 400.

226. *Id.*

227. *Id.* at 401. SPREP has 27 member nations. *Id.*

228. *Id.*

229. Priya Powell, *South Pacific: Forest Loss Threatens Livelihood and Culture*, Inter Press Service, December 18, 1992.

230. *Id.*

231. *Id.*

232. HOTSPOTS, *supra* note 4, at 99.

233. *Id.*

234. The World Wildlife Fund, Nature Conservancy, Conservation International, and Wildlife Conservation Society. *Id.*

235. *Id.*

236. Howard LaFranchi, *Giving Animals Room to Roam*, The Christian Science Monitor, April 30, 1998.

237. *See generally* Diego Cevallos, *Environment—Latin America: Tremendous Biodiversity Under Siege*, Inter Press Service, June 2, 2000; *Latin America—Environment: Latin America Responsible for Major Rainforest Loss*, EFE News Service, November 24, 1999; *World Environmental Fund Finances Reforestation Project*, Xinhua General News Service, March 25, 2000. (Noting that the Mesoamerican region annually loses 400,000 hectares to deforestation, or the loss of 50 hectares of forest every hour.)

238. *See* Jack Epstein, *Giving in High Gear; Silicon Jack*, Latin Trade, February, 2001.

239. *Costa Rica—Environment Poachers Sack World Heritage Site, Costa Rican Rangers Say*, EFE News Service, April 13, 2001. (Describing damage in Cocos Island National Park, a UNESCO World Heritage Site.)

240. Nfer Muoz, *Costa Rica: 500-Year-Old Tress Felled for $100*, Inter Press Service, September 25, 2000.

241. *Id.*

242. *Id.*

243. *Id.*

244. *Panama: Country Profile*, Quest Economics Database, Americas Review World of Information, September 4, 2000.

245. *Id.*

246. *Id.*

247. William Allen, *Preserving, Exploring "Central America's Amazon," St. Louis Biologist's Mission Is to Save the World's Endangered Wildlife*, St. Louis Post-Dispatch, January 28, 2001, at A1. Bosawas covers about 2,900 square miles in area, slightly smaller than Yellowstone National Park, and amounts to more than 6 percent of Nicaragua's land mass. Combined with an adjacent reserve across the border with Honduras, it is the Western Hemisphere's largest rainforest outside of the Amazon. Created in 1991 by President Violeta Chamorro, Bosawas was declared a United Nations international biosphere reserve in 1997. *Id.*

248. *Id.*

249. *Id.*

250. *Id.*

251. Juan Jose Dalton, *Environment: Lack of Laws Speeds Destruction in El Salvador*, Inter Press Service, July 19, 1996.

252. *Id.*

253. Roberto Sanchez, *Environmental Challenges in Mexico*, News World Communications, Inc., March 1, 2000.

254. *Id.*

255. *Id.*

256. Pilar Franco, *Environment—Mexico: Area of Strategic Biodiversity in Danger*, Inter Press Service, September 28, 1999.

257. *Id.*

258. *Id.*

259. *Id.*

260. *Id.*

261. *Id.*

262. *Id*.

263. *Worldwatch: Political Will to Save Global Environment Falters*, Environment News Service, January 15, 2001; *see also Environment: IMF Policies Damage Ecosystem*, Inter Press Service, March 7, 2000. (Linking International Monetary Fund initiatives to deforestation in nations such as Cameroon, Guyana, and Nicaragua, where the IMF's and local governments' targets for economic growth depend on the extraction of natural resources through logging and mining.)

264. HOTSPOTS, *supra* note 4, at 119.

265. *Id*. Jamaica's Forest Act of 1996 is an attempt to gain some measure of control over the situation.

266. *Id*. The key statute is the Act on Forest Conservation and Fruit Trees, Dominican Republic No.5856 (1962).

267. Dominican Republic No.55 (1992).

268. No. 52 (1952). This act provides that all birds except listed game species are protected; provides for closed seasons for game species; regulates hunting methods; prohibits trade in wild birds; prohibits the possession of wild birds during the closed season; establishes a bag limit for game birds; provides for the issue of hunting licenses; and provides for enforcement measures and penalties.

269. An Act to Make Provision for the Control of the Taking and Export of Wild Animals, No. 21 (1968). This applies to all wild animals, defined as animals found living in a natural or feral state in The Bahamas; prohibits, except under a license from the Minister, the taking or capturing of animals specified in the schedule; prohibits, except under a license from the Minister, the export or attempt to export any wild animal from The Bahamas; and empowers the Minister to amend the schedule by ministerial order and to make regulations prescribing the form of application for licenses and the form of licenses.

270. An Act to Incorporate and Confer Powers upon the Bahamas National Trust for Places of Historic Interest or Natural Beauty, No. 21 (1959).

271. Pursuant to Statutory Instruments in 1965 and 1969, respectively.

272. HOTSPOTS, *supra* note 4, at 119.

273. *Id*.

274. *Id*.

275. *Id*. at 154.

276. *Id*.

277. *Id*. at 262.

278. *Id*. at 265.

279. EC Directive on the Conservation of Natural Habitats and of Wild Fauna and Flora, Council Directive 92/43/EEC of 21 May 1992. *See* PHILIPPE SANDS, PRINCIPLES OF INTERNATIONAL ENVIRONMENTAL LAW I: FRAMEWORKS, STANDARDS AND IMPLEMENTATION, 398–401 (Manchester, 1995).

280. Habitats Directive, Art. 1(c), defines these as those areas within the jurisdiction of the EU which "(i) are in danger of disappearance in their natural range; or (ii) have a small natural range following their regression or by reason of their intrinsically restricted area; or (iii) present outstanding examples of typical characteristics of one or more of the five following biogeographical regions: Alpine, Atlantic, Continental, Macaronesian and Mediterranean."

281. These are defined in Art. 1(d) as those habitats within the EU's jurisdiction which are "in danger of disappearance, . . . and for the conservation of which the

Community has particular responsibility in view of the proportion of their natural range which falls within" the EU's territory. These habitats are designated by an asterisk in Annex I.

282. *Id*. Art. 3(1). The lists in Annex I and II can be viewed on-line at <http://www.ecnc.nl/doc/europe/legislat/habidire.html>.

283. This takes place in two stages. During stage one, there is an assessment at the national level of the relative importance of sites for each natural habitat type in Annex I and each species in Annex II. For natural habitats, the criteria are: (a) Degree of representativity of the natural habitat type on the site; (b) Area of the site covered by the natural habitat type in relation to the total area covered by that natural habitat type within national territory; (c) Degree of conservation of the structure and functions of the natural habitat type concerned and restoration possibilities; and (d) Global assessment of the value of the site for conservation of the natural habitat type concerned. For species, the criteria are: (a) Size and density of the population of the species present on the site in relation to the populations present within national territory; (b) Degree of conservation of the features of the habitat which are important for the species concerned and restoration possibilities; (c) Degree of isolation of the population present on the site in relation to the natural range of the species; and (d) Global assessment of the value of the site for conservation of the species concerned. Then, in stage two, there is an assessment of the Community importance of the sites included on the national lists. *Id*. Annex III.

284. *Id*. Art. 6.1.

285. *Id*. Art. 6.2. Cofinancing is provided for the assistance of member states in meeting their Article 6 obligations. *Id*. Art. 8.

286. *Id*. Art. 6.3.

287. *Id*. If, in spite of a negative assessment of the implications for the site and in the absence of alternative solutions, a plan or project must nevertheless be carried out for imperative reasons of overriding public interest, including those of a social or economic nature, the member state "shall take all compensatory measures necessary to ensure that the overall coherence of Natura 2000 is protected." It shall inform the commission of the compensatory measures adopted. And where the site concerned hosts a priority natural habitat type and/or a priority species, the only considerations which may be raised are those relating to human health or public safety, to beneficial consequences of primary importance for the environment or, further to an opinion from the European Commission, to other imperative reasons of overriding public interest. *Id*. Art. 6.4.

288. HOTSPOTS, *supra* note 4, at 261.

289. *Id*. at 261–2.

290. *Id*. at 273.

291. *Id*.

292. *Id*.

293. Law on the System of Protected Territories, available at <http://faolex.fao.org/faolex/index.htm>.

294. HOTSPOTS, *supra* note 4, at 273. *See* Fred Strebeigh, *Across the Russian Wilds*, 33 SMITHSONIAN, No. 3 (June 2001), 88, 93–96.

295. *See* Azerbaijan Land Law of 10/91. Article 5 provides, inter alia, land for "natural conservation," "forests," and "land reserve." Available on-line at <http://faolex.fao.org/faolex/index.htm> website.

296. Agreement between the Republic of Turkey and the Republic of Georgia on co-operation in the field of environment. *See* <http://faolex.fao.org/faolex/index.htm>.

297. An Act to consolidate and amend certain enactments relating to public reserves, to make further provision for their acquisition, control, management, maintenance, preservation (including the protection of the natural environment), development, and use, and to make provision for public access to the coastline and the countryside.

298. This act establishes a Department of Conservation, which controls conservation areas, specially protected areas, and marginal strips. It also establishes the New Zealand Conservation Authority, Conservation Boards, and Fish and Game Councils, and controls freshwater fisheries.

299. HOTSPOTS, *supra* note 4, at 386.

300. *Id.* Additionally, New Zealand protects about 10,987 square kilometers of the sea. *Id. See* INTERNATIONAL ENCYCLOPAEDIA, *supra* note 87, Vol. 4, 235, 263 et seq.

301. *Id.*

302. *Environmental Shock*, The Press (Christchurch), October 3, 1997.

303. *Not Much New in Massive Audit*, The Evening Standard (Palmerston North), October 3, 1997.

304. Act No.57 (1976). Under this act there are also Regulations for the Control, Management and Maintenance of the National Parks and for the Conduct of the General Business of the Board, No. R 2006/1978.

305. HOTSPOTS, *supra* note 4, at 234.

306. *Id.*

307. *Id.* at 233.

308. *Id.*

309. *Id.* at 303.

310. *Id.* at 303–4.

311. *Id.* at 304.

312. *Id.* at 303.

313. *Id.*

314. Jon H. Goldstein, *The Prospects for Using Market Incentives to Conserve Biological Diversity*, 21 Envtl. L. 985, 1005 (1991).

315. For background information on Papua New Guinea, *see* <http://forests.org/ric/background/png.htm> (visited April 23, 2001).

316. Hardaway et al., *supra* note 11, at 939.

317. *Id.* at 938–9.

318. "PNG Government Tries to Greenwash Abysmal Review of Timber Industry, Overview and Commentary," 04/13/01, Item #2, http://forests.org/archive/png/minoplet.htm, (visited April 23, 2001).

319. Bob Burton, "WWF Eco-Forestry Project Operating Without Approval," Environment News Service, April 4, 2001, <http://forests.org/archive/png/fromcylo.htm> (visited April 23, 2001).

320. "Papua New Guinea Cabinet Orders Overhaul of Logging Industry, Overview and Commentary," May 24, 2000, <http://forests.org/archive/png/pngcaboo.htm> (visited April 23, 2001).

321. "PNG Government Tries to Greenwash Abysmal Review of Timber Industry, Overview and Commentary," April 13, 2001, <http://forests.org/archive/png/minoplet.htm> (visited April 23, 2001).

322. *Id.*

323. Goldstein, *supra* note 310, at 1008.

324. *Id.* at 1009.

325. *Id.* at 1010.

326. *Id.* at 1011.

327. ECOLEX, National Legislation of Papua New Guinea, <http://www.exolex. org/LE/LE/details/EN/024325.htm> and <http://www.exolex.org/LE/LE/ details/ EN/024397.htm> (visited April 18, 2001).

328. Environment Protection Act of 1991, No. 91–3.

329. RUSSELL A. MITTERMEIER AND CRISTINA GOETTSCH MITTERMEIER, MEGADIVERSITY: EARTH'S BIOLOGICALLY RICHEST NATIONS, 474 (1997).

330. *Id.* at 477.

331. Cindy Starr, *Zoo Spearheads Effort to Save Apes, Other African Wildlife*, Scripps Howard News Service, October 5, 2000.

332. *Id.*

333. *Id.*

334. *Id.*

335. HOTSPOTS, *supra* note 4, at 328–31.

336. *Id.* at 334.

337. *Indochinese Countries Cooperate to Protect the Environment*, Agence France Presse, May 30, 2001. (Describing recent attempts by the governments of Vietnam, Laos, and Cambodia to work together to protect the badly threatened environment in Indochina.)

338. Ron Moreau and Richard Ernsberger Jr., *Strangling the Mekong*, Newsweek, March 19, 2001. (Describing how dam construction along the Mekong has led to massive deforestation, the destruction of wildlife, and the displacement of tens of thousands of poor people who live along the river, mostly ethnic minorities.)

339. HOTSPOTS, *supra* note 4, at 328–31.

340. *Id.*

341. *Flash Flood Kills at Least 22 People in Northern Thailand*, Deutsche Presse-Agentur, May 4, 2001. In 1989, Thailand banned the granting of new forestry concessions nationwide following a devastating flash flood in the southern province of Chumpol that covered a village in mud and killed more than 100 people. The tragedy was blamed on the indiscriminate cutting of trees on neighboring hills surrounding the village. *Id.*

342. HOTSPOTS, *supra* note 4, at 334.

343. Michael Mathes, *Vietnam's Final Frontier Buckles Under Migrant Pressure*, Deutsche Presse-Agentur, March 27, 2001.

344. *Vietnam: Sectoral Analysis*, Quest Economics Database, World of Information Country Report, February 19, 2001.

345. *See, e.g., Gold Rush Overwhelms Vietnam Province, Rivers Poisoned by Mercury*, Deutsche Presse-Agentur, March 24, 2001.

346. HOTSPOTS, *supra* note 4, at 334. Cambodia's major applicable statute is the Law on Environmental Protection and Natural Resource Management of 1996.

347. *Id.*

348. *Id.* at 332.

349. *Id.*

350. John Pomfret, *China's Lumbering Economy Ravages Border Forests; Logging Industry Taps Unregulated Markets for Wood*, Washington Post, March 26, 2001. (Blaming the deforestation on a combination of the military-backed junta in Burma and enormous needs for lumber in China.)

351. *Id.*

352. *Id.*

353. *Id.*

354. *Id.*

355. HOTSPOTS, *supra* note 4, at 334.

356. *Laos's 7th Party Congress Sets Five-Year Goals*, Deutsche Presse-Agentur, March 12, 2001.

357. HOTSPOTS, *supra* note 4, at 334.

358. *See generally* ANTONIA H. CHAYES and ABRAM CHAYES, THE NEW SOVEREIGNTY: COMPLIANCE WITH INTERNATIONAL REGULATORY AGREEMENTS, at 250–70 (1995); Dan Tarlock, *The Role of Non-Governmental Organizations in the Development of International Environmental Law*, 68 Chi.-Kent L. Rev. 61 (1992); Kal Raustiala, *The "Participatory Revolution" in International Environmental Law*, 21 Harv. Envtl. L. Rev. 537 (1997); Steve Charnovitz, *Two Centuries of Participation: NGOs and International Governance*, 18 Mich. J. Int'l L. 183 (1997).

359. Edith Brown Weiss, *Understanding Compliance with International Environmental Agreements: The Baker's Dozen Myths*, 32 U. Rich. L. Rev. 1555, 1579–80 (1999); *see generally* Peter J. Spiro, *New Global Communities: Nongovernmental Organizations in International Decision-Making Institutions*, 18 Wash. Q. 45 (1995).

360. Weiss, *supra* note 355 at 1579–80 (citing examples of Greenpeace, World Wildlife Fund, TRAFFIC, and the IUCN).

361. <http://www.conservation.org/>.

362. THOMAS G. WEISS and LEON GORDENKER, NGOS, THE UN, & GLOBAL GOVERNANCE 217–19 (1996); Weiss, *supra* note 355 at 1580–81.

• 5 •

A Legal Proposal for Saving the Planet: The Vital Ecosystems Preservation Act

THE NEED FOR HOTSPOTS LEGISLATION

Chapters 3 and 4 set forth, in painstaking and often painful detail, the multiple reasons why the legal status quo is grossly inadequate for purposes of hotspots preservation. Neither existing international agreements nor any mosaic of internal laws of the various nations that are home to the hotspots have stopped the devastation.

We have seen that this is not only a matter of lax enforcement, although that is part of the problem. There are structural defects in the legal regime, and fundamental errors in approach, that make for a recipe for mass extinction. Let us briefly summarize the reasons why.

First, one of the bulwarks of legal conservation efforts within individual nations and internationally is a one-by-one listing and protection of imperiled species. Internationally, CITES serves this function, and many nations have enacted legislation along the lines of the United States' ESA to do likewise. These laws do have merit, because sometimes focusing on a single species in danger is the only way to prevent its extinction, and every extinction should be resisted to the extent possible. There are failing species that exist outside of well-defined ecosystems, and beyond hotspots, that we should try to save because they are ecologically significant, or of symbolic importance, or might offer practical advantages for people to exploit, or simply because it is the right thing to do. Every species is significant in some sense and worthy of legal intervention in the event of approaching extinction. CITES, ESA, and similar species-oriented laws in many nations must be retained and improved to serve in this vital work.

But from a global biodiversity perspective, it is far more important to preserve the greatest number of species and the greatest number of members of each species. It is actually irrelevant for this purpose whether humans have ever laid eyes on the species. We may not have identified a particular species; it may not have a name by which we would call it; we may not know what it is if it walked, crawled, flew, swam, or slithered in front of our face. No matter. What matters is its place within its ecosystem, the niche it occupies there, and the potential benefits it carries within its phenotype and genotype for human beings and for the natural environment now and in the future.

If, as credible scientific opinion holds, many species now in existence have never been formally introduced, as it were, to the human race, what can we do to boost their chances for survival? How can we protect what we cannot detect? If truly there are many thousands, even millions, of species now living on earth yet unknown to us, how can we keep them alive long enough to

1. learn of their existence;
2. discover their role within their ecosystem;
3. determine any current practical value for people; and
4. attempt to assess potential future practical value?

Certainly the CITES/ESA method is not the answer to these questions, because even to qualify for these dubious protections, a species must be listed, and to be listed it must be known to humans. We cannot list species we do not know exist; it is akin to trying to call a stranger who has an unlisted telephone number. The entire thrust of the CITES/ESA approach is protecting species of which we are aware, not those hidden within the black box of the world's less traveled places, deep within the womb of the unknown species.

The second major problem with the current legal regime centers around international law. I examined in Chapter 3 the various major international agreements, including CITES, that relate in some way to biodiversity preservation. This is the obvious place one would search for an overarching global legal response to the worldwide biodiversity crisis. A mass extinction crosses all national and international boundaries, sparing no nation from its effects, and a multilateral legal agreement is the default option when such threats confront the world's nations. There are several such instruments, of varying degrees of applicability to global biodiversity preservation.

The CBD and WHC both at least address the concept of biodiversity and/or the need to save unique natural wonders as a global resource. Philosophically, they are a decent starting point for hotspots protection. But they lack teeth, and they are more aspirational, educational, and inspirational than legally compelling.

Other international agreements fall even farther from the mark. CITES, Ramsar, and a host of additional international legal regimes touch in some way on biodiversity protection, either on a species-by-species level or on the basis of certain types of ecosystems. As with the CBD and WHC, there are generally problems with weak enforcement and inadequate or utterly absent sanctions for noncompliance. Plus, legal instruments such as CITES that focus on individual species, especially species already on their deathbed, are burdened with the same flaws that plague the ESA—they miss the forest for the trees, and they often wait until it is too late.

All of the international agreements share the difficulty that they rely on each individual nation to sign on to them; no nation can be forced to become a signatory. Thus, even at a threshold level, any nation that does not desire to be constrained by such a treaty or convention may simply refuse to become a party. And once a nation does become a signatory, what is the downside if it fails to abide by the terms of the agreement? Typically, not so much as a slap on the national wrist. What is the benefit to the nation for forgoing economic opportunity? Not so much as a nickel in the national pocket.

The third major defect in the existing legal regime resides, like the first, primarily in the laws of the individual hotspots nations. Each nation typically has a legal system for setting aside protected areas of varying descriptions and degrees of protection. In this manner, one might reasonably suppose that, failing an effective overarching international legal regime, key centers of biodiversity might have been identified and safeguarded, one nation at a time. But this is not the case. In Chapter 4, I considered the legal protections on the books, nation by nation. There were certain recurring themes that haunted this story like a Wagnerian leitmotif.

First, no country has legally recognized the hotspots concept per se, nor any of the other major approaches to establishing scientifically sound priorities for conservation I described in Chapter 2. Instead, there is typically some national system of parks, reserves, preserves, and other types of "protected" areas, sometimes supplemented by state, regional, or local enclaves. These are not always chosen on the basis of sound scientific evidence as the most vital pockets of biodiversity. Rather, they may be convenient, not suitable for development, or otherwise relatively easy and cheap. But the low-hanging fruit is not always the choicest. Sometimes it remains available because no one else wants it.

The areas that are set aside, even if part of the actual hotspots region, are often too small and/or too fragmented to be effective in safeguarding biodiversity. Isolated, minuscule parks are no substitute for the hotspots. When only tiny fractions of the hotspots regions are placed within protected areas, and there are no corridors to allow migration and genetic transfer, the long-term prospects for biodiversity are not good.

Moreover, even the legally protected areas in each nation, small and unconnected as they often are, are frequently not well protected in actuality. Some parks formally allow for multiple use, including logging, mining, and other destructive human activities. There is a lot of money to be made from development and exploitation of the hotspots, and, very often, greed trumps need. Other parks officially ban such threats but lack the means or the will to enforce the restrictions effectively. When a handful of park rangers with meager resources are asked to defend against financially motivated, numerous, heavily armed poachers, illegal loggers, and a veritable army of other intruders, it is anything but a fair fight. And the big losers are the hotspots.

Thus there is, in fact, no system of national statutes, international agreements, or any synergistic combination thereof that even comes close to addressing in any effective way the conundrum of preserving the womb of the unknown species. Several multilateral environmental agreements and the internal laws of many individual nations, whether considered alone or in combination, have proved woefully ineffective.

The problem is extremely significant because there may well be millions of species at risk, any one of which could hold the key to the next penicillin, a cure for cancer, or a new source of inexpensive nutrition. Putting aside the weighty moral issue of failing to safeguard such a huge portion of the planet's biodiversity, it would be foolhardy to assume that none of these myriad unknown species is worth saving as a practical matter. There is no reason to suppose that, by sheer random chance, all of the medically and economically useful species in the world are numbered among the species—perhaps the small minority of species—that happen to have been already discovered by us. To make that supposition and, as a result, do nothing to preserve the unknown species is to gamble with the future of humankind and the entire planet. That is a gamble at the highest possible stakes, with no way of knowing the correct odds. The Ark is too precious to place at such risk.

SAVING THE HOTSPOTS

I propose a new statute specifically designed to save the Ark of the Broken Covenant.[1] A descriptive name would be the Vital Ecosystems Preservation Act (VEPA), although the term "ecosystems" could well be replaced with "hotspots," "eco-regions," "habitats," or a number of other appropriate alternatives.

The focus of VEPA could be on the hotspots of the world. If VEPA succeeds in preventing the destruction or degradation of these hotspots, there is a good possibility that at the same time it would succeed in preserving the continued viability of many of the planet's known endangered species. It would also protect the nameless throng of still unidentified species by safeguarding their habitat.

I have mentioned the idea of the black box, a common metaphor for something that happens within a certain area but is only poorly understood. One can adapt this metaphor and conceptualize the situation confronting VEPA as follows. Suppose you were given a beautiful black box and were told that it contains at a minimum certain amounts of valuable crystal and other delicate treasure as well as some unspecified number of unnamed items that may be of great value to you and to your neighbors sometime in the future. Suppose further that you were also told that there are other black boxes in the possession of your neighbors, and that these "foreign" black boxes contain some mysterious items that someday could be very important to you. You were informed that all of these black boxes and at least some of their contents are extremely fragile, and, if broken, can never be repaired or replaced. What would you do with your box? What would you do with regard to your neighbors' boxes?

Some difficult decisions would demand the attention of anyone faced with such a scenario:

1. How can you safeguard your treasure most effectively?

2. How can you realize any tangible benefits from ownership of your box without destroying the box and/or its contents?

3. How can you learn more about the contents of your box without causing irreparable harm?

4. What if any duty do you owe to your neighbors with regard to the way you spend or conserve your treasure?

5. What if any similar duty do your neighbors owe you?

6. How can you legally influence your neighbors to preserve their treasure for the common good?

VEPA would deal with this Gordian knot of tangled issues as did, according to legend, Alexander the Great—by cutting through all the tangles and twists, cleanly and clearly. In developing the idea of VEPA, I have attempted to avoid as many as possible of the defects that have plagued the ESA and CITES. In the process, I have no doubt created a few new defects, but that is inevitable in an imperfect world. The most important feature of VEPA, in fact, is not in any of its details. It is in the overarching concept, which selectively focuses positive incentives on saving the richest pockets of biodiversity in the world.

The first step is to identify the black boxes. What are the at-risk regions that contain the most previously identified species and may contain the most unidentified species? Regardless of whether or to what extent these ecosystems/ecosystem networks or any of the species living within them are currently in grave and imminent danger of destruction, these are the places that shelter the greatest abundance of diverse life-forms. If these areas can be identified and protected, there is a very good chance that we will also succeed in saving a large portion of the planet's biodiversity.

The hotspots are the black boxes. These relatively few, often geographically small regions are the mother lode of life on earth. The imperiled hotspots examined in Chapter 2 account for over 60 percent of the planet's biodiversity but only 1.44 percent of the land surface.[2] This is a phenomenal density of living things and an unparalleled target of opportunity for conservation efforts.

It makes sense from an efficiency standpoint to focus the effort to preserve biodiversity on the hotspots, at least initially. The number of different endemic species, and the number of individuals from each species, would be much higher than in most other regions. The higher taxa are also disproportionately concentrated here, with more genera and families than in other areas. Given limited conservation resources, both financial and political, it is prudent and rational to devote these resources to the endangered places where they will do the greatest good for the greatest number.

This is particularly important for the unknown species. The best available scientific evidence is that a large majority of the unidentified species reside in the hotspots, just as do most of the species we have already named. If in fact there are millions—perhaps many millions—of unknown species currently living beyond the outer limits of human scrutiny in the hotspots, the only feasible way to protect them is to protect the black boxes that conceal them. Save the black boxes, and we will also, in the blind, save the bountiful yet mysterious biodiversity hiding within them. It is impossible to list these species individually, as required under the ESA or CITES, for the very good reason that we do not know they exist. They might share the need for critical habitat with some listed species, but this is mostly a matter of happenstance. Moreover, most of the hotspots are outside the United States, where the ESA does not provide for critical habitat designation. VEPA is certainly needed to save the unknown species overseas, but even within the United States an ecosystem focus would avert many of the flaws in the ESA/CITES approach.[3]

It is, of course, not a simple matter to identify and delimit the boundaries of the hotspots of the world. We have seen that there is controversy within the scientific community both as to the magnitude of the threat to biodiversity and the number of species yet to be discovered—the latter on a scale of an order of magnitude variation in the estimates. Likewise, there would be some disagreement as to which regions should qualify for designation as a hotspot, as evidenced by the several differing approaches to setting priorities for biodiversity conservation discussed in Chapter 2. And there would be some difficult scientific and political line-drawing problems associated with determining and managing the official borders setting off the hotspots from the surrounding areas.[4] An important part of the process would be to ensure that the areas surrounding, bordering, or near the actual hotspots also receive some degree of protection so as to prevent such devastation that the hotspots would become veritable islands, with all the limitations and risks that isolation entails.[5]

It is important to note that VEPA need not focus exclusively on the hotspots paradigm. In Chapter 2, I mentioned several major alternatives to hotspots in biodiversity preservation, including Global 200, Centers of Plant

Diversity, and Endemic Bird Areas. VEPA could be the framework within which any of these approaches, or some combination or variant thereof, serves as the mechanism for identifying priority areas for conservation. The key point is to set priorities in a systematic, scientifically sound manner, with maximum global biodiversity the focal point of all efforts.

The preservation task is made somewhat easier by the fact that credible scientific evidence exists that a relatively small number of nations (17 countries out of more than 200 total) are home to a disproportionately large share of the world's biodiversity. Some estimates indicate that these 17 countries account for about 60 to 70 percent of the total global biodiversity, including terrestrial, freshwater, and marine species (when 200 mile zones are considered).[6] These 17 nations are:

1. Brazil[7]
2. Colombia[8]
3. Indonesia[9]
4. China[10]
5. Mexico[11]
6. South Africa[12]
7. Venezuela[13]
8. Ecuador[14]
9. Peru[15]
10. United States[16]
11. Papua New Guinea[17]
12. India[18]
13. Australia[19]
14. Malaysia[20]
15. Madagascar[21]
16. Democratic Republic of the Congo[22]
17. Philippines[23]

Conservation International (CI), which has taken the lead on advocating for hotspots protection, has used the degree to which an ecosystem or ecosystem cluster is endangered as one of the criteria in determining whether to consider it a hotspot.[24] Both Norman Myers and CI employ a threat criterion consisting of degree of habitat loss. To qualify as a hotspot, they suggest that an area must have lost 75 percent or more of its primary vegetation.[25] Eleven of the hotspots listed in Chapter 2 have already lost 90 percent of their primary vegetation, and three have lost 95 percent.[26]

Under VEPA as envisioned, hotspot designation would be performed by the regulators on the basis of the best available information at the time. As more information becomes available, the list may evolve to some extent. But it is likely that most of the hotspots mentioned in Chapter 2, or some variants thereof, would appear on the VEPA list, at least initially.

HOW SHOULD HOTSPOTS LEGISLATION BE STRUCTURED?

How would VEPA be structured? I propose an outline of its general terms as follows, although there is much room for variation in the details.

One agency, such as the EPA or the U.S. Fish and Wildlife Service (FWS), or perhaps an entirely new entity, should be made responsible for administering VEPA. It is important that a single agency have clear authority to make the key decisions necessary to implement this, or any other, statute. EPA obviously has a great deal of environmental experience and expertise, albeit not so much in the biodiversity sphere as FWS. If EPA were to be the lead agency under VEPA, there could be a role for other agencies with extensive wildlife preservation experience as well, such as FWS and NMFS, but there must be one organization with overarching authority.

The lead agency would, in consultation with a panel of recognized scientific experts worldwide, including experts from each nation involved, determine which ecosystems qualify for VEPA protection. As indicated, the focus would be on the hotspots of the world or a credible alternative. The lead agency would need to exercise great care to make the correct decisions on VEPA designation. Because of the nature of VEPA protection, it would be very costly, both in the political and in the economic sense, to designate the wrong areas, or to designate too many of them. It would be wise to limit VEPA designation to very few regions—perhaps no more than 30 or so—in order to avoid the problems of diminishing returns and political backlash that have plagued other attempts to legislate within the international sphere, in the environmental context or otherwise. The years of debate and rancor over the Kyoto Protocol and the Law of the Sea should serve as a warning and a guide.

Even if practical resource limitations and political resistance forced us to limit VEPA designation to only 5 or 10 hotspots, the effective protection of those would still constitute a colossal contribution to the cause of biodiversity preservation if we chose the hotspots well. Some hotspots are much richer than others in biodiversity. For example, each of five hotspots—the Tropical Andes, Sundaland, Madagascar, Brazil's Atlantic Forest, and the Caribbean—contain endemic plants and vertebrates amounting to at least 2 percent of total species worldwide.[27] Together, these five hotspots harbor 20 percent and 16 percent, respectively, of earth's species of plants and vertebrates in only 0.4 percent of the planet's land surface—an amazing rate of endemism.[28] Such is the beauty and power of the hotspots phenomenon, yielding tremendous efficiency and economy of preservation effort. If we are to be limited to a very small Ark, this would be a propitious place to begin.

Indeed, when we analyze them in terms of five key factors—numbers of endemic species and endemic species/area ratios for both plants and vertebrates, plus extent of habitat loss—it is possible to rank the hotspots in an ecologically meaningful and legally useful way. Madagascar, the Philippines, and Sundaland are in the top 10 for all five categories, while Brazil's Atlantic Forest and the Caribbean are similarly ranked in four of five categories.[29] Indo-Burma, the Western Ghats/Sri Lanka, and the Eastern Arc/ Coastal Forests of Tanzania/Kenya are close behind, in the top 10 in three categories.[30] We could reasonably use many variations on the theme of ranking methods, and these would result in somewhat differing priorities, but certain regions would probably rise to the top regardless of the precise system employed.[31]

The best possible scientific evidence should be used to make these determinations.[32] Moreover, there must be objective, scientifically defensible criteria for designation.[33] The problem of capricious listings under the ESA has undermined its efficacy and both its political and popular support. VEPA designations should not be driven by sentiment or uninformed popular demand. Ecosystems should not receive special treatment on the basis of their location close to "home" in the sense that Americans spend more time in, and are more familiar with, some nations than others. A hotspot in Madagascar should be on equal footing with a comparable hotspot in the United States or Mexico. Nor should the fact that some ecosystems are known to harbor certain favorite species—charismatic megafauna such as the bald eagle—qualify them for VEPA designation if they fail to meet the threshold criteria. The focus must be on the true hotspots of the planet, those comparatively few areas that are home to far more biodiversity and species endemism than the average ecosystem. These are the black boxes that contain the greatest "treasure" and are therefore the most appropriate focal point for our conservation efforts.

VEPA designation would be equally available for ecosystems located in nations anywhere in the world. This is another key distinction between VEPA and the ESA or other national laws. Given that habitat destruction or modification is the primary cause of extinction now, as generally throughout history, global reach is essential.

Is an overarching legal solution to the hotspots problem necessary? Is VEPA a return to imperialism, a recrudescence of the United States' bid to dominate other nations? Why not rely on each individual nation to enact and enforce whatever legislation it deems appropriate for hotspots conservation within its own borders? The short answer is that we have tried the "let a thousand flowers bloom" method, and it has not worked. The outcome has been more like "let a thousand flowers die." And many of those flowers cannot be found anywhere but within a hotspot. The hotspots are in large part a global resource. Their loss is a global tragedy. Their preservation is a global challenge.

A total of 800,767 square kilometers within the hotspots listed in Chapter 2 (about 38 percent of the overall total area) is currently already "protected" in parks and reserves within these other nations;[34] only about 5.1 percent of the original extent of the hotspots is protected in any way, which illustrates the urgency of safeguarding the roughly 40 percent of the remaining intact natural vegetation that does have some legally protected status.[35] Some of these ostensibly protected areas are not much better than "paper parks," offering very little protection, and all of them are in urgent need of stronger safeguards.[36] Moreover, the areas without any current legal protection at all amount to 1.3 million square kilometers, or about 62 percent of the total area of the hotspots.[37]

From a scientific standpoint, it is indisputable that most of the world's hotspots are not within the United States; only three are even partially within its borders. Although the United States is among the 17 nations that are home to the greater part of the biodiversity on the planet, it would be bad science to pretend that the United States is home to as many or as important hotspots as the other countries on the list. The hotspots concept does not recognize political boundaries; it deals with the habitats that support far more than their proportionate share of life on earth. It cannot be denied that most of these hotspots happen to be situated in lands that are outside the territorial limits of the United States.

For VEPA to be effective in preserving the Ark, it must have the power to designate vital centers of biodiversity, that is, hotspots, wherever they are located. The EPA or some other single lead agency should be given the legal authority, in consultation with the best available scientific experts, to grant VEPA designation without restriction to foreign and domestic hotspots. If it accomplished nothing else, this action would focus public attention on designated hotspots, along the lines of the WHC and its List of World Heritage in Danger, and perhaps would be useful in shaping public opinion within the applicable nations in a manner favorable to conservation efforts therein. But much more than that is needed.

Once a hotspot is officially designated for VEPA protection, the acceptable uses of that ecosystem should be subject to strict scientifically determined limits in consultation with local experts. The chief reason why so many key ecosystems are at risk today is that, especially in developing nations, there are severe pressures to derive maximum short- and near-term economic gain from all available natural resources. That can mean virtually unregulated deforestation for purposes of farming, development, and construction; primitive and inefficient agricultural practices; destructive mining techniques; widespread use of highly toxic pesticides; hunting/harvesting of species for profit; poorly controlled air and water pollution; inadequate regulation of toxic chemicals and hazardous wastes; conversion of wild lands to grazing of livestock; deliberate extermination of wild species deemed a threat or a nuisance to humans or their crops and domesticated animals; diversion of sources of water for human use; and lax enforcement of existing internal conservation laws, such as those directed toward preventing and punishing already illegal actions such as poaching.[38]

Some of these environmental stressors directly and obviously affect a particular ecosystem and lend themselves to specific ecosystem preservation methods. Others, such as air pollution (together with its ramifications, which include ozone-layer depletion, acid rain, and global warming) present more diffuse and distant, but nonetheless real, problems.[39] This latter category of stressors makes it impossible for any nation to safeguard its own vital ecosystems in total isolation from other nations. Less developed nations seek to gain some measure of prosperity through exploitation of their natural resources, even as industrialized nations seek cheap sources of food, energy, and raw materials from poorer countries and inflict part of their fossil fuel pollution on other nations. It is a new version of the tragedy of the commons, but this time on a global scale.[40]

VEPA must counter all of these formidable threats and pressures. Left unchecked, these activities will likely continue, or even intensify, and the world's hotspots will be inexorably consumed by human actions. One difficulty, however, is in determining what if any activities can safely be allowed to impact a VEPA-designated hotspot, consistent with its preservation, and at what level such activities can proceed.

Ideally (and idealistically) the determination of what human activities to allow and on what level would be made on the basis of the best available expert scientific information, case by case. It is highly unlikely that the same number, type, and degree of activities would be ecologically acceptable for all hotspots across the board. It is also unlikely that the same number, type, and degree of pressures and threats would imperil all hotspots, given that they are located in nations of widely varying stages of economic development and divergent political systems. Developing nations with rapid rates of population growth present very different challenges from those that exist in prosperous nations such as the United States where population size is essentially stable. Plus, nations with unstable governments, with real dangers of civil war, foreign war, and intense terrorist activity, are prone to political hazards of a decidedly different order.

VEPA should employ a flexible approach. While a rigid, uniform set of regulations has the virtue of being readily accessed and understood, it fails to account for important variables in ecological circumstances and political context.

It would be tempting, perhaps, to paint with a very broad brush and craft VEPA in such a way as to prohibit all further modifications of, or harmful impacts on, designated ecosystems. The designated hotspots or portions thereof could be set aside as wilderness preserves, in essence, and insulated from virtually all human activity. This would be the ultimate in "black box" treatment. Because the hotspots contain, or are thought to contain, so much biodiversity that we know little or nothing about, some might argue that the best policy would be to adopt a hands-off approach under the Murphy's Law theory that anything that can go wrong will insofar as human impact on nature is concerned. Aside from carefully limited scientific experiments and exploratory forays into the hotspots, these regions would be off-limits to all additional development, modification, destruction, and exploration. Even indirect stressors such as air and water pollution would be closely regulated.

Purely from a theoretical scientific standpoint, the hands-off method might be optimal in light of the great uncertainty inherent in hotspots ecology, although given the drastically reduced condition of the hotspots this is certainly debatable. A hands-off approach would insulate fragile, poorly understood hotspots from essentially all human influence, with the exception of limited scientific study. When you are presented with a black box containing mysterious and delicate treasure, the best way to ensure that you cause no harm is to leave the box alone. Let some experts explore the contents for you and try to add to your knowledge of what they are, how much handling they can tolerate, and what value they might have for you and for others, but take no other action to disturb the box. A fortiori, when dealing with living things the very identities of which are unknown,[41] not to mention their specific environmental needs, it may be most prudent to allow nothing to change the status quo. It is reasonable to presume that whatever species are currently living within any hotspot are adequately served by the nutrients, shelter, web-of-life symbiotic species, and climatic conditions that now exist there. It is impossible accurately to predict the consequences that would flow from further altering any of the above.

On the other hand, and more realistically, where human activity is currently encroaching on, or is likely to encroach on in the future, the preserved area (that is, just about everywhere), valid scientific principles may well call for some departure from a strict hands-off policy.[42] Active management efforts may be required to counteract the effects of past, current, or future human actions beyond the boundary of the protected area. For example, people may need to counteract competition with or predation by nonnative species, which, once introduced into an ecosystem, often spread rapidly and are very difficult to eradicate.[43] Protecting a hotspot ecosystem from the threat of such intruder species will often require active management. Human management may also be needed to offset changes in fire patterns and other aspects of the natural environment. Because of these and other ramifications of a wilderness reserve system, prominent ecologists believe that most areas dedicated to wilderness preservation should not be left entirely "undisturbed," but rather require active human management.[44]

Some guiding principles have become well accepted in the field of ecosystem management, and these principles and future advancements in the state of the art should be incorporated into the VEPA process. Specifically,

1. Species well distributed across their native range are less susceptible to extinction than species confined to small portions of their range;
2. Large blocks of habitat containing large populations of a target species are superior to small blocks of habitat containing small populations;

3. Blocks of habitat close together are better than blocks far apart;

4. Habitat in contiguous blocks is better than fragmented habitat;

5. Interconnected blocks of habitat are better than isolated blocks, and dispersing individuals travel more easily through habitat resembling that preferred by the species in question; and

6. Blocks of habitat that are roadless or otherwise inaccessible to humans are better than roaded and accessible habitat blocks.[45]

In addition, threats to biodiversity should be addressed at the core. In many instances, greater attention to setting aside well-managed protected areas should be accompanied by aggressive focus on air pollution, water pollution, population growth, and severe poverty, among other factors. If these less immediate/less obvious stressors are not tackled, progress in the protected area program may be insufficient to counter the assault on biodiversity.[46] Acid rain, widespread contamination of air, water, and soil, and unrelenting pressures to develop natural resources will continue to take an enormous toll.

VEPA could make use of an international panel of prominent experts in ecology, biodiversity, and natural resource management. For each ecosystem designated for VEPA protection, this panel would be responsible for making detailed recommendations as to acceptable and unacceptable activities relating to that ecosystem. This would need to be an ongoing process, accomplished in stages. For example, a preliminary set of guidelines could be required within one year of designation, with continued scientific research thereafter and annual revisions of the guidelines as more information becomes available and conditions change. The range and extent of permissible activities could be adjusted depending on the results of continuing research in each hotspot.

How would we effect restrictions on activities that impact VEPA-designated hotspots? This question is complicated by the fact that so many hotspots fall outside of the jurisdiction of the United States, as will be discussed in Chapter 6. Short of an enforceable international treaty that includes as signatories each of the nations that hosts a hotspot—something that has proved to be extremely elusive in a variety of contexts—how could the environmental laws of the United States regulate human actions in other lands?

The lead agency could, based on input from the applicable scientific panel, draft a set of proposed regulations for each designated hotspot. The proposed regulations would be discussed and negotiated with the political and scientific leadership of the nation that is home to each hotspot. This should involve the direct participation of indigenous people and other communities that actually live in and near the hotspot. It is extremely important that meaningful involvement of local people be required in all cases. The "top-down" approach to conservation in which the people on the ground are dictated to by the people in charge has been tried many times in many places, and the result is many failures. We must learn the concerns and needs of the local people, obtain their input on what can and should be done to help them, and solicit their advice on what can and should be done to halt destruction of the natural habitats. There are many people living within the hotspots now, and poverty is the norm. This is the reality we must confront if we are to oppose the destruction of natural resources by people desperate to survive.

After this interactive evaluation process is concluded, the host nation would then have a period of time in which to implement, by legislation or executive order, enforceable legal provisions within its own jurisdiction substantially consistent with the lead agency proposal and taking into account the input derived from the consultation phase. Although there should be a mechanism by which the host nation can contest certain aspects of the proposed restrictions on the basis of scientific principle or practical infeasibility, this cannot be allowed to delay indefinitely the effectuation of meaningful VEPA protection in the interim. One of the most serious flaws in the ESA, for example, is its vulnerability to lengthy delays at multiple key stages—listing, designation of critical habitat, and development of recovery plans. VEPA must be structured so as to impose at least some automatic requirements as proceedings continue, lest ecosystems be plundered while legal protections are mired in a bog of procedural delays.

By referring the lead agency proposal to each host nation for whatever legally binding implementation is deemed appropriate by that nation's leaders, VEPA would allow for a variety of approaches while still helping to ensure that these approaches do not become toothless in their implementation. Some nations might opt for more restrictive measures than recommended by the lead agency. Some might favor positive inducements over civil and criminal penalties for violators, or vice versa. In time, there would be sufficient empirical data resulting from a multiplicity of approaches to enable each nation to make more informed choices. The progressive diminution in uncertainty should be one of the primary goals of the VEPA process—to learn more about biodiversity, to peel away the mysteries of the hotspots, and to advance the state of the art in ecosystem conservation.

The conservation choices would, in some instances, be extremely difficult. Here is one more reason why, and one chief reason why, it is crucial to involve local communities in the VEPA process. If the boundaries of the hotspots listed in Chapter 2 are defined as broadly as proposed by CI, sometimes including large islands in their entirety, a surprising fact emerges. The hotspots are not only home to most of earth's biodiversity; they are also home to almost 20 percent of the world's human population.[47] In 1995, more than 1.1 billion people were living within the hotspots.[48] Moreover, the population growth rate in the hotspots was roughly 1.8 percent per year from 1995 to 2000, substantially higher than the 1.3 percent of the world as a whole.[49] Even the three major tropical wilderness areas were home to nearly 75 million people in 1995, and the growth rate of 3.1 percent per year was more than twice the global average.[50] That many people cannot be ignored, and cannot be written out of the planning and implementation process. Sadly, that is exactly what has happened many times in many places, with predictably horrid results. The people "on the ground" in and near the hotspots are the ones with the most direct impact on biodiversity, and are in the greatest need of positive inducements to refrain from destructive behavior.

This substantial intersection of hotspots and human habitation could require a variety of conservation measures, depending on the proximity and extent of human population centers to the key ecological regions.[51] Although it may arguably make scientific sense to designate all of Madagascar as a hotspot, for example, it would be utterly impossible to impose uniform restrictions on human activity throughout the nation, cities and forests alike; some areas would have to be more open to development, while relatively undisturbed areas could receive much more comprehensive protection. In any event, the problem underscores the nexus between human need and the imperilment of the hotspots.

VEPA designation and the ensuing nation-specific legal protections, of course, would be of only symbolic and informational significance unless they carried with them real and substantial consequences for human actions relating to the designated hotspots. But what should those consequences be? Again, we must learn from the mistakes made with other approaches to international environmental law if we are to craft an efficacious plan for protection of the most vital ecosystems in the world.

The typical approach to enforcement is to carry a very big "stick" while maintaining a red-meat diet utterly free of "carrots." For example, the onerous land use restrictions that accompany ESA designation of critical habitat are exacerbated by severe penalties for takings and other violations. No incentives built into the ESA in any way soften the impact on a landowner who happens to have listed species or their critical habitat on her property. No positive consequences, no benefits flow to such a landowner. The result is the "shoot, shovel, and shut up" (3-S) syndrome. Why should a private landowner react with anything but dismay when she discovers a listed species inside her fence? The manifest unfairness of making private individuals shoulder the burden of preserving a public resource has generated damaging controversies under the ESA, on top of the perverse incentives the ESA creates to "3-S" the problem.

Consider the example of the rainforests. They are slow growing and, once destroyed, they may be irreplaceable. Guarding them is very expensive, if not impossible, given their enormous size and inhospitable terrain. And while they contribute enormously to the planet's health through photosynthesis and biological diversity, if left standing, they present few immediate, tangible benefits to the local people and the nations in which they grow. But they can yield quick profits to the opportunists who chop them down. In fact, governments have actively encouraged deforestation by giving tax credits that allow land speculators to offset the costs of clearing forest land for cattle ranching against their income tax; by providing subsidized credit for crops and livestock; by building roads; and by supplying underpriced electricity.[52] A Brazilian law, now rescinded, long allowed a farmer who cleared an acre to claim title to two acres.[53] With such powerful perverse incentives at work, it is inevitable that the destruction will continue unless adequate rewards can be made available for those who preserve and manage the forests on a sustainable yield basis.

VEPA must combine positive incentives for compliance with penalties for noncompliance if it is to be effective.[54] If it relies excessively on command-and-control measures—that is, if it is all "stick"—it will produce the same type of perverse incentives and costly controversies as the ESA and other similar laws. There must be real, significant *benefits* that redound to the affected nation *and its citizens at all levels* when a hotspot is selected for VEPA designation.

This is particularly crucial in light of the fact that VEPA would apply equally to all designated ecosystems irrespective of which nations happen to contain them. Extraterritorial application of environmental statutes is a sensitive legal issue, with implications under GATT/WTO as discussed in the next chapter, as well as a politically controversial issue. If the United States attempts, through legislative rewards and penalties, to regulate the internal affairs of other nations through VEPA or any other environmental law, there would be serious legal and political obstacles. That is why the approach recommended here is to convey the lead agency's proposed restrictions to each host nation for modification and implementation through the legal mechanisms available there, and to do so in a spirit of bilateral or multilateral negotiation and give-and-take. This is not a call for a new imperialism. It is a proposal for sharing—of money, information, people, and expertise—to save a global treasure.

Rather than unilateral legal action attempting to force another nation's hand, VEPA should entail interactive negotiation between the applicable United States lead agency and each other nation designated under VEPA. To head off legal challenges under GATT/WTO as well as political charges of latter-day imperialism, VEPA must mandate meaningful exchange of views and information between the United States and the other VEPA nations along the road to a plan of action for each hotspot. Each host nation ultimately would then be responsible for creating, implementing, and enforcing its own means of preserving its VEPA-designated hotspots.

How would VEPA ensure that other nations

1. enact appropriate legal protections substantially consistent with lead agency proposals in a timely manner, and

2. actively, consistently, and effectively enforce such legal protections with respect to the people within its jurisdiction?

How can the dangers of perverse incentives and lax enforcement be addressed? How can the political and international legal issues be handled?

I suggest that Congress support VEPA implementation through authorization and appropriation of a fund specifically dedicated to this purpose. Although unlike the Superfund used under CERCLA[55] to pay for remediation of past environmental contamination in that it would not be replenished from money recovered from violators, the VEPA fund would be similar to Superfund in its focus on a particular environmental concern. Indeed, there is already a federal international-oriented environmental version of this approach on the books, in the Tropical Forest Conservation Act of 1998,[56] in which the U.S. Congress noted the role of economic debt carried by certain developing nations in driving destruction of their tropical forests.[57] The Tropical Forest Conservation Act allows for debt relief in qualifying countries and the targeting of U.S.-provided funds for the protection of tropical forests therein. VEPA could build on this foundation and benefit from our experiences with this act.[58]

Once an ecosystem is designated for VEPA protection in a foreign country, that country would become eligible for a portion of the VEPA fund, contingent upon compliance. Before any funds are available to a nation, that nation should demonstrate that it has taken all necessary steps to enact and implement the legal controls called for in the lead agency proposal. If, in the judgment of the lead agency administrator, the host nation has set in place the appropriate legal regulations to preserve the hotspot in question, VEPA funds should be provided to assist in the implementation and enforcement of those regulations. Often, the host nation will be much less wealthy than the United States and may lack the wherewithal to launch effective protective measures.[59] Through VEPA payments the United States would alleviate a substantial part of that burden. But VEPA funds should do more than aid in implementation and enforcement.

To create an incentive for other nations to comply, and to counteract any perverse incentives that restrictions on development could generate, VEPA funds should be used to compensate for lost opportunity costs. Developing nations would be understandably resentful of U.S. efforts to restrict their economic advancement; after all, during the expansion phase of American history, there were few if any environmental hurdles to overcome. The America of today was built on top of felled forests, plowed grasslands, and drained wetlands. Biodiversity was food on the table or game to be hunted for sport. American history does not afford the United States the moral high ground for biodiversity preservation. To be fair to developing nations, which tend to be in far less favorable economic condition, the United States must pay for the modernization and economic enhancements that might have been achieved by exploitation of the protected hotspots. Indeed, Norman Myers has identified poverty/lack of economic development as the greatest threat to the world's remaining vital ecosystems.[60] He summarizes the situation as follows.

Plainly, and humanitarian considerations apart, we should bear in mind that there is no greater threat to protected areas than the destitute person who disregards the boundaries of the best-protected park if he or she feels there is no other place to gain a livelihood. . . . Of course, our first and overriding concern for the region must be human survival. But the prospect has ominous implications for protected areas. . . . [T]he principal threat to protected areas comes from multitudes of impoverished people practicing rudimentary agriculture. An underdeveloped region will be unable to modernize its agriculture, so the small-scale farmer will continue to practice extensive rather than intensive agriculture. . . . In other words, the biggest threat of all for protected areas is lack of development.[61]

In light of this, and in stark contrast to the ESA approach, VEPA should ensure that affected nations and their often rapidly growing number of individuals[62] benefit rather than suffer from its provisions. It is crucial that a meaningful portion of the benefit be directed toward, and actually reach, the people who live in and near the key habitats. They are the people who have been compelled, by urgent subsistence-level personal need, to consume vital natural resources for their own survival. These people, usually severely impoverished, are the ones who must know that they have not been forgotten and that it is in their interest not to poach, slash-and-burn, or otherwise harm the targeted enclaves of biodiversity. Perhaps a system of tiered funds, devoted to national, regional, local, and individual aid, would be one way for VEPA to direct its resources where they will be most effective.[63]

It is not enough to transfer funds directly to the national government, or to relieve a portion of national debt owed to the United States, in any given hotspot nation, although that should be part of the solution. Sometimes the central government and its officials are precisely the cause of both the poverty of the common citizen and the depredation of the hotspots. Corrupt, exploitative, acquisitive, and oppressive officials cannot be allowed to divert VEPA funds to their own selfish purposes. Rather, people at *each* major level within the nation must receive a share of the VEPA funds, to motivate, energize, and enable them to act in compliance with the VEPA plan. And the most vital tier of all is the bottom, where most impact on biodiversity takes place.

VEPA funds, properly disbursed, must make it the demonstrably, palpably prudent option of a rational utility maximizer on the ground *not* to poach, *not* to practice slash-and-burn agriculture, and *not* to assist others in illegal logging, mining, hunting, or other harmful activities. VEPA funds should be targeted, at the bottom tier, toward creating permanent and preferable alternatives to the old means of survival for the local communities in and near the hotspots. In this way, VEPA is in reality an economic stimulus package aimed at helping the poor in other nations, with prerequisites related to biodiversity preservation. VEPA could change people's lives for the better and help them permanently shift to ecologically responsible ways of earning a decent living.

The amount of VEPA funds transferred to host nations could be determined in each case by the lead agency, in consultation with Congress. Funds should be sufficient to replace any revenues lost to the host nation due to

1. cessation of activities that impinge on designated hotspots;
2. enforcement costs; and
3. costs of other affirmative measures instituted to protect the hotspots.

At a minimum, enough funds should be transferred to place each host nation in no worse an economic posture than it would have been in without VEPA. Beyond this, it is quite desirable to provide some substantial amount of additional funds that could be used by each host nation for whatever internal improvements it deems necessary, along the lines of traditional forms of foreign aid. Such additional funds would reduce the risk of perverse incentives and foreign resistance to VEPA restrictions. Funds of either type should be sent to host nations in relatively small installments, at frequent periodic intervals, so as to provide a means by which payment can be tied to compliance.

To be effective, VEPA must contain a mechanism by which host nation compliance is independently assessed by the lead agency on a frequent, regular, recurring basis, and there must be predictable, significant consequences of both compliance and noncompliance. If inspections show substantial compliance, VEPA payments to that nation would not need to be reduced in the next payment cycle. But if there are uncorrected and serious violations of the applicable regulations, the next payment cycle should bring a meaningful diminution in revenue for the host nation targeted to the source of the noncompliance. A standard framework for calculating the percent reduction in transfer payments, akin to those in use for other environmental statutes, could base penalties on factors such as the severity of the environmental harm, the seriousness of the risk, the degree of intentionality involved, the extent to which the regulated entity profited from the violation, and whether there have been repeated violations.

Conversely, if a particular nation is demonstrably doing an outstanding job preserving its designated hotspot, well beyond the minimum level of compliance, additional VEPA funds could be awarded to that nation, above the usual amount. If these supplemental payments were linked to genuine, verifiable excellence in conservation, and if the payments were large enough to be perceived as significant by the host nation and other nations, they could supply a useful further incentive for innovation and initiative in effectuating compliance with VEPA. VEPA should make wise and effective stewardship a rewarding enterprise, not only in the sense of satisfaction over a worthwhile job well done but also in terms of financial benefit.

It may be advisable to build into VEPA some other penalty provisions in the event that withholding of VEPA funds proves to be an insufficient deterrent for noncompliance. With care to avert potential pitfalls with GATT/WTO, some portion of non-VEPA foreign aid funds that otherwise would have gone to the noncomplying nation might be withheld in the event of especially egregious violation. This is analogous to the practice within the United States whereby federal highway funds can be withheld from states that fail to comply with certain provisions of the Clean Air Act, albeit significantly complicated by the international dimension in light of key GATT/WTO decisions previously discussed. The potential loss of such funds would be a powerful "stick" that might be necessary to complement the "carrot" aspects of VEPA,[64] but if the incentive/reward portions are properly implemented, there should not be many occasions on which the harshest punitive sanctions are called for.

NOTES

1. There have been some other proposals for a new statute focused on ecosystem protection within the United States. *See, e.g.*, Julie B. Bloch, *Preserving Biological Diversity in the United States: The Case for Moving to an Ecosystems Approach to Protect the Nation's Biological Wealth*, 10 Pace Envtl. L. Rev. 175, 218–222 (1992); Holly D. Doremus, *Patching the Ark: Improving Legal Protection of Biological Diversity*, 18 Ecology Law Quarterly 265, 323–26 (1991); J.B. Ruhl, *Biodiversity Conservation and the Ever-Expanding Web of Federal Laws Regulating Non-federal Lands: Time for Something Completely Different?*, 66 U. Colo. L. Rev. 555, 662–671 (1995); Jacqueline Lesley Brown, *Preserving Species: The Endangered Species Act Versus Ecosystem Management Regime, Ecological and Political Considerations, and Recommendations for Reform*, 12 J. Envtl. L. & Litig. 151, 219–263 (1997); Patrick Parenteau, *Rearranging the Deck Chairs: Endangered Species Act Reforms in an Era of Mass Extinction*, 22 Wm. & Mary Envtl. L. & Pol'y Rev. 227, 304–09 (1998).

2. Russell A. Mittermeier, Norman Myers, and Cristina Goettsch Mittermeier, Hotspots: Earth's Biologically Richest and Most Endangered Terrestrial Ecoregions at 7 (2000) (hereinafter Hotspots).

3. *See generally* Continental Conservation: Scientific Foundations of Regional Reserve Networks (Michael E. Soule and John Terborgh, eds., 1999).

4. *See* Holly D. Doremus, *The Rhetoric and Reality of Nature Protection: Toward a New Discourse*, 57 Wash. & Lee L. Rev. 11, 57–61 (2000).

5. If the hotspots were protected, but unrestricted development allowed on all other nearby lands, the protected areas would become living museums of declining biodiversity. *See* Bloch, *supra* note 1, at 208. Unprotected lands would likely be developed and would become uninhabitable to many species. Species within the protected hotspots would then be, in effect, jailed within their confines. Evidence from islands suggests that as areas surrounding the protected lands become uninhabitable to species living within the protected lands, such protected lands can support fewer species, which in turn may inhibit evolution and consequently contribute to species extinction. Therefore, these key ecosystems should be strictly preserved in conjunction

with adequate protection for buffer areas near the ecosystem. *Id.* at 209. *See also* Sahotra Sarkar, *Wilderness Preservation and Biodiversity Conservation—Keeping Divergent Goals Distinct,* 49 Biosci. 405, 409 (1999) (opining that a strategy of strict and absolute wilderness preservation "may result in compromises in which regions outside the reserves are entirely unprotected").

6. RUSSELL A. MITTERMEIER AND CRISTINA GOETTSCH MITTERMEIER, MEGADIVERSITY: EARTH'S BIOLOGICALLY WEALTHIEST NATIONS at 17–37 (1997).

7. *Id.* at 39–55.

8. *Id.* at 109–27.

9. *Id.* at 75–97.

10. *Id.* at 257–71.

11. *Id.* at 141–58.

12. *Id.* at 407–17.

13. *Id.* at 449–58.

14. *Id.* at 315–24.

15. *Id.* at 283–97.

16. *Id.* at 387–96.

17. *Id.* at 363–74.

18. *Id.* at 337–51.

19. *Id.* at 179–92.

20. *Id.* at 425–36.

21. *Id.* at 209–23.

22. *Id.* at 469–77.

23. *Id.* at 237–49.

24. Conservation International employs a two-factor approach to hotspot designation. The biological criteria (primarily the degree of species endemism, i.e., the percentage of total global species diversity endemic to a given area) are used for establishing the first layer of analysis. Secondarily, the degree of threat to an area is considered in determining whether an area will qualify for high conservation priority as a hotspot—generally that there be no more than 25 percent remaining of the original vegetation cover. HOTSPOTS, *supra* note 2, at 27–30.

25. Norman Myers, Russell A. Mittermeier, et al., *Biodiversity Hotspots for Conservation Priorities,* 403 Nature 853, 855 (Feb. 2000). This piece suggests 70 percent loss, rather than 75 percent, as the benchmark.

26. *Id.*

27. Myers, Mittermeier, et al., *supra* note 25, at 855.

28. *Id.*

29. *Id.* at 856.

30. *Id.* at 856–57. For complete hotspot rankings based on species diversity and endemism for birds, mammals, reptiles, amphibians, and nonfish vertebrates, *see* HOTSPOTS, *supra* note 2, at 38–42. For similar rankings of these taxa for all hotspots based on diversity per unit area of original extent of natural vegetation and diversity per unit area of remaining intact natural vegetation, *see id.* at 46–50.

31. HOTSPOTS, *supra* note 2 at 40–44. One method yields a "top nine" list of the following hotspots, in order: (1) Tropical Andes; (2) Sundaland; (3) Madagascar; (4) Caribbean; (5) Brazil's Atlantic Forest Region; (6) Mesoamerica; (7) Mediterranean Basin; (8) Indo-Burma; and (9) Philippines. These nine hotspots together house 88,536 of a global total of 300,000 species of vascular plants (29.5 percent)

and 6,804 of 27,298 nonfish vertebrates (24.9 percent) in just 0.73 percent of earth's land surface. *Id.* at 40. Other credible methods might place Chocó-Darien-Western Ecuador, Wallacea, the Guinean Forests of West Africa, or the Mountains of South-Central China among the hottest of the hotspots, with one or two of the above moving down a few notches in the list. *See id.* at 40–44, 50–55 for a variety of approaches to ranking the hotspots.

32. As noted in Chapter 2, it is encouraging that although several organizations have attempted to gauge which of the world's regions are most significant and most in need of intensified conservation measures, substantially the same areas tend to receive top priority. The International Union for Conservation of Nature and Natural Resources, the World Wildlife Fund, the World Resources Institute, and BirdLife International have each prepared their own lists, along the lines of those compiled by CI. A comparison of the various lists reveals that they all focus on the Tropical Andes, Madagascar, the Atlantic Forest region of eastern Brazil, the Mesoamerican forests, the Philippines, most of Indonesia, the Cape Floristic Region of South Africa, and New Caledonia, among others. Russell A. Mittermeier, Norman Myers, et al., *Biodiversity Hotspots and Major Tropical Wilderness Areas: Approaches to Setting Conservation Priorities*, 12 Conserv. Biol. 516, 519 (Jun. 1998).

33. As one workable standard, Myers has proposed that to qualify as a hotspot, an area must contain at least 0.5 percent (or roughly 1,500) of the world's approximately 300,000 identified plant species as endemics. Of the hotspots listed in our book, 15 of them contain at least 2,500 endemic plant species, and 10 harbor 5,000 or more. Myers, Mittermeier, et al., *supra* note 25, at 854.

34. *Id.* at 856.

35. HOTSPOTS, *supra* note 2, at 53.

36. Myers, Mittermeier, et al., *supra* note 25, at 856. *See also* HOTSPOTS, *supra* note 2, at 53–58.

37. *Id.* at 857.

38. Poaching, of course, only directly influences individual members of certain species rather than ecosystems themselves. Nonetheless, poaching often affects prominent components of the ecosystem, such as particularly large carnivores or herbivores (elephants, lions, etc.), and if these species are decimated there can be impacts beyond the species level. *See* HOTSPOTS, *supra* note 2, at 62–65.

39. Norman Myers, *Saving Biodiversity and Saving the Biosphere*, in THE LIVING PLANET IN CRISIS: BIODIVERSITY SCIENCE AND POLICY, at 237 (Joel Cracraft and Francesca T. Grifo, eds., 1999).

40. *Id.* at 243–44. The term "tragedy of the commons" was coined by Garrett Hardin and ever since has been used, and misused, countless times. Garrett Hardin, *The Tragedy of the Commons*, 162 Science 1244 (1968).

41. Unknowns are omnipresent. For example, there is no current account of Brazil's plant species, although Brazil is believed to contain the earth's richest flora— at least 50,000 plant species, one-sixth of the planet's total. Myers, Mittermeier, et al., *supra* note 25, at 854.

42. *See* Doremus, *supra* note 4, at 55–58.

43. *See* David S. Wilcove et al., *Quantifying Threats to Imperiled Species in the United States*, 48 Biosci. 607, 608–09 (1998).

44. *See* Donald A. Falk and Peggy Olwell, *Scientific and Policy Considerations in Restoration and Reintroduction of Endangered Species*, 94 Rhodora 287, 303 (1992).

45. REED. F. NOSS AND ALLEN Y. COOPERRIDER, SAVING NATURE'S LEGACY, at 141 (1994).

46. Norman Myers, *Questions of Mass Extinction*, 2 Biodivers. & Conserv. 2, 11–12 (1993).

47. Richard P. Cincotta, Jennifer Wisniwski, and Robert Engelman, *Human Population in the Biodiversity Hotspots*, 404 Nature 990 (Apr. 2000).

48. *Id.*

49. *Id.*

50. *Id.* at 991. In general however, and in contrast to the listed hotspots, which often feature large numbers of people living within them, the major tropical wilderness areas are much less sparsely populated (generally fewer than 5 to 8 people per square kilometer on average). *Id. See also* Myers, Mittermeier et al., *supra* note 25, at 857.

51. *See* Andrew Balmford et al., *Conservation Conflicts Across Africa*, 291 Science 2616–2619 (2001) (describing the tendency for areas of outstanding conservation importance to coincide with dense human settlement).

52. FRANCES CAIRNCROSS, COSTING THE EARTH: THE CHALLENGE FOR GOVERNMENTS, THE OPPORTUNITIES FOR BUSINESS 142–45 (1991).

53. *Id.* at 145.

54. *See generally* Jon H. Goldstein, *The Prospects for Using Market Incentives to Conserve Biological Diversity*, 21 Envtl. L. 985 (1991).

55. The Comprehensive Environmental Response, Compensation, and Liability Act, 42 U.S.C. § § 9601–9675.

56. Tropical Forest Conservation Act of 1998, 22 U.S.C. 2431 (1998) (amending 22 U.S.C. 2151 (1961)).

57. 22 U.S.C. 2431(a)(2)–(7).

58. Jennifer A. Loughrey, *The Tropical Forest Conservation Act of 1998: Can the United States Really Protect the World's Resources? The Need for a Binding International Treaty Convention on Forests*, 14 Emory Int'l L. Rev. 315, 328–37 (2000) (discussing the merits and shortcomings of this act). *See also* Nancy Knupfer, *Debt-for-Nature Swaps: Innovation or Intrusion?*, 4 N.Y. Int'l L. Rev. 86, 88 (1991); Paul J. Ferraro and Randall A. Kramer, *Compensation and Economic Incentives: Reducing Pressure on Protected Areas*, in LAST STAND: PROTECTED AREAS AND THE DEFENSE OF TROPICAL BIODIVERSITY, 187–211 (R. Kramer et al., eds., Oxford, 1997).

59. For example, the problem of poachers is a serious one that threatens the survival of prominent species such as elephants, gorillas, and lions. In certain nations that harbor such wildlife, poaching has proved to be a persistent and intractable threat, even within putatively protected nature preserves. Poaching can be very profitable, and legal alternatives often cannot offer anything approaching that level of income for most people. As a result, poachers may pursue their illegal trade with violent tenacity. Armed with automatic weapons, grenades, and other military-type armaments, poachers are the equivalent of a formidable insurgent force, capable of and willing to use whatever means are necessary to continue their activities. *See* R. W. Johnson, *Plan for Giant New African Game Park Raises Fears of Poachers' Paradise*, Sunday Times (London), Dec. 3, 2000; *Creatures Common Contraband in Cold Weather*, Toronto Star, Edition 1, Dec. 27, 2000. It is totally unrealistic to expect struggling governments within developing nations to counteract such dangerous and deadly threats effectively without a great deal of assistance.

60. Norman Myers, *Saving Biodiversity and Saving the Biosphere*, in LIVING PLANET, *supra* note 39, at 241–42.

61. *Id.* at 241.

62. Cincotta, *supra* note 47, at 990–91.

63. *See* R.I. Vane-Wright, *Identifying Priorities for the Conservation of Biodiversity: Systematic Biological Criteria Within a Socio-Political Framework*, in BIODIVERSITY: A BIOLOGY OF NUMBERS AND DIFFERENCE, 309, 322–28 (Kevin J. Gaston, ed., Blackwell, 1996).

64. The Federal Swampbuster Program, for example, denies federal farm subsidies to farmers if they convert wetlands to agricultural uses. *See* Bradley C. Karkkainen, *Biodiversity and Land*, 83 Cornell L. Rev. 1, 66–68 (1995).

• 6 •

To Be or Not to Be

IS HOTSPOTS LEGISLATION REALISTICALLY POSSIBLE?

To maintain the legal status quo for the hotspots is to sign a death warrant. This would be a death warrant unlike any other. In fact, it would closely resemble a blank check. It would have only a blank line for the date of execution and the name of the condemned. We would probably never know what species were becoming extinct or on what date the last remaining member of each species died. In many cases, even if we were aware what was happening, we would be unable to fill in the name of the dying species—because we had never given it a name. If the hotspots are the Ark of the Broken Covenant, it is beyond dispute that the Ark, as a lifeboat for earth's living things, is as badly in need of protection and repair as it is overcrowded.

We have seen in Chapter 4 the extent to which the hotspots have already been decimated, despite the phalanx of multilateral environmental agreements and domestic laws that purport to shelter biodiversity. The borders of the hotspots have been pushed back again and again. Each time new economic and political pressures mount, something has to give—and that something has very often been the hotspots. When the question within a developing nation is framed as jobs versus rainforests, or agriculture versus wilderness, the answer is foreordained. The Ark is cannibalized for its most instantly and obviously valuable parts, or torn apart bit by bit and burned as scrap to make room for more "productive" things.

The existing system of parks, reserves, and preserves often misses the target. Nations understandably may choose to pick mainly the low-hanging fruit, setting aside land with limited ecological significance that is not suitable for development, while permitting encroachment in much richer pockets of biodiversity—the true wombs of the unknown species—that promise a rich payback from logging, grazing, farming, mining, and urbanization. They protect that which does not need it and fail to protect that which does.[1]

Even areas with putative legal protection are not safe. Where the territory is vast and the available law enforcement resources are meager, it is not possible to provide effective security for the natural resources. Heavily armed poachers, motivated by the prospect of great profits from their illegal commodities, are a formidable foe. Indeed, trade in illegally taken wildlife is a huge moneymaker internationally, behind only drugs and armaments,[2] and that level of profit motive generates the equivalent of wartime resistance to regulation. Similar conditions can prevail where the treasure is timber, or minerals, or other Golden Eggs offering the promise of quick wealth . . . from a goose that is being bled to death.

Moreover, in nations where the central government itself is unstable and/or in constant danger of violent revolution, coup, or civil war, the efficacy of internal legal protection for nature preserves is questionable. Where the government is in mortal danger, it is understandable that political leaders choose to devote most of their scarce military and law enforcement resources to their own immediate self-preservation instead of the more altruistic preservation of nature. Some governments may also be plagued with corruption, and their leaders can be persuaded to tolerate poaching, logging, and other destructive activities in exchange for a share of the profits. Paper laws are no match for paper money.

We may feel compelled to step in and take control of the train before the wreck. Yet national sovereignty is one of the firmest pillars of the international legal system, as embodied in the CBD, WHC, and other major international laws.[3] This is a primary reason for the paucity of effective legal measures that allow foreign governments to impose their will on the internal domestic activities of a sovereign nation. This is why United States statutes such as the ESA allow the listing of threatened or endangered species within other lands but stop short of authorizing the designation of critical habitat therein.

How would Americans react if the situation were reversed? If we were failing to protect Yellowstone National Park adequately in the face of rampant poaching and developmental encroachment, would we resist the efforts of other governments to clamp legal controls on our ability to manage, or mismanage, Yellowstone? Certainly. Would other nations have a right to be outraged that we were allowing the devastation of an irreplaceable and unique natural wonder of the world? Certainly.

There are, of course, other types of internal affairs that traditionally fall within the proper ambit of a nation's sovereignty but nonetheless provoke intense disapproval in other countries. Human rights abuses are a classic example. Some nations tolerate, or even actively engage in, appalling atrocities within their borders. There are contemporary horrific cases in some areas of the world of large-scale religious persecution, slavery, genocide, forced genital mutilation of females, compulsory abortion or infanticide, mass murder, mass confiscation of private property, and other severe deprivations of human rights. We, in the United States, might occasionally see news accounts reporting such things and become upset, but there is usually not much in the way of official action by our federal government or by the international community. National sovereignty provides an effective shield for other governments as they use, or allow the use of, the sword on their own citizens.

It is in recognition of this that I have posited the idea of an incentives-based United States statute aimed at influencing (through encouragement, persuasion, and, most importantly, financial and technical assistance) other nations to develop and implement effective and consistent measures to protect the hotspots.[4] This statute, which I call the Vital Ecosystems Preservation Act (VEPA), would respect national sovereignty while still offering the benefits of sound biodiversity planning and a powerful, carrot-based approach to shaping conservationist actions.[5] I suggested in Chapter 5 that a single agency, such as EPA or the U.S. Fish and Wildlife Service (FWS) or some new alternative, be made responsible for administering VEPA and that this agency would, in consultation with recognized scientific experts world wide, determine which eco-regions qualify for VEPA protection.

At present, of course, VEPA remains only a theoretical option, somewhere on the continuum between pipe dream and forthcoming legislation. The idea has the virtues of avoiding the perverse incentives of unsuccessful statutes such as the ESA and respecting traditional notions of national sovereignty.[6] It would also directly and demonstrably help people who desperately need help, which may make it more politically palatable than the ESA, which only seeks to aid plants and animals and has often been seen as unfair to human beings. Through an organized, scientifically sound mechanism and an array of positive incentives, VEPA could give developing nations an infusion of scientific expertise and the money to translate it into effective actions, while enabling each nation to retain much control over the details of the process.[7] I can confidently and with studied understatement declare that the only things standing between VEPA and reality are the U.S. government, several billion dollars a year, and GATT/WTO.

VEPA would be a unilateral attempt by the United States to influence environmental actions within other nations, and as such would fall within a category of measures traditionally disfavored by GATT/WTO panels. The Appellate Body's opinion in the key Shrimp-Turtles case contains discussion of the general preference for multilateral solutions to international environmental problems, as opposed to unilateral actions. The Appellate Body pointed to the Inter-American Convention as evidence that "an alternative course of action" featuring "cooperative efforts" rather than "the unilateral and non-consensual procedures of the import prohibition" under the Marine Mammals Protection Act "was reasonably open to the United States."[8] But the opinion carefully avoids the suggestion that unilateral measures generally fall outside Article XX of GATT. Such a claim would be inconsistent with earlier passages in the same opinion implying that such a rule would render "most, if not all, of the specific exceptions of Article XX inutile" and thus would be "abhorrent."[9] Such a claim would also be inconsistent with the use of the singular noun in Article XX, which permits "any contracting party" to adopt the measures in question, and with GATT case law, which has often found unilateral measures to fall within Article XX. Nothing in the language of Article XX suggests that unilateral measures are illegal solely on the basis that they are directed at resources outside the jurisdiction of the importing country.

Thus, when the Appellate Body referred to the alternative of "cooperative efforts,"[10] it did so only to underscore the feasibility of serious negotiations with all affected parties prior to the imposition of ETMs. It identified a "cooperative" alternative to unilateral ETMs only to criticize the failure of the United States "to negotiate similar agreements with any other country or group of countries."[11] A failure to negotiate with all countries on an equal basis may render a subsequent ETM "a means of arbitrary or unjustifiable discrimination" against the targeted imports, but a unilateral measure would not violate GATT if *evenhanded negotiations* do in fact precede the imposition of the measure.[12] VEPA could certainly be designed to accommodate these concerns, and may well survive WTO scrutiny.

Without question, the financial and political burdens of protecting the hotspots would be considerable. If, as seems likely, the United States is the only nation that might shoulder most of this burden, we must ask whether it could or would do so.

This question evokes two layers of analogy, both involving the mythic figure of Atlas. First, according to ancient Roman mythology, Atlas quite literally carried the weight of the entire world on his titanic shoulders. In perpetuity he was doomed to support the globe and, with it, all living things, preventing the earth from falling to a disastrous end. This onerous duty was punishment for Atlas's prior misdeeds.

The burden of Atlas can be analogized to the responsibility the United States must bear with regard to the hotspots. Because of its leading role in development and exploitation of the earth's natural resources, and because of its unmatched wealth and strength, the United States can justly be expected to carry much of the load for the entire planet in preserving biodiversity. But would it? Would the United States, in essence, pay reparations to the planet for our misdeeds, from which have benefitted enormously in the economic and political arenas, and which have created in us a duty to spare the world more of the same kind of devastation that we used to help us grow rich? These questions lead to the next analogy.

The second layer of analogy is more modern. In her epic novel *Atlas Shrugged*,[13] Ayn Rand argued that self-interest is the force that moves the world. She viewed the relatively few innovative, visionary, entrepreneurial individuals as the key to the effective functioning of human societies. Driven by selfish considerations, such people were collectively portrayed as the Atlas that supports the whole planet. In the book, when governments interfered too much with their activities, the entrepreneurs eventually ceased to provide their vital spark, and the system broke down. In effect, Atlas shrugged under the terrible weight he was asked to bear, and the earth shook with violent upheaval.

Is the United States the modern Atlas? Will Atlas shrug under the burden of carrying hotspots preservation on his shoulders, reject the burden of paying reparations for past misdeeds, and refuse to bear the load? Or will our moral sense and the prospect of a share of the profits—direct or indirect—to be derived from present and future economically valuable commodities that emerge from the hotspots be sufficient to motivate and sustain the long-suffering but self-interested Atlas? As I have established, the myriad species, known and unknown to humans, contained within the hotspots may hold the secrets to unimaginable new benefits in medicine, food, ecosystem services, genetic engineering, and other potentially lucrative fields.[14] It may be that self-interest in the discovery and exploitation of these new sources of wealth can overcome the reluctance of Atlas to shoulder the hotspots, once the facts are more widely known.[15]

Certainly there is ample cause for pessimism. A great deal would need to be done to persuade the American taxpayers to foot the bill for another major conservation/environmental program, especially one that will deal almost entirely with other nations. In the current political climate, no president or Congress is apt to champion VEPA to the voters in the United States, given all the difficulty in maintaining support even for environmental protection within their home country. There will always be many other competing proposals for the federal budget, from A to Z, from artistic support to zoo grants, and many of these will appear to be of much more immediate concern and benefit to the American people.

However, there is some evidence to the contrary. In enacting the Tropical Forest Conservation Act of 1998,[16] Congress determined that the United States should protect tropical forests because they benefit humankind through biodiversity, agricultural resources, balancing global climate, and regulating hydroelectric cycles, and recognized that one of the causes of rampant deforestation is the enormous debt load carried by some poorer countries, which impels them to exploit their tropical forest resources.[17] The Tropical Forest Conservation Act is intended to protect tropical forests by alleviating debt in qualifying countries and to target money for the protection of tropical forests, using "debt for nature swaps." Although hampered by numerous qualifications unrelated to biodiversity issues,[18] dependent on continuing appropriations of necessary and meaningful amounts of debt-forgiveness funds by Congress, and largely left to the discretion of the president of the United States, this statute is at least a step in the right direction. It stands as proof that the United States is aware of both the value of global biodiversity and the power of economic incentives to drive appropriate remedial measures in other sovereign nations, just as economic conditions have been a powerful force driving poorer nations to overexploit their natural resources.[19] It is encouraging to note that the 1998 act was overwhelmingly approved by the House and passed the Senate with unanimous consent.

The Tropical Forest Conservation Act authorizes the president to allow eligible countries to use debt swaps, buybacks,[20] or debt reduction/restructuring[21] in exchange for protecting threatened tropical forests on a sustained basis. The president can use the act to reduce some bilateral government-to-government debt owed to the United States under the Foreign Assistance Act of 1981 or Title I of the Agricultural Trade Development and Assistance Act of 1954, or to restructure debt to an amount equal to or lower than its asset value. The Secretary of State is empowered to negotiate these bilateral agreements. In return, each of the recipient nations is to put its own money (in local currency, as opposed to the usually required hard currency) into a tropical forest fund to pay for preservation, restoration, and maintenance of their forests. The act allows private organizations/NGOs to contribute their funds as well in what are called "three-party swaps."[22]

The Tropical Forest Conservation Act attempts to ensure accountability through establishment of an administrative body within each beneficiary country. This group is to consist of one or more U.S. government officials, one or more persons appointed by the recipient country's government, and representatives of environmental, community development, scientific, academic, and forestry organizations of the beneficiary country. These groups are all overseen by the preexisting Enterprise for Americas Initiative Board, which was expanded by four new members under the act.

The act was reauthorized in 2001, through fiscal year 2004, an indication of some initial successes, the continuing support of Congress, and the endorsement of President George W. Bush.[23] The first actual debt-for-nature agreement under the act was concluded in 2000, with Bangladesh, and with Belize, Thailand, and El Salvador following close behind in 2001. Several more nations have expressed significant interest in negotiating their own agreements. Between enactment and February 2002, $24.8 million had been used under the act to restructure loan agreements in four countries.[24] The reauthorized act has appropriations of $50 million, $75 million, and $100 million for fiscal years 2002, 2003, and 2004 respectively—a sizable increase from the $13 million appropriated for both fiscal year 2000 and 2001.[25]

There is the potential for much more to be done with debt-for-nature swaps, with the important hotspots nations of Brazil and Peru indebted to the United States in an amount totaling over $1 billion each,[26] although some analysts have criticized debt-for-nature swaps as doing little actually to diminish the rate of deforestation and natural exploitation in developing countries.[27] Also, the swaps have been faulted for being inadequately enforced (particularly in three-party debt swap situations), generating insufficient money to make a significant improvement in the environment, and possibly infringing on national sovereignty.[28] But for our purposes, irrespective of its limitations, the Tropical Forest Conservation Act is noteworthy because it demonstrates contemporary congressional and presidential recognition of

1. the vital importance of tropical biodiversity;
2. the role of economic hardship in spurring destructive development and exploitation of key habitats in other nations; and
3. the utility of providing positive incentives for host nations to implement meaningful conservationist reforms.

These same factors could spell a favorable climate for VEPA at the highest levels of American government. But what about the voters? How would VEPA play in Peoria, or in its sister cities from Madagascar to New Caledonia?

Fair or not, many people would be skeptical of VEPA because of the perception that other federal conservation and environmental laws have been ineffective, inefficient, counterproductive, and/or wasteful. The various flaws in the command-and-control panoply of statutes such as the ESA have generated considerable resistance to environmental regulation. Even a law along the lines of VEPA, which is specifically designed to avoid these mistakes of the past, would likely be lumped in with the tried-and-failed bunch and rejected out of hand.

Of course, there are responses to this opposition. In this chapter I will posit the Hotspots Wager and its accompanying decision matrix as a method of analyzing the issue of whether to pay for hotspots preservation.[29] If decision makers gather sufficient information about the hotspots phenomenon, especially the potential tangible value to be derived from the biodiversity at risk, and consider it in light of the Hotspots Wager, they may recognize that a significant benefit is likely to come to the United States if we take meaningful action. Properly understood, hotspots preservation is not entirely altruistic, even if funded solely by the United States; ultimately, all nations can reasonably expect to benefit, and dominant economic superpowers such as the United States would be apt to reap their traditionally large share. But this analysis requires patience, vision, and a long-term perspective. These are three commodities that are not always found in abundance in people, whether politicians or the general public. Of course, the fact that you are reading this book is virtually conclusive evidence that you are an exception to the rule.

The hotspots legislation I have proposed would face formidable political opposition, both in the United States and in the other nations VEPA would affect. The reasons for this opposition center around the same factors that render hotspots so important and so elusive. To illustrate, I will return to the metaphor of the black box.

Americans are in the position of a person who is comfortably well-off in terms of creature comforts and is asked to contribute significantly to the aid of numerous less-fortunate individuals, each of whom is in possession of a black box. This hypothetical prosperous American is already accustomed to paying burdensome taxes, with a substantial portion of those taxes going to people in other countries. Hotspots legislation would compel this person to dig even deeper into deep pockets to compensate foreigners—some would say bribe them—not to harm their black boxes. Why? Because those black boxes might hold treasures that on multiple tangible and intangible levels might benefit people, might help the environment, and might even be vital to people all over the world. To tax-weary Americans, that might be one or two mights too many.

From the perspective of the other nations in which almost all of the hotspots are situated, there is a different set of practical obstacles. The typical circumstances are those of a poor person who is struggling to feed and clothe the immediate family. This person is wrestling with the bottom levels of Maslow's hierarchy of needs, fighting to obtain and retain even the basics of life. At or near the subsistence level, the person has no time for worrying about the long term, and no room for global concerns. This person has, as perhaps the only possession of much practical value, a black box. At present, the choices are altruistically to preserve and protect the black box and thereby realize virtually no profit from owning it, or to sell or break into and use at least part of the black box to stave off life-threatening privations. Even the acts of preserving and buying insurance covering the black box would cost this person money and resources that can scarcely be spared, and the benefits, if any, of this sacrifice would not redound only or even primarily to the benefit of those at home, but would be enjoyed by the whole world. What would you do in this situation? Probably the same thing millions of other people who live in the hotspots are doing everyday. They do what they must do to feed their families.

To counter the natural tendency to exploit the black boxes for the benefit of self and family, hotspots legislation must make it worthwhile for a poor person/nation to forgo the very real short-term benefits that can be derived from cracking into and selling/using the black boxes and their contents. The legislation must also provide the wherewithal to safeguard the black boxes. And the legislation must make continued exploitation of the black boxes, clearly and demonstrably, the significantly more expensive option. Given the exigencies that confront most of the developing nations, this would require a substantial array of incentives and penalties.

There are two very different sets of haves and have-nots in the world. In terms of material goods and financial wealth, the United States and a few other nations are the haves, with the developing, hotspot-host nations largely empty-pocketed. But in terms of biodiversity richness, especially at the hotspots level, the situation is essentially reversed. The developed nations are the have-nots of biodiversity, while the developing nations are the rich ones. This is in large part the *very result* of the exploitation of biodiversity in which the developed nations have indulged on the road to riches; they have attained material wealth at the cost of their natural resources and formerly immense wildernesses.

In a very real sense, the developed nations have traded their birthright, that is, the once vast natural resources within their boundaries, for a "mess of pottage," the material wealth they now enjoy. The analogy to the biblical Esau[30] is powerful, because the actions of these nations have truly relinquished priceless and timeless treasures in order to satisfy a craving for far more transient gut-level gain. Moreover, the "mess" they have received is indeed a mess in more ways than one—not only a sizable amount of material goods but also a huge and unruly problem. Like Esau, who "despised his birthright,"[31] they have dealt with the wonders of nature as if they were nothing but means to an end, of value only if they could be exchanged for something they can quickly consume.

The developed nations now point the finger of blame at the developing ones that are exploiting their own natural resources, including hotspots, to try to raise their standard of living and enter the community of modern nations. When they do, the response from those poorer lands is entirely predictable and justifiable on the basis of equitable treatment and, if you will, equal opportunity for all nations.

The developing nations accuse their wealthy relatives of hypocrisy for condemning them for doing the same things that brought the "First World" countries to that status. They allege that it is easy for rich nations to spout preservationist sentiments now, because their wilderness areas are already mostly destroyed—forests cut down, rivers dammed, prairies plowed, mountains leveled, soil mined. Developed nations have little to lose by calling for a cease-fire in the war on the wilderness at this point because they have virtually nothing left to shoot at. The developing nations see the First World[32] countries as having made their fortune by exploiting the natural resources that they once found within their territorial boundaries. These nations now want the same advantages for their people—adequate food, health care, sanitation, education, and an economy that can compete in the modern marketplace.

When these poorer nations look at the United States, they see what gains are possible from using, and using up, the natural wonders within their grasp. Why, they ask, should they shoulder all the burdens of preserving hotspots that happen to exist inside their borders, when the entire world would benefit? Why, they ask, should they suffer all the economic deprivation brought on by lost opportunities to sell, cultivate, harvest, clear, mine, or build on the land that is theirs, when that forbearance redounds to the advantage of all the globe's people? Why, they ask, should their national sovereignty not entitle them to just compensation when they perform a highly valuable service for all the peoples of the planet by preserving the hotspots that belong to their nation and to them alone? They correctly assert that the United States did not hesitate to develop its own resources from sea to shining sea as it toiled to become a world power.

Now that the United States has achieved its manifest destiny, we smugly castigate less developed countries for their wanton destruction of rainforests and other key habitats. And why not? We already have our material treasures, purchased largely at the cost of our own hotspots. The onus of preservation today must necessarily fall disproportionately elsewhere, where there are still hotspots remaining, where there is still something to preserve.

The twin national epidemics of convenient myopia and historical amnesia allow the United States and other developed nations to decry the devastation of the world's hotspots while doing nothing to stop it. I have shown that no existing domestic statute in the United States or any other nation, nor any multilateral environmental agreement, is even remotely adequate to save the hotspots. Yet any potentially effective measure such as VEPA would almost certainly encounter huge political opposition. It is easy to anticipate the arguments that would be brought against VEPA: It would be a colossal waste of money that we desperately need to spend at home on social programs, defense, combatting terrorism, or reduction of the national debt. Why should we be the world's zookeeper, especially when we do not even know what species are in the zoo? If hotspots are so important, let the whole world contribute a fair share of the expense for preserving them. Why should we bribe other sovereign nations not to destroy their own countries? The foreign hotspots are an internal problem for those other governments to solve. And how do we know for certain that there are millions of unknown species hidden inside these hotspots, let alone that some of them could be valuable to us now or at some nebulous time in the far-off future? We have better things to do with our tax dollars than gamble them on so much speculation. Other nations do not appreciate all the aid we give them now; why should we give them more?

To be fair, there is some power in the arguments of both the developing nations and the United States. The hotspots pose a problem of great difficulty and complexity, and the solutions are neither readily apparent nor facile. This is precisely why nothing has been done. This is precisely why, if nothing is done, the hotspots will continue to be decimated inexorably until, inevitably, they cease to exist. Yet there is a way to analyze the hotspot issues and all the unknowns in the hotspot preservation equation in a rational manner that takes into account all the areas of uncertainty and the magnitude of the risks and benefits that flow from various circumstances.

THE HOTSPOTS WAGER

With billions of dollars at stake and gigantic consequences possible from certain particularly wise or unwise decisions, how should we choose what to do about hotspots preservation? Table 6.1 is our attempt to simplify the main issues relevant to the question of whether a VEPA-like legal solution to the hotspots puzzle should be implemented. The table distills the primary question marks in the hotspots equation into three unknowns that may never become knowns. These unknowns form the core of most of the objections to VEPA outlined above. In essence, they are

1. the actual extinction risk faced by the species, whether identified or not, within the world's hotspots;
2. the true number of different species that live in the hotspots, including any and all unidentified species; and
3. the "real" practical value of all hotspots species, both known and unknown species, in terms of current or future practical benefit for humans and/or the environment.

Critics would argue that these unknowns probably cannot be ascertained and that in light of so much uncertainty it would be irresponsible and imprudent to risk billions of tax dollars on safeguarding hotspots. Are they right? The table can help us decide.

Obviously, the table is intended as a simplification. We recognize that the true situation as to each unknown, if we could somehow determine it, would be some complex and shifting position along a continuum of possibilities. Nevertheless, for purposes of framing the issues, I have boiled these down to two polar opposites at the extremes of each continuum, either "low" or "high." Anything between these limits would merely be variations on the general theme. Within a given variable, there can also be complicating factors. For instance, some species are at much higher extinction risk than others within any hotspot; some hotspots as a whole are in greater danger than others and/or would cost more to preserve; some species have much more current or future practical value than others; and some hotspots contain far greater numbers of species and/or more valuable species than others. Also, much of the practical value of a particular hotspot could theoretically be confined to one species among the hundreds of thousands that reside therein. Such factors as these could and should be used to craft individually tailored regulations and management plans for each hotspot under VEPA, but they need not detract from our use of the table as an illustrative tool to shape decision making.

One other point deserves explanation. The variable for practical value of all species within hotspots encompasses both identified and unidentified species. It also includes both currently known uses and those that still wait to be discovered or needed. It may be centuries before we learn about certain benefits we could derive from some particular species' genotype or phenotype. Plus, new diseases, new environmental stressors, changed atmospheric conditions, mutations, and other unpredictable future events could be many years away at present, but someday they may confront us, and a previously "insignificant" species could suddenly take on great value by offering the solution. I could have designed the table with separate columns for current and future value of species and/or for known and unknown species, but this would have complicated the table without real gain in utility. Our decisions as to hotspot preservation would not be altered much, if at all, by separating the categories of species value in this manner, so I have placed them in one variable.

The "results" column represents the principal types of consequences that flow from a decision whether to invest heavily in hotspots preservation, depending upon all possible permutations of the three primary unknowns. There are eight different ways in which the true value of three unknowns can be combined, and those eight concatenations yield some dramatically different results. I have used very abbreviated shorthand labels to describe the various possible results, along the lines that might be used in game theory or in analyzing a game of chance in which wagers are placed. I use the terms "first order" and "second order" to denote respectively, in broad terms, the more significant and less significant variants within a particular category of impact.

Let us explain the bad news outcomes first. A "serious error" is a failure to protect hotspots when there is in fact a major extinction risk in general for the species therein but the tangible value of those species overall is low. This is a serious error because presumably some species will go extinct due to our inaction, and they will have intangible value. If there are many unknown species, this value is multiplied greatly, resulting in a "first-order serious error," while if that number is actually low, we have a low multiplier effect and a "second-order serious error."

Similarly, a "grave error" is a failure to protect hotspots when there is in fact both a major extinction risk for whatever number of species live therein and high actual tangible value for those species. This is a grave error because some species will die out that could have provided people or the planet with great benefits, such as cures for disease, valuable genes, ecosystem services, new sources of nutrition, and the like.

The accelerating and potentially catastrophic loss of biodiversity is quite unlike all other environmental threats because it is utterly irreversible.[33] That is why I chose the term "grave error." Unlike air pollution, water pollution, toxic waste dumping, or any other form of environmental harm, the destruction of life is a wrong that can never be righted no matter how much money we spend and no matter how hard we try we cannot resurrect the extinct species, *Jurassic Park* films not withstanding. Once the living product of millions of years of evolutionary refinement is shattered, no subsequent penalties, no matter how severe, can ever restore it. There is no remediation possible,

Table 6.1

Enact VEPA and Fund Major Hotspots Protection?	True Degree of Extinction Risk in Hotspots	True Number of Unknown Species in Hotspots	True Tangible Value of All Species in Hotspots	Results of VEPA Funding Decision
No	Low	Low	Low	Lucky wager, money saved
No	High	Low	Low	Second-order serious error
No	Low	High	Low	Lucky wager, money saved
No	High	High	Low	First-order serious error
No	Low	Low	High	Lucky wager, money saved
No	High	Low	High	Second-order grave error
No	Low	High	High	Lucky wager, money saved
No	High	High	High	First-order grave error
Yes	Low	Low	Low	Unused insurance
Yes	High	Low	Low	Second-order moral victory
Yes	Low	High	Low	Unused insurance
Yes	High	High	Low	First-order moral victory
Yes	Low	Low	High	Unused insurance
Yes	High	Low	High	Second-order jackpot
Yes	Low	High	High	Unused insurance
Yes	High	High	High	First-order jackpot

no cleanup except for the bones. It is a harm without redress, a deficit that can never be recouped, a break beyond repair. Prevention is the only cure.

Again, if there are large numbers of unknown species hidden inside these hotspots, this result is magnified, and we have a "first-order grave error," whereas relatively low numbers of unidentified species yield a low multiplier effect and a "second-order grave error." However, even if, contrary to all indications, there were no unknown species—no species at all remaining to be discovered—both the number and value of the species already identified are incalculably high.

Now for the good news. This comes when we invest in hotspots preservation and the (unknown and unknowable) facts show that this was the right move. A "moral victory" obtains when there is actually a high risk that whatever species exist in the hotspots will become extinct unless we act but the tangible benefits those species offer are relatively low. This is a moral victory because our actions will presumably save some species from extinction, and those species will confer intangible benefits in terms of a sense of well-being, moral satisfaction from having done the right thing, and the like.[34] If there are many unknown species, this is multiplied and we have a "first-order moral victory," while the converse yields a "second-order moral victory." And where our investment in hotspots preservation finds both a high overall risk of extinction for species therein and high tangible overall value for those species, we hit the "jackpot." Our dollars will buy the preservation of species that will pay us back manifold. If there are multitudes of unidentified species in the hotspots, the tangible value of these will be multiplied further, rewarding our investment with a "first-order jackpot," while small numbers of such species would present a "second-order jackpot."

There are two other possible consequences, each of which can spring from four different combinations of variables. If our decision is not to spend significant amounts of tax dollars on hotspots preservation, and it turns out that there is actually a low extinction threat facing the species in the hotspots, we have in effect made a "lucky wager." We have not squandered billions of dollars trying to save species that were not going to go extinct anyway. The sky was not falling, the earth's resiliency enabled it to weather the storm, and life found a way to endure—it was all a false alarm, and we were right not to throw money at a nonexistent problem. This is true regardless of the number of unknown species in existence within the hotspots or the practical value all the species in the hotspots, both identified and unidentified, hold for people and the planet. There is no need to spend money saving something that does not need to be saved.[35]

Along similar lines, if we do opt to fund VEPA-like legislation to the tune of billions of dollars, it might again be the case that there is no great threat to the existence of whatever species inhabit the hotspots. Under these circumstances, the money we spend protecting the hotspots could be considered wasted, because we did not really need to be concerned about the extinction situation.[36] More accurately, I choose to call it "unused insurance," because it is somewhat akin to money we personally spend on various forms of insurance—life, health, homeowners, automobile collision—for any period in which we do not actually need to file a claim. We spend insurance money to cover ourselves for harmful, even disastrous, eventualities that might befall us. The fact that we may not suffer any misfortune that leads to a payout from our insurance policy does not mean that we were foolish to buy insurance in the first place. After all, how were we to know that we would be so lucky? The saying is "Better safe than sorry."

If we could accurately foretell the future in our own lives, we would never buy insurance until shortly before we actually will suffer a loss that needs to be covered. But we can never know this, and for that lack of a crystal ball all insurance companies are quite grateful. No, we must pay for insurance dutifully every year because we will not be able to predict when we will need it. To skimp, to do without insurance, is literally to live life on the edge of disaster and gamble at extremely high stakes—so much so that, in some instances, we are *required by law* to maintain certain current levels of insurance. If the law can demand that we buy insurance for ourselves, one life, home, and vehicle at a time, then why not require insurance for the hotspots, which are in large part the life of the world?

If we examine the table and all of the ways in which the variables can be combined, we can develop a game theory for optimal decision making regarding the hotspots question. The results column holds the key. The dramatic outcomes follow from the situation wherein the hotspots are in fact at high risk and contain species (known or unknown) with great tangible value; where these factors are combined with a third factor, large numbers of unknown species nestled within the hotspots, we find the most extreme outcomes of all.

None of the other results approach the magnitude of either a "jackpot" or a "grave error." Although VEPA could easily cost several billions of dollars each year, neither the "needless" expenditure nor the "lucky" saving of such amounts of money is on the same level of importance as a jackpot or a grave error. A jackpot would mean incalculable benefits to people and planet for countless years, while a grave error would spell disaster from irretrievably and permanently lost solutions to major health and environmental problems. Similarly, where "only" intangible value is available from hotspot species, saving or losing these species in numbers large or small can be a matter of considerable importance, but of a different and lower order of magnitude than a jackpot or grave error.

What would a rational decision maker do? If one accepts the premises, the decision whether to fund hotspots legislation is similar to the situation at issue in Pascal's wager.[37] We have two main options, and some unbridgeable gaps in our knowledge of crucial facts. The consequences for guessing wrong and making the wrong wager are far more momentous on one side than on the other.

First, consider the less consequential outcomes. The worst that can happen if we fund hotspots legislation where there is only a low extinction risk is that those billions of dollars are spent to protect species that would not have gone extinct even without our intervention. Certainly, those funds could have been spent on other things that might have yielded significant benefits, but most likely they would have been no more efficacious than any other tax dollars. This is arguably a negative outcome, but no worse than any other governmental spending that eventually proves to be suboptimal. In fact, even this is really a positive outcome, in that some of the VEPA funds will go to help impoverished people in other nations improve their lives—essentially, VEPA is a global economic stimulus package with some conservationist strings attached. Thus, even if very little biodiversity is aided by VEPA dollars, there will still be a human benefit, and that cannot be dismissed as unimportant.

The corollary of this is the impact of a decision to refrain from funding VEPA, where we find that no disasters result because there was only a low risk of extinction. We would have that money available to spend on other governmental programs or on debt reduction, but again, probably no world-changing benefits would result. This is a positive outcome, but not of the earthshaking variety, literally or figuratively. And the benefits to the American taxpayer must be weighed against the counterbalancing loss of economic stimulus funds to the poor people in the hotspots nations. The money we save is money that will not go to those who need it most.

It may seem strange to dismiss either the expenditure or saving of billions of tax dollars annually as inconsequential, but relative to the most extreme results possible, that assessment is exactly right. This is because there is, in effect, *no limit* to the magnitude of either a "grave error" or a "jackpot" result. The magnitude in either direction approaches infinity.

A grave error situation is the ultimate example of the "penny wise, pound foolish" syndrome expanded to a global scale. If we gamble that the hotspots are not facing a major extinction threat and that the tangible value of the species within them is not high, there is a chance that we could be wrong. We would do nothing to stop the extinction of species, perhaps millions of species, that hold the keys to conquering deadly diseases (some of which may not yet even exist), improving food production, reducing toxic pesticide use, and a vast array of other vital benefits. It would be difficult to place a dollar value on such losses, but many human lives could easily be part of the casualty list. If the 21st century counterpart to penicillin were one of the lost opportunities, billions of dollars per year could not begin to measure the gravity of our error. Our decision not to fund hotspots preservation would be literally dead wrong.

In the same way, the upside potential of a decision to protect hotspots is essentially unbounded. If our funds block the extinction of numerous species with great practical value, we could save the source of the next penicillin and many other colossal benefits from disappearing. If again we liken VEPA to insurance, this would be an insurance premium well spent indeed. No one could accurately assign a dollar value to such treasures. This "wager" on hotspots preservation, with all the variables aligned in this way, could be the wisest choice humans have ever made with regard to the environment, an infinitely worthwhile decision.

This set of options is analogous to those weighed in Pascal's wager. We have basically two choices—to fund hotspots preservation or not.[38] There are important unknowns relevant to the issue of which option is preferable. The unknowns cannot be known, at least not without a huge amount of work over a long period of time. But we do know that a decision to protect hotspots has the possibility of paying immense, even infinite dividends, with only relatively minor negative consequences under the worst-case scenario. We also know that a decision not to protect hotspots could lead to horrific, nearly infinite harm to people and this planet but could only offer comparatively small rewards even under the best of circumstances. In this situation, the rational decision would be to protect the hotspots, judiciously applying a carefully measured amount of our limited conservation resources on a priority basis to those areas where they will do the most good. This option eliminates the possibility of ruin while opening the door to limitless gain.

Could the hotspots wager matrix actually change minds and make a difference? The antidote for the inertia that has so firmly mired hotspot protection in the mud of inaction is education. The hotspots concept is still very new, even within the scientific community. This book is the first within the legal community to focus entirely on hotspots. And political leaders, legislators, and members of the general public are unlikely to have had much if any exposure to the hotspots concept as yet. The evidence as to the immense importance of hotspots and the threats to their continued viability is formidable and would probably prove persuasive to many people if they were aware of it, particularly if they view all the factors in context, along the lines of the proposed variation of Pascal's wager. There is much work to be done in that regard, and there is no time to waste.

Yet all is not lost, and ideas do have the power to transform history. In the same pivotal year of 1776 in which the United States was born, Adam Smith published his famous and tremendously influential book, *An Inquiry into the Nature and Causes of the Wealth of Nations*. That pivotal book gave wings to key ideas about the prerequisites for "the necessaries and conveniencies of life" that Smith believed constituted the wealth of a nation. The United States and other nations pursued Smith's ideas and shaped their political, legal, and economic systems accordingly. Now, more than two centuries later, the world must deal with some of the same challenges that existed in Smith's time, but also with some new, dramatically different, issues on a global scale.

The wealth of nations is the real topic of this book. We have discussed the recurring theme in which, nation by nation, the preservation of biodiversity has been subordinated to the pursuit of wealth—economic wealth, in the form of more income, more industrialization, more infrastructure. But today we should understand that this planet's irreplaceable biodiversity is a also very real form of wealth, which may be as necessary as any other treasure for the preservation and progression of humankind. The hotspots are the crown jewels of planet Earth, the wealth of nations in its rarest and most precious form. And it is quite fitting that Adam Smith crafted his famous title in the plural, using the word "nations" rather than "nation," because the hotspots must be understood as belonging in some sense to all the world, all nations, all peoples.

They are our mutual inheritance, and our mutual responsibility. If the leaders and citizens of the world's nations can be shown the evidence of the promise and perils of the hotspots, the enigmatic black boxes that grace some of the most exotic places on the globe, then there may still be time for another great shift in the course of civilization.

ALTERNATIVES TO VEPA

What if VEPA cannot be enacted? If Atlas shrugs off this added burden and opts for respite, what else might be done? Other measures might also further the cause of hotspots preservation, if those who hold the keys choose to use them. Some of these keys are in the hands of governments, or groups of governments, while others belong to individuals.

A proponent of Critical Legal Studies (CLS) theory[39] would argue that the World Heritage Convention (WHC), VEPA, or any legal instrument, be it domestic statute or international treaty, is in and of itself of at best minimal utility as an outcome determining factor. The aforementioned realities are consistent with CLS thought, because they spotlight the impotence of international laws such as the WHC to (1) compel nations to sign and ratify, and (2) induce signatories to take actions which they are not otherwise willing to take. Nations may sign on for reasons very divergent from the purposes of the convention, e.g., to curry favor with other nations, to appease political factions at home, or to use the treaty as an instrument to extract benefits from other nations. Once a State Party, a nation may comply with the provisions of the treaty to a greater or lesser extent along a broad continuum, but it will not do so because the treaty compels this outcome. Rather, it will take actions in some degree consistent or inconsistent with the convention's strictures because it deems it in the nation's self-interest to do so. This can be because its leaders fear the disapproval of other nations, or they expect more resources to flow into their nation than out of it, or they see intangible benefits to their nation arising from a public perception of it as a good global citizen.

CLS theory questions whether rules or laws actually decide cases even when they have apparently clear, precisely defined meaning and effective teeth, i.e., vigorous enforcement mechanisms with real penalties for noncompliance. There is often, perhaps always, a way around the rule for a judge or jury looking for a different answer from the one the rule seems to mandate.

The judge or jury can decide, either explicitly or sub rosa, that the key terms are not so clearly defined after all. There could be legal precedent external to the text of the law/rule that must be superimposed on its terms, whether from the common law of other cases or from other codified laws. Maybe there are multiple provisions of the same law in conflict, requiring a creative solution that harmonizes the competing sections. Or the unique facts of the instant case (and the facts are always unique to each case, in some detail or another distinguishable from all other cases no matter how superficially similar) must be dealt with on their own merit, because they implicate concerns unanticipated by the text itself. Perhaps the rule is clear, but under the circumstances of the case public policy requires that an exception be carved out. Or the rule was created too long ago and/or under conditions significantly different from those that confront us today, and thus the law must bend and change with the times, lest the dead hand of the past rule us from the grave. This incantation of excuses could be extended indefinitely, but further examples are not needed; one gets the picture.

These ideas, which have considerable validity even as to the internal domestic law of a given nation state, are even more powerful when applied to the international law context. In international law, there is no sovereign with the power to dictate particular policies or procedures or to attempt to ensure they are followed. There is no universally recognized judicial body empowered to decide disputes and impose enforceable outcomes on unwilling litigants. There is no standing army or functional police force charged with and capable of enforcing the law and punishing malefactors. Unlike the states of the Union with regard to federal law, the nations of the world are able to determine unilaterally whether a particular treaty applies to them, by deciding whether to become and remain a State Party. And although there is a concept of customary international law analogous to the common law of an individual nation, absent an efficacious judicial and enforcement system it is quite difficult to remedy violations.

Attempts to rectify some of these shortcomings have been sporadic, controversial, and of dubious efficacy. The recent experience with the International Criminal Court (ICC) is illustrative. The United States has refused to agree to allow its citizens to be subject to ICC jurisdiction, partially out of fears that American military servicemembers could be brought before the ICC for politically motivated prosecutions arising out of the proper performance of their duties outside the United States. As a result, the United States has decided not to play the ICC game, and there is little or nothing that the other nations of the world can do about it, individually or collectively. It is as if the governor and state legislature of Wyoming decided that its citizens would not to be bound by the decisions of the Federal District Court in that state, and then got away with it. This is inevitable in a world with many independent nation states and no overall government.

World government is not a new idea. The dream of uniting the entire planet under one unified, comprehensive, consistent form of rule is as old as humanity. Our history has recorded noteworthy examples of people who actually attempted to reify this dream. Often, great leaders justified the steps they took by asseverating that world government, with them as the head, was necessary to effectuate such lofty stated ambitions as ending war, spreading civilization to all peoples, bringing the true religion to all unbelievers, and facilitating prosperity and peace across the globe. Some may have used such rationales as rationalization, mere window dressing for the ugly truth, but others evidently held these beliefs very sincerely and were convinced that they were on the side of the angels in their work.

And what work it was! The utopian ideal of One World, united and peaceful, harmonious and Edenic, has in reality only been seriously pursued by running the rapids in rivers of blood.

Alexander the Great came as close as anyone to unifying the whole world, at least that part of it that was known to him. Schooled by no less a teacher than Aristotle, he explained that his goal was brotherly love and enlightened civilization for all. But his phenomenal successes in bringing many peoples together under one ruler (i.e., Alexander the Great himself) were achieved through conquest, not conciliation. With sword and spear, bristling phalanxes and brilliant tactics, extraordinary personal courage and much good luck, he annihilated far larger armies, repeatedly, methodically, and brutally. Mighty Persia and many other nations fell to him and joined, involuntarily, his brotherhood of love. Alas, his unsurpassed military triumphs were counterbalanced by his paranoia, megalomania, delusions of divinity, and cruelty. The world government he established did not long outlive its founder's very brief but eventful lifetime.

To a greater or lesser extent, Alexander the Great's example was followed by a succession of others who had visions of a united world. Julius Caesar, Saladin, Napoleon Bonaparte, and Adolf Hitler are among those who longed for the good (as they saw it) that could be done in a world ruled by a single overarching government. The millions of human lives lost or ruined in the process were seen by them as a price that must be paid for such a pearl. Whether one views these people as heroes, villains, or something else depends on one's perspective, but two things are clear. All of the most notable efforts to create One World were extremely bloody. And all of them ultimately failed at some point, despite some remarkable victories along the way.

If there could be a world government today, one might envision it as a global version of the American experiment, with a republican form of government, free and open elections, a system of "federalism" extrapolated to a worldwide scale that allowed for some diversity of approach from nation-state to nation-state, the universal rule of law, and vigorous protection of fundamental human rights for all people. Peace would be maintained by a single military under one leader, albeit with troops drawn from all over the planet. Compliance with the law would be enforced through a global police force under the overall direction of one person.

Under such a world government, the applicability of legal instruments such as the WHC would no longer be hostage to the voluntary choices of nations to sign, or to comply after signing. Once enacted into law, they would apply universally, and would be enforced with real force. If there were disputes as to the meaning of a term, or the proper way to interpret a requirement, they would be resolved by a body with the jurisdiction and authority to ensure that its judgments are followed.

But reality continues to intrude upon our dreams, and wishful thinking is often heavy on the wishful and light on the thinking. It is likely that all serious attempts to unite the world will be violently launched in the time-honored fashion by bloodthirsty, ruthless lunatics, fanatics, and racists, not by peace-loving, biodiversity-hugging, global versions of Mister Rogers who stroll together into the woods and rainforests to hold hands and sing "Kumbaya." Even if, somehow, the nations could be brought together, how could they be kept together for long? Powerful, ancient centripetal forces of nationalism, tribalism, and core differences in religion, culture, race, ethnicity, language, and political tradition would constantly pull on the components, prying them apart again. Absent an unprecedented transformation in the nature of the world and its people, what could possibly bind the nations together beyond the near term? The greatest empires of the world's history eventually crumbled (often very quickly, as with Alexander's vast conquests), and brute force cannot be the permanent bond that overcomes our fragmentational propensities.[40] And so, we are left again with hordes of incalcitrant cats to herd, if we can.

It may be discomfiting for some people to contemplate the powerlessness of international law to direct the most momentous actions of the world's nations. As young children, we were taught the importance of rules—rules set for us by our parents, rules to playground games, rules to games that came in a box, schoolroom games, God's commandments—and the very real consequences of disobeying them. We chafed and resisted at times, but there was a sense of comfort, certitude, predictability, and reliability that the rules provided for us. They made us feel safe. If we followed the rules, everything would be fine. This aura of security made life more manageable and less threatening. Certainty was a palliative for our fears.

But as we grew older we learned that some, perhaps all, rules were less clear and less predictable than we had first been taught. We discovered that sometimes we could get away with breaking our parents' rules, and that the rules to our playground games could be altered on the fly by the consent of the players. We even found that people could disagree about what the rules meant and what they required in any particular situation. Unless there was an ultimate authority (such as our mother, or God), disputes over rule interpretation could become an impasse that halted the entire enterprise. Without a definitive, powerful arbiter, the rules were subject to as many divergent interpretations as there were individuals involved.

We learned, eventually, that the rules called "laws" by adults had many of the same features as the other rules in our lives. Laws were not the unquestioned and unquestionable, omnipotent, for-our-own-good, never-to-be-broken Laws with a capital "L" that we were first taught they were. They could be unfair, unclear, contradictory, difficult to enforce, and inconsistently interpreted or applied by judges and police officers. And there were some things that laws (now with a lower-case "L") could not do, no matter how hard people tried to make them do it, and regardless of how much we longed for a deus ex machina to solve our worst problems. Laws could not end violent crime, stop all drug abuse, or make people be good to one another. The world became a much more challenging, frustrating, frightening, uncertain, and unsafe place for us.

It seems wrong that the law should not be able to protect the hotspots. We have so many laws, in so many nations, all devoted to tackling a piece of the problem! There are entire treaties and conventions, like the WHC and the CBD, that are specifically intended to save living treasures such as the hotspots. Why have all these laws and all the people who wrote them and live with them been unable to do more to stop the devastation of our planet's most vital living jewels? Why, we have international laws with the very words "biological diversity" in their title! We have many statutes, and many police officers and park rangers, in many countries, all pointing at the problem and commanding it to go away! What is wrong?

What is wrong is that reality has crashed our party. Laws, in individual nations and in great aggregations of nations, have not been capable of saving the hotspots. Neither have they ended war, eliminated starvation, banished genocide, swept away terrorism, wiped out all slavery, stamped out religious persecution, or halted the brutal degradation of women throughout the world. If we no longer expect our parents' rules to be the final word in our lives, why do we persist in our child-like faith that laws can be a panacea to the world's greatest tragedies? Although we often speak of "the rule of law," it is not truly law that rules—it is people, power, and politics, all fueled by money. Law can guide, inform, inspire, and place some limits on each of these forces, but it cannot rule in and of itself.

Top-down, command-and-control, stick-wielding laws can be effective under some limited circumstances, if they are clearly and unambiguously written, free of escape hatches, vigorously enforced by sufficiently numerous, vigilant, and powerful people, and subject to the final interpretative rulings of an authoritative and power-laden ultimate judge. This situation might present itself at times in some individual nations or empires—unfortunately, often ones markedly low on the civil liberties scale. It does not and cannot ever happen on a global scale, at least not unless and until the world is drastically transformed. And if it takes another Alexander the Great to do the job, with world government and its laws imposed at the point of a sword, we are much better off with things as chaotic as they are.

This does not mean that laws are worthless. It does not mean that noble efforts such as the WHC and CBD should be discarded. It only means that we must use laws, including these, in whatever way they can be most useful. If the WHC can teach people to value the hotspots, and shape world opinion as to the significance of hotspots preservation, that will be a very real, very valuable contribution. We should not be chagrined, as disillusioned children, to learn that the law cannot solve all our problems. We can be realists, and use the law as one instrument that, along with many others, can make a difference.

The WHC, in its current form, still has value as one tool for hotspots preservation. But, as we have seen, it is primarily a tool of education and motivation, not a tool of direct action. It is more akin to a pointer than a billy club. And, as Jerry Seinfeld might say, "Not that there's anything wrong with it." By offering the prospect of official, highly visible, international recognition of the hotspots as some of the most precious natural treasures of the entire planet, by prodding further scientific and technical research into them, and by facilitating targeted fundraising for their rescue, the WHC can do more to save the hotspots than any other extant international law. It is by no means a perfect, all-encompassing solution, but neither is it inconsequential. For want of anything better, and with no deus ex machina in sight, it is a place to begin.

I have argued in this book and elsewhere for a new United States statute, VEPA, that could effectively deal with the hotspots crisis better than more conventional international legal means.[41] By allowing the United States to take the lead, and by providing much-needed substantial financial incentives and technical support where it is most needed, VEPA would avoid some of the intractable problems that have stopped international law from saving the hotspots. However, I understand that my proposal faces formidable practical obstacles no less daunting than those in the path of using the WHC to guide more progressive international preservationist actions. At least for the near term, the WHC is the best we have. If we can use it to help teach people about the value of the hotspots and change minds, we might succeed in changing the gloomy fate that now awaits so many of these global treasures, and perhaps enable the enactment of VEPA or an effective alternative in the future. We cannot afford to let the better be the enemy of the good, for perfection in the law is as impossible as resurrecting from extinction the species we have already lost as the hotspots dwindle away.

There are also non-legalistic options familiar to anyone who has studied the actions of the United States and the international response to various disfavored actions within other nations. When a nation, either officially or unofficially, takes citizens of another nation hostage, or sponsors deadly terrorist assaults, or attacks an embassy, or invades another nation, or engages in egregious human rights abuses, a menu of responses is available. They may be implemented in combination or one at a time. Often there is a graduated response, in which ever more serious measures are employed if the offending nation fails to react appropriately to less severe alternatives. The following are the standard options:

1. Shame.
   This includes expressions of disapproval, orally or in writing, by the head of state or by diplomats. These can begin as private actions, and shift into the public sphere if private measures fail. In the public area, they may be addressed directly to the offending nation or simply made one of the topics in a speech or press conference addressed to a general audience. Private citizens also can contribute in this area by organizing and participating in protests, demonstrations, letter-writing campaigns, and other forms of political action.

2. Most Favored Nation Status/Trade Sanctions.
   A nation can use Most Favored Nation (MFN) status as a tool to shape the behavior of other nations with which it deals. MFN recognition affords a nation tangible economic advantages in its international commercial transactions, which can mean sizable increases in revenues. Because of this, a nation may condition a new MFN determination on certain actions by the other nation. Similarly, where the offending nation already enjoys MFN status, the other nation or nations may threaten to revoke MFN status unless the offending nation mends its ways.

   There is also the possibility of employing specific trade measures, such as sanctions, as a means of influence. These are legally and politically controversial, but trade sanctions have been employed successfully in several instances to obtain positive environmental results.[42] Unfortunately, GATT does constitute an obstacle to such environmental trade measures, as we have discussed, and it is somewhat unclear exactly how ETMs must be designed in order to pass muster under current WTO/GATT interpretations of the law.

3. Divestment/Boycott.
   Private entities within any nation may resolve to refuse to do business with their counterparts in an offending nation and/or divest themselves of stock holdings and other investments in business organizations therein. Reinvestment is conditioned upon a suitable response. Corporations, educational institutions, nonprofit organizations, and individual citizens may collectively put meaningful economic pressure on the offending nation in this manner. Such efforts were partially responsible for ending apartheid in South Africa, for example.

4. United Nations Pronouncements.
   The United Nations may resolve to single out one or more individual nations for official criticism. Such international obloquy, although intangible, may be an important motivator for some nations. This may be particularly so in the case of relatively new nations that may crave international respect; the prospect of UN disapproval might move such nations to modify their disfavored behavior.

5. United Nations Sanctions.
   The UN may impose formal sanctions on nations. These can take a variety of forms and may be more effective than the actions of any one nation. The tangible impact of UN sanctions can hit an offending nation in the pocketbook as well as in the ego.

6. Humanitarian Intervention.
   This type of direct action can be undertaken either by an individual nation or by the UN. In what the U.S. military calls "operations other than war" (OOTW),

military forces can be deployed for missions such as peacekeeping, nation build-ing, and other humanitarian concerns. Protection of the hotspots could fit into the OOTW category, and ground troops may well be necessary for effective implementation of comprehensive preservation measures in large, remote, and dangerous hotspots. Of course, there is often public opinion against any commit-ment of troops, and the nation in need would have to be receptive, but under some circumstances it is the only way to accomplish an important objective.

A UN force, or a stand-alone U.S. force, would be the most effective—if not the only—means by which we could ensure that funds are being spent for the in-tended purposes and that applicable preservation measures are being actively en-forced. From the comfort of our ivory towers it may be difficult for us to imagine the daunting practical challenges that confront any efforts to conduct meaningful protective operations in some of the developing nations. Particularly where species of animals or plants are present that yield high rewards for poachers or illegal log-gers, the situation is akin to a brutal, all-out guerrilla war. Heavily armed poachers and loggers who have a great financial incentive to reject all opposing laws, includ-ing the law of armed conflict, can be an overwhelming opponent for the domestic law enforcement forces of developing nations. Outside assistance is essential under such circumstances—unpopular and highly controversial, but essential.

Means of persuasion such as these can be directed at various desired out-comes with regard to the hotspots. The goal may be to induce individual nations to sign on to one or more international legal conventions, such as the CBD, WHC, Ramsar, or CITES, in the hope that this may at least incre-mentally lead to better protection of their portions of the hotspots. Of course, the United States is not in a position to exercise effective moral per-suasion in this regard, at least in the case of the CBD, even if it were inclined to do so, because it has not even ratified this convention itself. This creates a serious leadership gap at precisely the point where global suasion is most es-sential. And even if the United States were prepared to launch a multipronged diplomatic campaign to prod the world toward hotspots preservation, it would be far preferable to use this political will to enact and implement VEPA. These other measures have long been available and have not been used. They have not worked, and even if pursued with great vigor, they would not be a good substitute for VEPA.

For the many nations that are already states parties to the biodiversity-related conventions, outside pressure could be brought to encourage them to abide by their preexisting commitments and to strive actively to conform to the spirit as well as the letter of the law. However, as we have seen, these international legal mechanisms are burdened with caveats, exceptions, reser-vations, excessive discretion, gaps in coverage, narrowly defined ambits, and/or the lack of solid enforcement provisions, and thus would not be a satisfactory solution to the hotspots problem no matter how many nations ratified them. There is ample if not excessive wiggle room within these con-ventions that enable states parties to avoid meaningful restrictions on their capacity to expand and develop their economies at the expense of natural resources such as the hotspots. Only if signatories could be persuaded to view their treaty commitments expansively and proactively in furtherance of scientifically sound preservationist goals could these international agreements serve as a satisfactory solution to the hotspots problem.

Alternatively, or in combination with this approach, international persuasion might be focused on enactment of more stringent natural resource legislation, one nation at a time, or, more likely, enhanced enforcement of the laws already on the books. I have noted in Chapter 3 the many biodiversity-related laws currently in force in the hotspots nations, particularly in the area of parks, reserves, refuges, and other natural enclaves. In theory, these laws could serve as the legal instrument that enables each nation to set aside additional land within its hotspot, with little or no amendment to the basic statutory scheme. Perhaps in response to international pressure, some countries could be moved to use their existing laws to carve out more territory for wilderness preserves, wildlife refuges, and the like, consistent with the characteristics and boundaries of each individual hotspot. In most if not all nations that harbor hotspots, a significant amount of undeveloped land is still both part of the hotspot and currently devoid of legal protection, so there is ample room for improvement along these lines.

But there are good, practical reasons why these nations have not already set aside a larger portion of their hotspots. Most fundamentally, it costs money. There are costs associated with erecting and maintaining fences, ranger stations, and other structures needed for a protected area. It is expensive to hire, train, arm and equip the extra people necessary to manage and guard the enclaves. And there may be immense lost-opportunity costs incurred as the nations forgo lucrative logging, mining, farming, grazing, and other developmental enterprises they could otherwise pursue in the regions to be set aside.

Some of these obstacles are identical to the concerns that have resulted in lax enforcement of the laws already on the books in many hotspots nations. Many of these countries are poor and struggling to develop, with shortages in the basic necessities of life. Money is scarce. There are often dire threats to the survival of the government, if not the people themselves, from civil wars, foreign wars, tribal conflicts, famine, rampant disease, and the like. Widespread corruption and weak commitment to the rule of law only exacerbate these plagues in many nations. The international community might exert pressure on developing nations to support more vigorous enforcement of their pre-existing natural resource protection laws, particularly in the case of protected areas that contain portions of the hotspots. But no amount of pressure will squeeze so much as one drop of blood out of a skeleton. If the resources simply are not there, or if more immediate and urgent human-survival threats demand every spare dime, what chance is there of increased spending on hotspots preservation? The missing ingredient is money, and no one is ready to provide enough of it to the right people in the right places.

For all of these reasons, this ad hoc, piecemeal method of international persuasive methods is unlikely to yield satisfactory results on a global level to preserve the womb of the unknown species. It may bring some success in individual cases, which is always better than nothing, but something much more comprehensive must be done, or the hotspots are destined to burn out after all. The political obstacles must be overcome, and the people must generate the will to change course. The hotspots phenomenon deserves and demands a unified, consistent, effective legal response. VEPA could be that response.

NOTES

1. C.R. Margules and R.L. Pressey, *Systematic Conservation Planning*, 405 Nature 243 (2000).

2. *See* Kathryn S. Fuller, Foreword to INTERNATIONAL WILDLIFE TRADE: A CITES SOURCEBOOK at vii (Ginette Hemley, ed., 1994) (stating that approximately $2–3 billion of world trade in wildlife annually comes from illegal transactions).

3. *See generally* Susan H. Bragdon, *National Sovereignty and Global Environmental Responsibility: Can The Tension Be Reconciled for the Conservation of Biological Diversity?*, 33 Harv. Int'l L.J. 381 (1992) (suggesting that effective conservation of global biodiversity will require modification of traditional principles of national sovereignty); Christopher D. Stone, *What to Do About Biodiversity: Property Rights, Public Goods, and the Earth's Biological Riches*, 68 S. Cal. L. Rev. 577 (1995).

4. John C. Kunich, *Preserving the Womb of the Unknown Species with Hotspots Legislation*, 52 Hastings L.J. 1 (2001).

5. *Id.* at 1226–39.

6. This is not to say that subsidies as incentives for hotspots preservation are free of any legal restrictions or potentially contentious issues. There are criteria and limits for such subsidies established in GATT, Art. XVI(1) and the EEC Treaty, Art. 92, for example. *See* PHILIPPE SANDS, PRINCIPLES OF INTERNATIONAL ENVIRONMENTAL LAW I: FRAMEWORKS, STANDARDS AND IMPLEMENTATION, 718–23 (Manchester, 1995).

7. There is evidence that this approach could work. For example, the Montreal Protocol's Multilateral Fund has distributed around $1 billion to compensate developing countries for the cost of phasing out ozone-depleting substances, significantly aiding in compliance with the terms of the Protocol. *See* David G. Victor, *Enforcing International Law: Implications for an Effective Global Warming Regime*, 10 Duke Env. L. & Pol'y J. 147, 160–3 (1999).

8. Report of the Appellate Body in United States—Import Prohibition of Certain Shrimp and Shrimp Products, Oct. 12, 1998, 33 I.L.M. 121 (Shrimp-Turtles Appellate Body), para. 171.

9. *Id.* at para. 121.

10. *Id.* at para. 171.

11. *Id.*

12. *See* Howard F. Chang, *Toward a Greener GATT: Environmental Trade Measures and the Shrimp-Turtle Case*, 74 S. Cal. L. Rev. 31, 41–43 (2000). The topic of unilateral ETMs remains disputatious, and, largely due to the confusing series of

WTO/GATT opinions, will probably continue to be until definitive clarification is available. *See, e.g.,* Eric L. Richards and Martin A. McCrory, *The Sea Turtle Dispute: Implications for Sovereignty, the Environment, and International Trade Law,* 71 U. Colo. L. Rev. 295, 340–41 (2000).

13. AYN RAND, ATLAS SHRUGGED, 35th anniversary edition (March 1992).

14. Kunich, *supra* note 4, at 1162–70.

15. *See* Alexander James, Kevin J. Gaston, and Andrew Balmford, *Can We Afford to Conserve Biodiversity?,* 51 Bioscience 43–52 (2001) (discussing the costs of various approaches to biodiversity conservation versus the benefits of conservation and concluding that the costs are dwarfed by both the rewards and the current subsidies for environmentally destructive practices).

16. Tropical Forest Conservation Act of 1998, 22 U.S.C. 2431 (1998) (amending 22 U.S.C. 2151 (1961) (the Foreign Assistance Act of 1961)).

17. 22 U.S.C. 2431(a)(2)–(7).

18. For example, to qualify for a debt-for-nature swap under this act, a nation must, inter alia, be one whose government (1) is democratically elected; (2) has not repeatedly provided support for acts of international terrorism; (3) is not failing to cooperate on international narcotics control matters; and (4) does not engage in a consistent pattern of gross violations of internationally recognized human rights. 22 U.S.C. 2430b(a)(1)–(4). Additionally, the nation must be either a low-income country (with a per capita income less than $725) or a middle-income country (with a per capita income more than $725 but less than $8,956). 22 U.S.C. 2431a(5)(A)(i)–(ii). It must also be "a country that contains at least one tropical forest that is globally outstanding in terms of its biological diversity or represents one of the larger intact blocks of tropical forests left, on a regional, continental, or global scale." 22 U.S.C. 2431a(5)(B). Other requirements include arrangements with various international funds, including the International Monetary Fund for adjustment loans, and formulation of financing programs with commercial bank lenders. The president has discretion to determine whether a nation meets the above standards and thus is eligible for benefits. 22 U.S.C. 2431f. The United States Secretary of State may enter into Tropical Forest Agreements with eligible countries to operate the funds created by this act for such purposes as establishing parks and reserves, promoting sustainable use of plant and animal species, and identification of medicinal uses of tropical forest plant life, as well as training programs for scientists and support of livelihoods of individuals living in or near tropical forests to prevent exploitation of the environmental resources. 22 U.S.C. 2431g.

19. Jennifer A. Loughrey, *The Tropical Forest Conservation Act of 1998: Can the United States Really Protect the World's Resources? The Need for a Binding International Treaty Convention on Forests,* 14 Emory Int'l L. Rev. 315, 328–37 (2000) (discussing the merits and shortcomings of this act). *See also* Nancy Knupfer, *Debt-for-Nature Swaps: Innovation or Intrusion?,* 4 N.Y. Int'l L. Rev. 86, 88 (1991); Paul J. Ferraro and Randall A. Kramer, *Compensation and Economic Incentives: Reducing Pressure on Protected Areas,* in LAST STAND: PROTECTED AREAS AND THE DEFENSE OF TROPICAL BIODIVERSITY, 187–211 (R. Kramer et al., eds., Oxford, 1997).

20. In a debt buyback, the debtor nation purchases its debt at a reduced price.

21. In a debt restructuring agreement, the original debt agreement is cancelled (a percentage of the face value of the debt is reduced) and a new agreement is

created that provides for an annual amount of money in local currency to be deposited into a fund for conservation projects.

22. A three-party swap works as follows. An NGO (usually a conservation group) buys on the secondary market a hard-currency debt owed to commercial banks, or a public/official debt owed to a creditor government at a discount rate, and then renegotiates the debt obligation with the creditor nation. The money generated from the renegotiated debt, to be repaid in local currency, is usually put into a fund that can allocate grants for conservation projects.

23. Public Law 107-26. *See* Report 107-119, Reauthorization of the Tropical Forest Conservation Act of 1998 Through Fiscal Year 2004, 107th Cong., 1st Sess., June 28, 2001.

24. Congressional Research Service Report for Congress, *Debt-for-Nature Initiatives and the Tropical Forest Conservation Act: Status and Implementation*, Feb. 13, 2002, Library of Congress Order Code RL31286.

25. *Id.* at 13.

26. *Id.* at 12.

27. *See* Dal Didia, *Debt-for-Nature Swaps, Market Imperfections, and Policy Failures as Determinants of Sustainable Development and Environmental Quality*, J. Econ. Issues 477–86 (2001).

28. *See* R.T. Deacon and P. Murphy, *The Structure of an Environmental Transaction: The Debt-for-Nature Swap*, LAND ECONOMICS 1–24 (1997).

29. Kunich, *supra* note 4, at 1243–50.

30. Genesis 25:29–34 (King James). The biblical account states that Esau willingly sold his birthright to his brother Jacob for a meal consisting of some stew, a "mess of pottage."

31. Genesis 25:34 (King James).

32. The term "First World" itself could be conceptualized as describing the actions of these nations during their developing phase. They were the first to use the world to the greatest extent possible to further their own national interests. They behaved as if they were first in line among all countries in terms of the right to exploit the resources of the world for their own ends.

33. Russell A. Mittermeier, Norman Myers, et al., *Biodiversity Hotspots and Major Tropical Wilderness Areas: Approaches to Setting Conservation Priorities*, 12 Conserv. Biol. 516 (Jun. 1998).

34. RUSSELL A. MITTERMEIER, NORMAN MYERS, AND CRISTINA GOETTSCH MITTERMEIER, HOTSPOTS: EARTH'S BIOLOGICALLY RICHEST AND MOST ENDANGERED TERRESTRIAL ECOREGIONS at 67 (2000).

35. However, short of actual extinction, the number of individual members of some or many of the species in the hotspots may be significantly reduced in the absence of major preservation efforts. Over time, this diminution of population size could lead to reduced vigor, lessened genetic diversity, and greater vulnerability to disease, predation, or changed habitat conditions. In the long run, the extinction rate may be exacerbated due to our inaction, even without a high current extinction risk.

36. The enhanced protection of such hotspots could still provide a positive outcome in the form of greater viability of some of the species therein. Although most species would not have become extinct even without the heightened preservation efforts, presumably the species would benefit from more protection. They may enjoy

an increase in population size, flourishing with more undisturbed habitat for breed-ing, feeding, and sheltering. This could prove important eventually, in the event of an outbreak of disease, or devastating fire, floods, earthquakes, etc. A rise in numbers could supply a crucial cushion against future threats. Thus, the analogy to unused insurance is imperfect; even absent a major extinction threat, hotspots preservation can be expected to yield worthwhile benefits.

37. Blaise Pascal (1623–1662) was a brilliant French mathematician, scientist, and philosopher. His famous "wager" is one of the most intriguing of his many contribu-tions. Simply put, Pascal's wager deals with our choice of whether to believe in God, or more accurately our decision whether to believe in God and to live as if God cares how we live. Given that we cannot definitively determine God's existence or nonex-istence nor discern the nature of God through objective, scientific means, what is the wise choice in light of the uncertainties? Pascal presupposed that God rewards belief and righteousness with eternal bliss and punishes disbelief and sinfulness with eternal anguish. Pascal posited that under these circumstances we should "bet" on God and believe/live a righteous life because if we do the rewards will be infinite for us if God exists, while our losses will be insignificant if there is no God. If God exists and we reject God, we have lost everything, but if there is no God and we have believed in a fiction, at least we have led a good life and have not truly lost anything. PETER KREEFT, CHRISTIANITY FOR MODERN PAGANS: PASCAL'S PENSÉES EDITED, OUTLINED, AND EXPLAINED (San Francisco: Ignatius Press, 1993), p. 292.

38. Of course, there are more than two options. We could fund VEPA at many different levels, and to a varying degree different spending levels may be adequate to protect some hotspots, or some portions of hotspots. Perhaps there would be a rough correlation between dollars spent and extent of preservation. But the underly-ing principles remain the same, and so for sake of clarity we are considering only the two extreme options—large-scale VEPA funding or none at all.

39. *See generally* ROBERTO MANGABEIRA UNGER, THE CRITICAL LEGAL STUDIES MOVEMENT, Harvard University Press (1983); CRITICAL LEGAL STUDIES, (James Boyle, ed.) New York University Press (1992). The Critical Legal Studies view, in a nutshell, is that rules do not decide cases or determine legal outcomes. Rather, the key stimuli are political power, hierarchical disparities in wealth and influence, the personal self-interest and predilections of the decision-makers, and other similar factors relating to the domination of some individuals, groups, and nations by others.

40. The Roman emperor Caligula had a favorite aphorism, "Oderint dum metu-ant." In English, this means, "Let them hate, so long as they fear." But this philoso-phy did not provide an enduring principle of success for him, and there is no reason to think it would be more effective now.

41. John Charles Kunich, *Preserving the Womb of the Unknown Species With Hotspots Legislation*, 52 Hast. L.J. 1149, 1212–17, 1226–39 (2001).

42. Leesteffy Jenkins, *Using Trade Measures to Protect Biodiversity*, in BIODIVER-SITY AND THE LAW, 93, 95–101 (William Snape, ed., 1996); *see also* Victor, *supra* note 7, at 162–3.

Conclusion

How could roughly half of all life on earth slip through the cracks of humanity's collective legal system? How could effective protection for numberless hosts of species and their habitats remain elusive amidst the thicket of domestic and international laws of the many nations that are hosts to the biodiversity hotspots? It is only a partial answer that the hotspots remained unrecognized even within the scientific community until 1988. There were other means of setting conservation priorities before the hotspots concept was posited, and yet the legal world failed to take up the cause of any of them. The remainder of the answer is in multiple parts.

First, the general public as well as the leaders of each nation, virtually without exception, continue to be oblivious to the fact that this planet's life is anything but evenly distributed around the globe. Citizens at all levels in all nations do not know that 44 percent of all plant species and 35 percent of all non-fish vertebrates live in, and only in, 1.44 percent of the earth's land surface. There is an appalling lack of cognizance of this phenomenal concentration of endemic species.

It is as if a person owned a 100-acre plot of land,[1] and there was information publicly available proving half of that person's wealth was hidden somewhere within a specific one-and-a-half acre parcel of the plot, yet the owner did not bother to notice. Why not? Maybe the information was not sufficiently publicized, and had not worked its way into the realm of common knowledge. Or maybe the owner did not know enough even to ask the right questions, never dreaming that there could be such a disproportionate share of riches in so tiny a parcel. Likewise, on a global scale, the scientific literature is certainly seldom read and even more seldom understood by the leaders and average citizens of any nation. Until/unless a scientific idea attracts significant attention beyond the perimeters of the specialized journals, it might as well exist in a parallel universe; laypersons will not be aware of it.

Second, people tend to be vaguely aware that there are laws in effect aimed at preserving endangered species and setting aside land for parks, preserves, national forests, and wildlife refuges—and they might assume that these laws have taken care of whatever needs might exist. To return to our 100-acre hypothetical, the owner might have complacently presumed that the existing laws were sufficient to protect everything on the land, irrespective of any imbalance that may obtain in the distribution of wealth from acre to acre. If, as the saying goes, ignorance is bliss, people may understandably derive comfort from remaining unaware of the gaps and flaws in the safety net of laws supposedly protecting them. To the limited extent that citizens, and even political leaders, are cognizant of the various laws that touch on living things, it is natural for them to gravitate to the default option of concluding that everything is under control. After all, there are so many laws, and so many words on so many pages—surely they must add up somehow to effective protection for something as valuable and irreplaceable as half of all life.

It can be quite discomfiting to learn that something we have relied on is unreliable. Such a revelation can provoke a crisis of confidence and shake a person's faith in the system. Moreover, when it requires considerable scientific and legal effort to discern the problem, it is far easier to relax and trust that all is well. Why go to all that trouble only to discover that we have a huge problem on our hands? If we do expend the effort to uncover the problem, we may also find out one of the reasons why it has not been solved: It is extremely difficult to do so.

This is the third part of the answer to the puzzle of legal neglect of the hotspots. For natural resources that are spread over so many nations, often very poor, developing nations, there are powerful local forces pushing for their exploitation, while the countervailing preservationist forces are weaker and more remote. If an impoverished nation chooses to develop its forests and fields to feed its people, how can other nations, alone or in concert, effectively intervene?

What more can we say after all we have said in this book? We can begin with this. There is credible scientific evidence for the following propositions.

1. The world is in the midst of an extinction crisis comparable to the most devastating epochs in the history of the planet.

2. Millions, perhaps many millions, of species currently live and die, thrive or go extinct, without ever being identified and named, let alone studied and understood, by human beings.

3. People—especially, in modern times, Americans—have derived enormous benefits, both tangible and intangible, from many of the species known to exist, and those species may yield more benefits in the future.

4. The species still unknown to humankind very probably hold the potential for similarly immense value.

5. Many species, known and unknown to humans, have great ecological significance to other species and to their ecosystems, apart from their direct utility for people.

Uncertainty—that which is now unknown and may always remain unknown—is a key aspect of the concept of biodiversity hotspots. We can, however, confidently add one more given to the above list of scientific facts: It is now well established that a few relatively small regions are home to a huge percentage of the previously identified species on earth today. It is reasonable to presume that the same is true for the unknown species, the life-forms that have never been catalogued by people. Most of the new species described each year live in or near these often poorly understood habitats. No one can say with certitude how many unknown species exist, but there is no reason to suppose that the hotspots contain a smaller share of them than they do of the known species, which is to say an enormous share.

Irrespective of the precise dimensions of the extinction threat and the extent to which the remaining hotspots of the world could be further reduced without drastically exacerbating the extinction rate, at some point human exploitation of the wild will cause a major and irreversible extinction spasm. I have argued that we are already there, or at least at the threshold. But that point of no return is not on any map. It is not spelled out in any book, statute, regulation, or conservation plan. It is unknown and probably unknowable. I have called the hotspots the Ark of the Broken Covenant. We do not know precisely how many living things are crowded into the myriad hidden places on the Ark. We cannot be certain how badly the Ark has been damaged, or at what specific point in time the many leaks will become catastrophic and the Ark will plunge violently, a global *Titanic*, throwing multitudinous species overboard at once, to sink into oblivion. The question is *what to do*, given that lack of certainty.

There are fairly predictable short-term gains available to people, at least on a local or national level, from conversion of portions of untamed areas into productive agricultural, mining, logging, developmental, and other enterprises. There is much less predictability as to the number and identity of species that would be lost due to any given additional amount of human exploitation, or the importance such lost species currently have for humans and for the web of life, or the value such lost species eventually might have under changed circumstances in the future. However, it is reasonable to presume that the current or future benefits offered by these species would not be limited to the local nation but rather would be diffused throughout all of the earth's people.

The developing nations that host so many of the planet's hotspots thus are faced with a dilemma. Do they exploit the ecological wonders within their territory for predictable, concrete, immediate economic gain to themselves directly and with less predictable, less tangible, and less immediate cost to the world as a whole? Or do they forgo development of these regions, thereby shouldering all of the lost opportunity costs themselves . . . while reaping no compensatory economic gain and conferring only some indeterminate benefit on humankind?

In light of the competing factors at work and their divergent degrees of predictability, it is not surprising that the world's hotspots already have been drastically reduced. Nations find it in their self-interest to develop their own natural resources for their own economic advancement, as they always have. When developing nations must struggle even for such basic needs as raising the life expectancy and standard of living for their citizens, it would be remarkable if they refrained from exploiting untapped natural resources within their control. Under the legal and political constraints now in place, the host nation would endure all of the very real disadvantages imposed by restraining its economic development, while the advantages would be both difficult to identify and diffusely spread out over the entire planet. That makes the rational option of choice quite obvious: the "shoot, shovel, and shut up" (3-S) syndrome on a grand scale.

Neither the Convention on Biological Diversity, nor the Convention on International Trade in Endangered Species, nor the World Heritage Convention, nor any other national or international legal mechanism now in place has been able to persuade developing nations not to "3-S" with regard to the destruction of their vital ecosystems. The incentives to exploit their natural resources are too powerful and too immediate, and the disincentives are either extremely weak, too remote, or nonexistent.

Worthy, even noble, sentiments are expressed in the various laws and international conventions applicable in some way to hotspots preservation. The aspiration of preservation is preferable to complete neglect. Unfortunately, in many instances, aspiration is all there is.

None of the existing legal mechanisms directly address the concept of biodiversity hotspots. At best, they attempt to create preserves, parks, and refuges within the boundaries of a particular nation, and sometimes these enclaves coincide with a portion of a hotspot. In no instance is anything approaching an entire hotspot protected, even on paper. This means that a large percentage of the most vital biodiversity habitats on earth are totally devoid of legal protection of any kind.

The hotspots phenomenon calls to mind the legend of Brigadoon, as immortalized in the musical play by Alan Jay Lerner and Frederick Loewe. In the play, a remarkable little village comes to life and becomes accessible to outsiders only for a single day every 100 years. After that one day, Brigadoon vanishes again for another century. A visitor can remain in Brigadoon only if he or she loves someone within it very much, because "if you love someone deeply enough, anything is possible—even miracles." So too, the hotspots are mostly out of sight and out of mind for virtually everyone on earth; most of us never have direct contact with any hotspot at all, and if we do it is usually very brief. The hotspots are also vanishing and may be near the end of their day. But if we care enough about the hotspots and what they mean, we can find a way to prevent them from disappearing. As in Brigadoon, with sufficient love, even miracles are possible. Time is running out, but it is not yet too late.

The hotspots are a global resource. They have immense importance not just for the nations within which they happen to be located but for the entire planet. The patchwork safety net of laws, stitched together with such good intentions nation by nation, yet full of gaping holes, will not save them. No laws now in existence can prevent the hotspots from burning out. The degree of destruction already suffered by the hotspots is appalling, and it will only worsen if nothing alters the status quo.

A unified, global solution to the hotspots problem is overdue. The United States has been a leader in the development and exploitation of the world's natural resources and in converting those resources to immense material wealth. We must now lead the way in recognizing the hotspots concept and committing significant resources to hotspots preservation. Absent this, the hotspots themselves may soon be absent.

This book has proposed a new statute, VEPA, to address the preservation of the hotspots. VEPA would rely on lessons learned from the failed experiments with other laws, both international and national, to avoid the practical and legal problems that have prevented the current legal regime from protecting the world's biodiversity. VEPA is designed to neutralize, and in fact reverse, the perverse incentives developing nations face when dealing with the hotspots within their jurisdiction.

VEPA would revolutionize the legal system for biodiversity protection. It would place the United States in the role of world leader in identifying, studying, and funding the preservation of the richest pockets of biodiversity on earth. Only the United States has the financial resources—amassed through many decades of exploitation of natural resources—necessary to counterbalance the formidable pressures that urge destruction of hotspots in developing nations. Certainly, this would be a considerable burden for the United States to bear, as it picks up much of the biodiversity preservation tab for the entire planet. But it is probable that no other nation, or group of nations, could or would intervene in this manner for the greater long-term good of all life on earth. Indeed, if not us, who? If not now, when?

In light of the multiple uncertainties that swirl around the hotspots phenomenon and the profound consequences for this planet and all of its people if the hotspots are lost, this book has put forth a variation of Pascal's famous wager to guide decision makers on a global scale. When the costs and consequences are analyzed using this approach, the appropriate choice is clear. The "Hotspots Wager" for rational decision makers is to preserve the hotspots. This decision forecloses potentially disastrous consequences and allows for potentially limitless rewards. The opposite decision does exactly the opposite.

VEPA would efficiently protect a substantial majority of the species in the world, regardless of whether those species have been given a name. By safeguarding the relatively small number of hotspots, this statute would shield far more species than any species-focused legal instrument such as CITES ever could. Moreover, the VEPA approach would take into account the paucity of knowledge humankind possesses about the web of life on earth, and would use that information vacuum as a factor in support of preservation of the hotspots. It would guard the hotspots—those few handfuls of black treasure boxes that are the womb of the unknown species and the true wealth of nations—in a way that no other law can do. VEPA would be a major advancement in the cause of global biodiversity preservation, and not a moment too soon. Before the Ark of the Broken Covenant is itself broken beyond repair and our chance to save the diversity of life vanishes forever, we must act. It is difficult to imagine another issue that is more truly a matter of life and death for the world as a whole.

NOTE

1. It may be helpful to conceptualize this parcel as the famous Hundred Acre Wood inhabited by such extraordinary creatures as Winnie the Pooh, Tigger, Eeyore, Owl, and Piglet. If the owners of such a 100-acre plot fail to check, who can say whether there might be living therein a small population of highly evolved endemic life forms capable of human speech and bipedal locomotion?

Index

About the Author

JOHN CHARLES KUNICH is professor of Law, Roger Williams University School of Law. He is the author of *Entomology and the Law: Flies as Forensic Indicators* with Bernard Greenberg (2002).

**Recent Titles in
Issues in Comparative Public Law**

Dignity and Liberty: Constitutional Visions in Germany and the United States
Edward J. Eberle